AFFAIRS AND SCANDALS

IN ANCIENT EGYPT

AFFAIRS AND SCANDALS IN ANCIENT EGYPT

by Pascal Vernus

Translated from the French by David Lorton

CORNELL UNIVERSITY PRESS

ITHACA AND LONDON

This translation was prepared with the generous assistance of the French Ministry of Culture—Centre national du livre.

First published 2003 by Cornell University Press

Printed in the United States of America

Library of Congress Cataloging-in-Publication Data

Vernus, Pascal.
  [Affaires et scandales sous les Ramsès. English]
  Affairs and scandals in Ancient Egypt / by Pascal Vernus ; translated from the French by David Lorton.
    p. cm.
Includes bibliographical references and index.
  ISBN 0-8014-4078-5 (cloth : alk. paper)
  1. Egypt—Civilization—To 332 B.C. 2. Egypt—Moral conditions. 3. Scandals—Egypt—History—To 1500. I. Title.
  DT61.V4413 2003
  932'.014—dc21
                         2003007905

Cloth printing   10 9 8 7 6 5 4 3 2 1

Contents

Foreword

Should we be surprised to learn that once upon a time, in the marvelous land of the pharaohs, there were what we today call "scandals"? Certainly not! Exceptions have always proved the rule: people are people, and life entails weaknesses, though we reprove them, and we often pursue and punish them. Would we want to ascribe to those Egyptians, to their brilliant and harmonious civilization, the total perfection that we are far from having attained in our own proud, modern world so filled with technological progress?

Perusing these fascinating texts and enjoying the discovery of their unexpected and instructive stories, readers will be surprised to learn how slowly mentalities evolve. History seems inevitably to repeat itself down through the millennia: the same ruses and evasions continue to occur, the same deals continue to be struck.

But the unexpected also occurs. First, after so many centuries, we have an exceptional selection of documents concerning legal hearings, in a state of preservation that permits the reconstruction of events. Another source of wonder: the justice of the land was solidly based on a moral law that those who dwelled along the Nile could be proud of. Even in the most turbulent periods, the "good old law" prevailed, and punishment sometimes rained down on the guilty. Still, many other developments could occur before the law triumphed, as confirmed in these stories, which are here entirely restudied and retold with all the rigor of France's most brilliant philologist.

The comical nature of the events depicted, the humor that

emerges from these thumbnail sketches of events, vividly brings to life the confused and troubled atmosphere of the end of the New Kingdom. Such an atmosphere proved to be propitious for the commission of felonies by cheerful and cynical rascals far from the seat of royal power in the capital, which was at that time located in the delta. These plunderers of the tombs of royalty and officials lived far away in Upper Egypt, on the west bank of Thebes. Reading these surprising and authentic stories, we discover the circumstances that led to the hatching and carrying out of one of the most astonishing plots against the crown.

The stories also depict a scandal that occurred at a late date in a province farther south; the story concerns a group of disreputable priests who held office on the island of Elephantine. Such accounts are otherwise lacking in the oft-evoked panorama of daily life in the land of Ramesses. This picture has been painted by the hand of a master.

Pascal Vernus concludes by giving us an incisive and heretofore unwritten historical outline of the change that occurred in the pharaonic realm around the beginning of the first millennium B.C.E. His final chapter is original and rich in both substance and finesse; it is to be read with the greatest of interest.

CHRISTIANE DESROCHES NOBLECOURT

Preface

No civilization has intuited the superhuman better than that of pharaonic Egypt. The overwhelming masses of the pyramids, the outsized dimensions of the hypostyle halls of temples, and the alien, hierarchical relationships found in representations can lead us to believe that the Egyptians had freed themselves from earthly contingencies and moved only in the ethereal slipstream of the divine. Indeed, certain writers have again and again credited the Egyptians with extraordinary powers and with knowledge that far surpassed that of modern science, elaborating ridiculous theories to the effect that they were experts in the liquefaction of rocks or virtuosos of antigravity. In search of the marvelous, these authors enter into the absurd. An imagination that needs such abracadabra to inspire it must be a poor one indeed!

For those who are able to study archaeological reports or to read the ancient texts, the Egyptians were people of flesh and blood, capable of both greatness and weakness, masters of ambitious projects but also slaves to banal preoccupations. They imposed their vision of the world on their environment, but they were weighed down by the burden of the human condition. In short, they were like any of us. And like ours, their society had its affairs, its scandals, its uncertainties, and its rifts. By presenting an account of five significant episodes, this book intends to shed light, through them and especially beyond them, on the crisis of values that eroded the New Kingdom at the very time when pharaonic Egypt was enjoying the acme of its prosperity and influence. This crisis was in some sense the dark side of an era too often recognized only for its triumphs and conquests, for the monumental splendor of Tuthmosis III and Ramesses II, for the fine and delicate reliefs of Amenophis III and Sethos I.

To describe the spectacular manifestations of this crisis and to explain its ins and outs is not to damage the prestige of the ancient Egyptians; rather, it reinforces the feeling of brotherhood that binds us to them across the millennia, and even increases our admiration of them. For the builders of the temples of Karnak and Luxor astonish us all the more in that they were but mere mortals, and pharaonic art arouses all the more emotion when we feel close to its creators. Their merit would have been less had they been demigods. Though they remained human, they were able to intimate the superhuman—and that is why they deserve our admiration.

P. V.

Translator's Note

The following conventions have been followed in the citations from ancient texts:

Parentheses ( ) enclose words or brief explanations that have been added for clarity.

Square brackets [ ] enclose words that have been restored in a lacuna.

Ellipses . . . indicate that a word or words in the original text have been omitted in the citation.

Ellipses in square brackets [. . .] indicate the presence of a lacuna for which no restoration has been attempted.

A question mark in parentheses (?) indicates that the translation of a word or phrase is uncertain.

English-speaking Egyptologists have no single set of conventions for the rendering of ancient Egyptian and modern Arabic personal and place names. Most of the names mentioned in this book occur in a standard reference work, John Baines and Jaromír Málek, *Atlas of Ancient Egypt* (New York, 1980), and the renderings here follow those in that volume. The only exception is the omission of the typographical sign for *ayin;* this consonant does not exist in English, and it was felt that its inclusion would serve only as a distraction to the reader.

The ancient scribes who wrote the texts quoted in this volume felt obliged to follow each mention of Pharaoh, whether by name or by title, with the pious wish "May he live, prosper, and be healthy." Here, I have followed the common Egyptological practice of abbreviating this lengthy and intrusive phrase as "l.p.h."

D. L.

AFFAIRS AND SCANDALS

IN ANCIENT EGYPT

1

The Plunder of Western Thebes

Economic Consequences of Funerary Beliefs

The crises that marked the end of the Ramesside Period were like the final groans of someone on a deathbed. To appreciate them fully, we must stress the exceptional importance of funerary beliefs in pharaonic civilization and their socioeconomic consequences. Like so many other peoples, the ancient Egyptians hoped that physical death was not just an annihilation. In fact, this hope[1] weighed so heavily on their earthly lives that it inspired many of their activities and their monuments. For the Egyptians, *postmortem* survival, however it was to be attained, was far from being a matter of individual faith. It entailed a number of preconditions, the fulfillment of which strictly constrained the organization and function of Egyptian society:

- The body had to be kept intact, which necessitated employing mummification techniques and keeping the body in a burial place designed to assure it an optimal chance of survival.
- At the time of interment, the body had to undergo complex rites and rituals designed to preserve its possibility of remaining alive and to ward off anything that could threaten it with a "second death"—that is, with total annihilation.
- The body had to be placed in a tomb with the most elaborate funerary equipment[2] possible, which had three functions: to eternize the effect of the rites and rituals; to restore, to the extent possible, the conditions of earthly life; and to assure the satisfaction of the body's needs in the afterlife by means of genuine and/or imitation food and drink. On the whole,

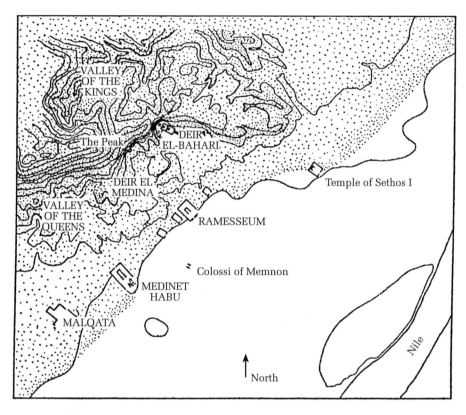

Map of Thebes

tomb furnishings were distinguished from their secular counterparts by the use of precious materials and extremely elaborate workmanship.[3] For the ancient Egyptians, their effectiveness was proportionate to their technical perfection.

- The deceased had to be sustained by a cult carried out by the living, consisting of food offerings, the recitation of appropriate formulas, and the celebration of rites, the cult being maximally effective when all three practices were combined. These practices entailed the provision of foodstuffs, the services of an officiant, and a monumental setting that included a funerary chapel, statues, stelae, and offering tables, set up wherever the deceased hoped to profit from his postmortem destiny.

These conditions the belief system imposed on individual survival had implications for what we might call *mutatis mutandis,* the savings they demanded. It would appear that each person devoting, in principle, as much of his resources as possible to his funerary provisions—a tomb and arrangements for a mortuary cult—reflected thereby his social position and standard of living. Though Cheops had the means to mobilize thousands of workers to raise a pyramid 481.4 feet in height, many others had to content themselves with a simple pit hastily dug in the desert sand.[4] But in any case, funerary beliefs had a profound effect on the economy of pharaonic Egypt.

For one thing, these beliefs affected social exchanges involving the circulation of goods and even of persons. A tomb was all the more suited to survival if it contained not just burial chambers but also a chapel that was open to visitors and in many cases decorated with bas-reliefs, paintings, and inscriptions. Creating such a tomb necessitated the cooperation of workers and artisans whose services were remunerated in one way or another.[5] Concerning oneself with one's tomb as early as possible was essential, for great resources had to be devoted to this end. A famous wisdom text attributed to Prince Hardjedef clearly expresses this practical imperative:

Make your dwelling in the necropolis,
perfect your place in the west!
. . .
The dwelling place of death is for life.[6]

Moreover, the funerary rites required the participation of specialized personnel at every level, including ritualists, mourning women, and embalmers, not to mention the materials and products they employed. Traditionally, Egyptians who could do so made contractual arrangements involving goods or fields to compensate officiants who undertook to guarantee their postmortem maintenance cult. What is more, the cult of deities and the cult of the dead entailed the same basic practices, and they were so closely connected that the resources mobilized for one could serve the other, according to a common practice. The divine offering was not destroyed in the course of the rite. According to the principle of the "reversion of offerings," it remained available after its consecration and could be put to another purpose, to benefit either a deity or a dead person; at the end of its rounds, it could be given to living individuals.[7]

The funerary beliefs ultimately had a debit effect on the economy. Enormous quantities of goods and precious materials lay wasted in tombs, removed in principle from use or enjoyment by the living.

Tomb Robbery in Pharaonic Egypt

The riches stored away for the self-serving and uncertain satisfaction of a dead person inevitably tempted the greedy, or those who were impoverished and famished. In fact, tomb robbery is attested early, both in texts and archaeologically, from the very dawn of pharaonic civilization. Many predynastic burials were profaned shortly after they had been carried out. Generally speaking, most of the pharaonic cemeteries suffered the attacks of robbers already in antiquity. Such attacks sometimes occurred soon after the burial, quite simply because they were carried out by people who knew the weak spots in the tomb, for they had witnessed or participated in its construction,[8] or in that of a neighboring tomb.[9]

That much said, the cases we are about to describe have a number of exceptional features. First, they are documented in extensive, detailed dossiers that were drawn up in the course of judicial investigations, and not just by vague textual allusions or fleshless archaeological observations.

Next, these tomb robberies occurred during the reigns of the last representatives of a prestigious dynasty, in a society that was organized and policed, or at least pretended that it still was, and at a time when literary tradition held that tomb robbery was a manifestation of revolutionary anarchy. A pertinent example is supplied by *The Admonitions of an Egyptian Sage,* where this theme is inserted into a lengthy description of a topsy-turvy world:[10]

What the pyramid concealed[11] has ended up emptied.
. . .
Alas, those who were in the embalming house are cast onto the hillside.[12]
Lo, those who had funerary chambers are cast onto the hillside, he who could not acquire a burial is [possessor] of a "white house."[13]

Here, tomb robbery is symptomatically correlated with inversion of the social order, and such robbery is only the consequence of the deeper scandal involving the overturning of institutions. The scandal of the sack of the west bank of Thebes, though, was that it occurred in a society in which the institutions were still in place, however weakened or corrupted they might have been.

Finally, these robberies contrast with many others by their very object: "the west of Thebes." This Egyptian expression designates the west bank of the Nile, opposite the temples of Karnak and Luxor, where there are several miles of tombs and sepulchers, along with cult buildings and grandiose funerary temples. The area includes the royal cemeteries, those of royal wives and royal children in the Valley of the Queens, and, of course, those of the kings, not only the pharaohs of Dynasties 11 and 17 and the beginning of Dynasty 18 at Deir el-Bahari and Dra Abu el-Naga, but also those of the New Kingdom in the Valley of the Kings.

During the New Kingdom conquests attracted unequaled amounts of precious products and objects, many of which in one way or another ended up in the tomb furnishings of the pharaohs. We could easily imagine what heaps of riches were stored within the mountain of the west bank of Thebes. But we need not stop to do so: we need only recall that Tutankhamun, whose treasure has so fascinated modern times, was undoubtedly one of the least important pharaohs. With that, we have an idea of what could have been contained in the tombs of kings such as Tuthmosis III, Amenophis III, or Ramesses II. This was thus a neighborhood of dead people that must have sorely tempted the living. And the judicial proceedings carried out against those who pillaged it at the end of Dynasty 20 must have been as striking to the ancient Egyptians as they are to us today, to the point of being, for them as for us, "causes célèbres," as the great Egyptologist Jaroslav Černý once called them.[14]

Though such robbery became a regular practice at this time,[15] official reaction to it led to two major series of investigations and trials,[16] the first in years 16 and 17 of Ramesses IX (c. 1124–1123 B.C.E.), and the second beginning in year 19 of Ramesses XI (c. 1084 B.C.E.), which corresponded to year 1 of the era called "Repeating of Births,"[17] though other judicial proceedings might have occurred as well.[18]

The Robberies in the Reign of Ramesses IX

The Deteriorating Conditions under Dynasty 20

In the course of Dynasty 20, we find numerous indications of what could anachronistically be called an "economic crisis"; such a term is imprecise for a microsociety such as that of the west bank of Thebes, and more specifically for that of the workers of (the institution of) the Tomb, where the laws that govern the modern marketplace evidently could not apply.[19] On the one hand, chronic crises regarding provisioning occurred, with the state unable to deliver rations that it owed its employees, who took to consulting oracles to learn whether they would be paid, as testified by this anguished plea: "My goodly lord, will [we be] given rations?"[20] From the reign of Ramesses III on, such failures to deliver rations led to strikes (see chapter 2). We also note, on the other hand, steep fluctuations in the price of basic grains, which practically doubled from the reign of Ramesses VII on, though most prices remained stable, as is to be expected in this sort of economy.[21] With the reign of Ramesses IX, the situation worsened. Interruptions in the deliveries of food supplies recurred, forcing the workers of (the institution of) the Tomb to go without food and to stand idle, as noted in the journal of (the institution of) the Tomb:[22]

> [Year 17, month 2 of winter, day 7]: Absence of the gang, because it was hungry, for its rations were not there. . . .
>
> [Year 17, month 2 of winter, day 9]: Absence of the gang, for it was hungry and found itself without its allocations.[23]

In addition, from that time on, a lack of security prevailed on the west bank of Thebes, thanks to the incursions of "foreigners,"[24] who were often designated as Libyans belonging to the Meshwesh or the Libu tribe.[25] Mentions of these incursions are concentrated in years 8 to 15 of Ramesses IX.[26] Though these were the wanderings of people on the move, not bloody raids, they struck fear in the locals and gave the workers of (the institution of) the Tomb, who lived in the isolated valley of Deir el-Medina, a good pretext for not reporting to work in the Valley of the Kings. Is it a coincidence that as early as year 13 of Ramesses IX, many people from various social groups were regularly turning to tomb robbery?[27] Without being the direct cause of the robberies, these incursions assured conditions favorable to the robbers, to the extent that they were less likely to be noticed when everyone preferred to hide at home or in the shelter of the high walls surrounding the funerary temples.

In any case, it was only in year 16, at least three years after they had become a regular practice, that the tomb robberies on the west bank of Thebes provoked a strong reaction by the authorities, including officials of the highest rank. That such an affair had at first been neglected and hushed up[28]—dare we say "buried"—only to cause such an uproar at a later date was the result of two related factors: the extreme corruption of institutions and the exploitation of the situation for purposes of settling scores between persons of high rank. God knows how different pharaonic society was from our own, in which, as we all know, such corruption and exploitation are entirely unthinkable!

Sources of diverse origin attest to the pathetic state of the administrative and judiciary institutions in the New Kingdom, in public opinion as much as in daily reality. To those anecdotes collected in chapter 6, we can add the following, which relates the confession of Amenpanefer, one of the most important accused:[29]

> In year 13 [of Pharaoh], l.p.h., our [Lord], l.p.h. . . . we set off to commit robberies in the funerary monuments according to the manner of

acting to which we quite regularly conformed. . . . Then, some days later, the guardians of Thebes learned that we had committed robberies in the west. They seized us, and they confined me in the seat of the governor of Thebes. I took the twenty *deben* of gold that had fallen to me as my share. I gave them to the scribe of the district of Tameniu, Khaemope; he freed me.[30] I rejoined my companions, and they repaid me a share. I returned to this practice of plundering in the tombs of the dignitaries and the men of the land who lie in the west of Thebes down to this day, along with the other robbers who were with me, a large number of men of the land also dedicating themselves to pillage, group by group.[31]

The confession is notable for the disarming candor with which Amenpanefer reports how, after his arrest, he escaped justice by greasing the palm of a scribe. Evidently, it was quite common for a representative of law and order to free a thief in exchange for his share of the loot! On another occasion of robbery, the same process was repeated; a guilty party was arrested, and then, for the price of his share, he was freed by the ridiculous Khaemope:[32]

When we [were] arrested, the scribe of the district Khaemope came to me. . . . I gave him the four *qite* of gold that had fallen to me.

The sum was different, because on this occasion, the thief who was freed had the right only to a smaller share. The robbers knew how to guard against the risks of their trade with clever arrangements; Amenpanefer's accomplices reimbursed him quickly, after which they all resumed their noble enterprise as though nothing had happened.

The Scandal Is Triggered

Under these conditions, the robberies could have continued for a long time, given that the indifference of the Theban authorities had been purchased. But, like a *deus ex machina,* a disagreement that arose in their midst lent these robberies the proportions of an affair of state. On one side of the dispute was Paser,[33] the governor of Thebes—the city on the east bank and its temples, such as those of Karnak and Luxor. On the other side was Pawero, the governor of the west bank of Thebes and chief of the Medjay of (the institution of) the Tomb—that is, the police chief who supervised the royal necropolis and the construction of the tomb of the reigning pharaoh.[34] In addition to a personal rivalry, the dispute involved a rivalry between factions. Pawero had not only the support of all the inhabitants of the west bank of Thebes, in particular the workers of (the institution

of) the Tomb, but also that of the vizier. This interlocking of powerful interests explains a certain fuzziness in the official documents
relating the proceedings that were set in motion on this occasion.[35]
Those that have come down to us are:

- the official account of a judicial investigation of robberies in the Valley of
  the Queens and the old royal necropolis of Dra Abu el-Naga from day 18
  to day 21 of the first month of the inundation season in year 16 (Papyrus
  Abbott);
- the official account of the proceedings carried out against the robbers of
  the pyramid of King Sebekemzaf-shedtawy in the old royal necropolis of
  Dra Abu el-Naga (Papyrus Amherst-Leopold II);
- "the interrogation of the thieves," the term applied to a series of depositions made by men who had robbed tombs of private persons; probably
  preparatory notes, perhaps written up well afterward (Papyrus BM
  10054);
- the account of the proceedings carried out to recover, from the thieves
  and receivers of stolen goods, precious metals and valuable objects taken
  during the robberies of year 16 (Papyrus BM 10068 and 10053).[36]

One anecdote regarding these documents reflects the disorder of
the times. At least two or three of these documents, as well as related
ones, had to be bought back from receivers of stolen goods more than
thirty years after they were written, in year 6 of the Repeating of
Births, undoubtedly because they had been stolen when the temple
of Ramesses III was taken during the civil war![37]

The matter also had echoes in the journals related to the activities
of the workers of (the institution of) the Tomb.

It was Paser, the governor of Thebes, who set the dispute in motion. Informed by two scribes of (the institution of) the Tomb, Hori
and Pabes, of five serious cases punishable by death, surely instances of tomb violation, he advised Pharaoh:

> The scribe Hori of (the institution of) the Tomb, a reserved domain,[38]
> son of Amennakht, came to this great riverbank of Thebes, to the place
> where I am. He brought three requests for inquiry regarding two very
> serious cases. My scribe and the two scribes of the district of Thebes
> wrote them down. Then the scribe Pabes of (the institution of) the
> Tomb reported two other cases to me, for a total of five cases. They
> also wrote them down, given that they could not be passed over in si-
> lence, for they are serious offenses punishable by mutilation, impale-
> ment,[39] and all sorts of like punishment. . . . I have reported on this
> before my Lord. For it would be an offense for someone in my position
> if I gained knowledge of an affair and concealed it.[40]

This zealous dignitary made it clear to the workers of (the institution of) the Tomb, who were responsible for the work in the Valley of the Queens,[41] that he well knew how to unleash the wrath of the state against them:

> I must write about them before[42] Pharaoh, l.p.h., my Lord, l.p.h., to cause Pharaoh, l.p.h., to send men to deal with you.

Pawero's Counterattack

Paser did not count on the disappointment that his imperious sense of duty would bring him. For his part, Pawero, the governor of the west bank of Thebes, who was immediately made aware of the agitation of his colleague and enemy, displayed signs of considerable anger on the pretext that the proper channels had not been followed:

> It was a mistake for these two scribes of (the institution of) the Tomb[43] to approach the governor of Thebes to make a report to him, given that none of their predecessors had ever made a report to him, and that it was the vizier, when he was in the southern region, to whom they made reports. And if he happened to be in the northern region, the Medjay and the retainers of His Majesty, l.p.h., from (the institution of) the Tomb went downstream with their memoranda to the place where the vizier was.

In reality, his pretended irritation masked a deep anxiety. The crimes had been committed in his own jurisdiction, and the fact that an external authority had reported them could raise a suspicion that he was covering them up, which in any event was probably the case. Thus, since he could no longer conceal them, like a good politician, he in turn hastened to denounce them. And it was in fact he, Pawero, who was officially presented as having, with all due diligence, originated the inquiry![44] In fact, here is the wording of one of the official reports that resulted:

> [Year 16], month 3 of the inundation season, day 18 under the majesty of the King of Upper and Lower Egypt, lord of the Two Lands, Neferkare-setepenre, l.p.h., the son of Re and lord of diadems [Ramesses-Khaem]wese-meryamun, l.p.h., beloved of Amun-Re, king of the gods, and of Harakhty, given life forever and ever.
> [On this day] the controllers[45] of the great and august Tomb, the scribe of the vizier, the scribe of the overseer of the white house of Pharaoh, l.p.h. [were dispatched to examine the] tombs [of the] former

kings, as well as the funerary monuments and the resting places of the praised ones [of past times that are located on] the west of Thebes, by the overseer of the city and vizier Khaemwese, (by) the royal cup-bearer Nesamun, the scribe of [Pharaoh, l.p.h., (by) the steward] of the domain of the Divine Adoratrice—may she live—of Amun-Re, king of the gods, (by) the royal cupbearer Neferkareemperamun, the herald of Pharaoh, l.p.h., [with regard to] the thieves of the west of Thebes, concerning whom the governor, the chief of the Medjay of (the institution of) the Tomb, great and august of a million years, of Pharaoh, l.p.h., Pawero had made a report to the vizier and to the officials and cup-bearers of Pharaoh, l.p.h.[46]

Thus, it is the report of Pawero that is explicitly presented here as having originated the inquiry. Another document associates some subordinate officials with Pawero in drawing up the denunciation:

The interrogation of the men who were found to have conducted excavations[47] in the funerary monuments of the west of Thebes, concerning whom the governor of the west of Thebes, chief of the Medjay of (the institution of) the Tomb, great and august of a million years, of Pharaoh, l.p.h., Pawero, [the scribe of the district], Wennefer, and the guardian of the west of Thebes, [Amen]nakht, had made a report.[48]

The commission that was put together after this denunciation consisted not only of the representatives of high offices (vizier, white house, domain of Amun), but also of local functionaries, with Pawero at their head:

the governor, chief of the Medjay of (the institution of) the Tomb, Pawero; [the chief of the Medjay] of this domain Bakwerel; . . . [49]
the chief of the Medjay of this domain, Mentuherkhopshef;
the scribe of the vizier, Paaenbik;
the scribe and chief of the storehouse of the overseer of the white house, Paynefer;
the prophet of the domain of Amenophis, Paankhaw;
the prophet of the wine department of the domain of Amun, Seramun;
the Medjay of (the institution of) the Tomb who are with them.[50]

The Report of the Commission

The commission began by inspecting the area of present-day Dra Abu el-Naga, the burial place of several pharaohs who, during the First and Second Intermediate Periods and the beginning of the

New Kingdom, had contributed to the reunification of the pharaonic realm. The commissioners submitted a report describing the condition of each of the funerary complexes they examined in the sector. Here is a sample:

> The pyramids, rock-cut tombs, and funerary monuments examined on this day by the controllers.[51]

> The horizon of eternity of King Djeserkare, the son of Re, Amenophis,[52] which is 120 cubits deep according to its stela, which is called Paaqa ("high access"), north of the domain of Amenophis, l.p.h., of the vineyard, concerning which the governor of Thebes, Paser, had made a report to the overseer of the city and vizier, Khaemwese, to the royal cupbearer Nesamun, the scribe of Pharaoh, l.p.h., to the steward of the domain of the Adoratrice of Amun-Re, king of the gods, to the royal cupbearer Neferkareemperamun, to the herald of Pharaoh, l.p.h., and to the great dignitaries in these terms: "The robbers have profaned it." Examined on this day, it was found intact by the controllers.

> The (complex of the) pyramid of the king, the son of Re Inaa,[53] l.p.h., which is north of the domain of Amenophis, l.p.h., of the forecourt, whose pyramid had been removed, but whose stela was found standing in front of it, while the representation of the king is on the stela, between his legs his dog named Behek.[54] Examined on this day, it was found intact.[55]

After inspection of the zone under consideration, the following assessment was made:

> Total. Pyramid (complexes) of former kings examined on this day by the controllers:
> Found intact: 9
> Found profaned: 1.
> Total: 10.
> Funerary monuments of the songstresses of the domain of the Divine Adoractrice of Amun-Re, king of the gods, may she live.
> (Tombs) found intact: 2
> (Tombs) found profaned by thieves: 2
> Total: 4.
> The funerary monuments and rock-cut tombs in which the favored of former times, the citizens and the men of the land, rest in the west of Thebes.
> It was determined that the robbers had profaned all of them, having removed the owners from their coffins and their sarcophagi, and having abandoned them in the desert after stealing the items of equipment

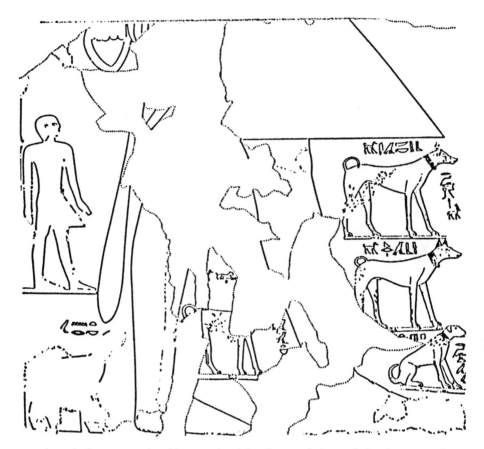

The stela depicting Wah-ankh Inyotef with his dogs, including Behek, who is one of the dogs standing in front of him. Drawing by W.-G. Legde.

that had been placed with them, along with the gold, silver, and adornments that were in their coffins.[56]

Thus, of the ten royal complexes that were inspected, nine were "found intact" in the official report. The formulation is clearly tendentious, for the "intact" category included two complexes that the robbers had invaded without reaching their goal:

> The (complex of the) pyramid of King Nubkheperre, l.p.h., the son of Re Inyotef, l.p.h. It was found in the course of being tunneled into by the robbers when they had penetrated two and a half cubits on its northern side, starting from the outer court of the tomb of the chief of the presentation of offerings in the domain of Amun, Iury,[57] who is dead. It was intact; the thieves were unable to reach it.

The (complex of the) pyramid of King Sekhemre-wepmaat, l.p.h.,
the son of Re Inyotef the Great, l.p.h. It was found in the course of
being tunneled into by the robbers in the place where the stela of his
pyramid had been set up. Examined on this day, it was found intact;
the robbers were unable to reach it.[58]

In fact, the demanding standards of this commission admitted of no
profaning worthy of being called such, except in the case of the
pyramid complex of King Sebekemzaf-shedtawy, which was considered important enough to warrant a special report[59] (see pp. 39–40
for the details of this tomb violation).

This assessment was completed by a confirmation of pillage in
two of the four tombs belonging to songstresses of the domain of the
Divine Adoratrice of Amun-Re, king of the gods, and, once again, of
pillage in a number of tombs belonging to private individuals,
though the commission did not trouble to indicate how many or the
names of the owners in this report. Its members apparently enjoyed
a clear conscience and the satisfaction of having fulfilled their duty,
after completing their task in the following manner:

The governor, chief of the Medjay of (the institution of) the great and
august Tomb, Pawero, along with the Medjay, the controllers of (the
institution of) the Tomb, the scribe of the vizier, and the scribe of the
overseer of the treasury who were with them made a report about it to
the overseer of the city and vizier Khaemwese, to the royal cupbearer
Nesamun, the scribe of Pharaoh, l.p.h., to the steward of the Divine
Adoratrice of Amun-Re, king of the gods, may she live, to the royal
cupbearer Neferkareemperamun, the herald of Pharaoh, l.p.h., and to
the great dignitaries. The governor and chief of the Medjay of (the institution of) the Tomb, Pawero, submitted a list of the robbers in writing to the vizier, to the dignitaries, and to the cupbearers. They were
seized, they were jailed, they were interrogated, and they told what
had happened.[60]

A Strangely Altered Deposition

The next day, the vizier himself, along with the personal
scribe of Pharaoh, the cupbearer Nesamun, came in person to verify
on the spot (in this case in the Valley of the Queens) the deposition
of the coppersmith Pakhar. When he had been arrested and interrogated two years earlier, this thief declared that he had entered the
tomb of the king's wife Isis, who was probably the wife of Ramesses
III, also known by the surname (Ta-)Heberdjet:[61]

The vizier and the cupbearer had the boilermaker led in their presence to the "Places,"[62] blindfolded like a prisoner. His sight was restored when he arrived there. The dignitaries said to him, "Go in our presence to the tomb from which you said that you removed the objects." In the presence of the dignitaries, the coppersmith went toward a group tomb[63] belonging to the royal children of King Usermaatre-setepenre,[64] l.p.h., the great god, where no burial had been made and which had been left open, and toward the home of a workman of (the institution of) the Tomb, Amenemone son of Huy, which is in this place, saying, "Behold the places where I was." The dignitaries had this coppersmith subjected to a very close questioning in the Great Valley. It was not determined that he was familiar with any place there other than the two places he had designated. He took an oath by the Lord, l.p.h., under pain of having his nose and ears cut off and being impaled, saying, "I know no other place here within the 'Places' except for the tomb which is open and this house I have shown you."

The dignitaries examined the seals of the great places in Tasetnefru, in which the royal children, the royal wives, the royal mothers, and the grandfathers and grandmothers of Pharaoh, l.p.h., rest. They were found intact.[65]

The coppersmith Pakhar thus supposedly accused himself of a crime he had not committed, declaring that he had violated a tomb that was found intact, when in fact, he had entered only an uncompleted tomb and the hut of a workman. This strange story leaves us suspicious, particularly because this tomb of Queen Isis (Ta-)Heberdjet was in fact damaged by robbers in year 17 of Ramesses XI—that is, scarcely a year later. This fact, determined by an investigative commission in that year, was unequivocally noted in the journal of the necropolis:

Going up to the august Tasetnefru by the royal cupbearer, the vizier Khaemwese, the gang of workmen of the tomb, and their foremen to inspect (the tomb of) the king's mother, the august king's wife, Isis, l.p.h. They opened her tomb. They noted the granite rock,[66] that the eight robbers[67] had smashed it in the *mnty*,[68] that they had seriously damaged everything that was there, and that they had smashed the western door.[69]

It is therefore not surprising that another robber, Bukhaaf, who entered this tomb at the time of the second sack of Thebes thirty years later, found it already profaned, much to his displeasure:

The vizier said to him, "Tell how you set out to assault the great and august places."

He said, "It was Paser, a man of the gang of (the institution of) the
Tomb who showed us the tomb of the king's wife (Ta-)Heberdjet."[70]

It was said to him, "As for the place to which you went, in what
condition did you find it?"

He said, "I found it already opened."[71]

The robber's trade was a tough one, for even his predecessors were
his rivals! Now that we have taken all due pity on this wretched
man, let us set aside his tale and return to year 17 of Ramesses IX,
when information regarding pillage in Tasetnefru, the Valley of the
Queens, was accumulating:

> Year 17, month 1 of winter, day 8 under the majesty of the King of
> Upper and Lower Egypt, Neferkare-setepenre, l.p.h., the son of Re,
> lord of diadems, Ramesses-Khaemwese, beloved of Amun-Re, king of
> the gods, given life forever and ever like his father Amun-Re, king of
> the gods, and Mut the great one, mistress of Asheru.
>
> Registering the depositions relating to the copper of the thieves who
> were determined to have pillaged Tasetnefru and whose interrogation
> was conducted by the vizier Khaemwese (and by) the first prophet of
> Amun-Re, king of the gods, Amenhotpe, in the domain of Maat in
> Thebes. (Depositions) set down in a document so that it (= the copper)
> might be recovered by the governor Pawero and by the scribe of the
> district, Wennefer, the foreman of the gang of (the institution of) the
> Tomb, Userkhepesh [. . .] Qadert, and the doorkeeper of the Tomb,
> Khonsmose.[72]
>
> The gold, the silver, the copper, and everything it was determined
> that the men of the gang (= the workmen of the royal tombs), [robbers
> of the necropolis],[73] had stolen . . . after it was determined that they
> had profaned Tasetnefru in the west of Thebes, the place where rest[74]
> [. . .][75]

Thus, in year 16 of Ramesses IX, in the third month of the inundation season, according to the report made at the instigation of
Pawero, the governor of the west of Thebes, it was determined
that:

- the tomb of Queen Isis was intact;
- Tasetnefru was free of serious damage;
- the workers of (the institution of) the Tomb were innocent of any accusation of robbery.

Yet in year 17 of the same Ramesses IX, a series of official reports at-
tests that:

- the tomb of Queen Isis had been violated;
- Tasetnefru had been looted to such an extent that the thieves were still in possession of more than 236 *deben* (i.e., nearly 50 pounds) of gold, electrum, and silver, above and beyond the enormous quantities of metals, products, and precious objects that they had given to a hundred receivers of stolen goods;
- eight men belonging to the workers of (the institution of) the Tomb were found guilty of these crimes.

Of course, it is possible that the robberies occurred during the interval between the inspections in years 16 and 17, but this is not very likely. Would the robbers have redoubled their efforts at just the time when the first scandal had drawn the attention of the authorities to their activity, and would they have done so in the very cemetery that had been involved?

In fact, it seems quite likely that the facts were manipulated to cover up the violation of tombs in the Valley of the Queens in year 16 of Ramesses IX, especially considering that the coppersmith Pakhar was curiously discharged when the scandal unraveled before the great tribunal, as though his freedom was the compensation for his retraction.[76] The continuation of the story reinforces this impression.

Paser's Defeat

The determination that the tombs in the Valley of the Queens were intact was exploited with more than suspect haste. Scarcely had it happened when the authorities invited the entire workforce of the (institution of) the Tomb, who had been implicated by Paser, the governor of Thebes, to make a display of rejoicing:

> The great dignitaries caused the controllers, the leaders, the men of the gang of (the institution of) the Tomb, the chiefs of the Medjay and the Medjay, and all the subordinate personnel of (the institution of) the Tomb to go from the west of Thebes to (the city of) Thebes for a great rally.[77]

When they reached their destination near the temple of Ptah, lord of Thebes, the true meaning of the rally did not escape the man who was its actual target, Paser:

> "As for this rally you have held today, it was not a rally, it was your triumph that you celebrated. . . . It was before the entrance to my house that you exulted against me. What does that mean, given that it is I, the governor, who report to the sovereign, l.p.h.? If you are exulting with regard to the place where you were, it was inspected and you found it intact; (but) [King] Sekhemre-shedtawy, the son of Re Se-

A funerary priest, head shaved and wearing a feline skin, holding a bouquet. Drawing by N. de Garis Davies.

bekemzaf, l.p.h., as well as Nubkha[es], his wife, have been violated. He was a great sovereign who made ten imposing works for Amun-Re, king of the gods; his monuments are in place in his central quarter to this day." Then the man of the gang Userkhepesh, who was under the supervision of the foreman of the gang of (the institution of) the Tomb, Nekhenmut, said, "As for every king and his royal wives, royal mothers, and royal children who rest in the great and august necropolis,[78] as well as those who rest in Tasetnefru, they are intact, they are preserved and safeguarded for eternity. The perfect care of Pharaoh, l.p.h., their son, guards them and watches over them rigorously."

This governor of Thebes said to him, "What you have done is a far cry (?)[79] from what you have said."[80]

Notwithstanding the uncertainties inherent in any translation of an Egyptian text, as well as the tendentious imprecision in the wording of this particular document,[81] the true dimensions of the scandal are clear. If Governor Paser manifested so much zeal for law and order, it was less because of the wounds that this pillaging inflicted on his delicate moral sense than because implicating the men of (the institution of) the Tomb gave him an opportunity to embarrass

Pawero, the governor of the west of Thebes, who was responsible for order in this region. It is in fact clear that they were actively involved in these robberies, if only as informers[82] or receivers of stolen goods, in the event that the thieves were not members of their group. Against this offensive, Pawero and his faction launched a clever strategy based on two main points.

Point one: minimizing the damage. When all was said and done, the commission recognized only the robbery of the tomb of King Sebekemzaf, not counting some private tombs that were barely mentioned.[83] In particular, the commission concluded that the Valley of the Queens was intact. It is clear that the violation of an obscure pharaoh who had lived more than five centuries earlier would have provoked less indignation than that of a queen, the wife of the glorious Ramesses III, whose funerary temple was still a major center of activity on the west bank of Thebes, and who was, moreover, the mother of Ramesses VI, who had died scarcely twenty years earlier. Paser, for his part, was interested in establishing the seriousness of the situation, hence his words in praise of King Sebekemzaf.[84]

Point two: taking advantage of the solidarity of the faction, which was a powerful one. Its lower echelon was the personnel of (the institution of) the Tomb, who were incited to demonstrate against Paser. At its head were important dignitaries, in particular the vizier. That a part of the upper administration supported Pawero is clear from the tendentious manner in which one of the official documents was written. This document, Papyrus Abbott, accords a positive role to Pawero by crediting him with denouncing the thefts, while the report sent by Paser to the pharaoh is mentioned only in the cases where the investigations invalidated it.[85] As for the complicity of the vizier, his speech before the great tribunal that was assembled to judge the affair illustrates it dramatically:

> And the vizier said to the great dignitaries of the great tribunal of Thebes, "This governor of Thebes has reported some cases regarding the controllers and the men of the gang of (the institution of) the Tomb in year 16, month 3 of the inundation season, day 18 before the royal cupbearer Nesamun, the scribe of Pharaoh, l.p.h., and it is regarding the great places that are in Tasetnefru that he made his deposition. But when I was there as vizier of the land with the royal cupbearer Nesamun, the scribe of Pharaoh, l.p.h. we examined the places about which the governor of Thebes had said to us, 'The coppersmiths of the House of Usermaatre-meryamun, l.p.h., in the domain of Amun attacked them.' We found them intact, and it was determined that everything he had said was false. Now, see, the coppersmiths are standing

before you. Make them tell everything that happened. Their depositions have been taken. It was determined that they did not know any
site in the place of Pharaoh, l.p.h. about which the governor had reported these things. He was proven wrong on this point. The great dignitaries released the coppersmiths of the House of Usermaatre-
meryamun, l.p.h. They were sent back to the first prophet of
Amun-Re, king of the gods, Amenhotpe, on that very day. A report
was made in writing; it is filed in the chancellery of the vizier."[86]

The affair thus ended with the defeat of Paser, who suffered the
supreme affront of being disavowed by his peers in the great tribunal, a high authority whose members included the vizier, the first
prophet of Amun, the scribe and the herald of Pharaoh, military
men, and high Theban officials—he being one of them! Of course,
those robbers who had had the bad luck of selecting tombs whose violation was of scant concern to the authorities were severely punished:

> The first prophet of Amun-Re, king of the gods, was ordered to bring
> them so as to place them as prisoners in the prison of the first prophet
> of Amun-Re, king of the gods, along with their accomplices in theft,
> until Pharaoh, l.p.h., our lord, decides their punishment.[87]

All evidence leads us to believe that this punishment, fixed by
Pharaoh,[88] was the death penalty.[89]

The Proceedings at the Dawn of the Repeating of Births

The Civil War

The first sensational affair caused by the pillage in the west
of Thebes was touched off by the enmity between two high officials.
Such was also true of the second scandal, but in this case, the quarrel turned into an armed conflict. In addition to economic problems
and chronic raids by Libyans, the reign of Ramesses XI experienced
the throes and destruction of a civil war.[90] The protagonists were
Panehsy, the King's Son of Kush—that is, the governor of the Nubian
province annexed to Egypt—and the adherents of the first prophet of
Amun, Amenhotpe, who thirty years earlier had been an *ex officio*
member of the great tribunal convoked in year 16 of Ramesses IX to
judge the tomb robbers. In the straitened circumstances of Dynasty
20 Egypt,[91] the tremendous resources commanded by their respective offices had enabled each of them to carve out a personal empire.

And, like two crocodiles in the same marsh, they ended by getting in one another's way, becoming rivals, and ultimately, entering into conflict with one another. The pretext could well have been control of the supplying of provisions. Panehsy received the title "overseer of the two granaries of Pharaoh,"[92] as would certain high military officers in the Third Intermediate Period,[93] and he was thus in control of the grain production on Upper Egyptian lands with a special administrative status. In the exercise of this office, he could not avoid encountering obstacles and entering into quarrels with the first prophet of the Temple of Amun, the largest landholding institution in this region. These two powerful men, whose respective influence made it impossible for them to get along with each other, must have encountered many opportunities to fan the flames of their discord. In any event, Panehsy bore so much animosity toward the first prophet that the outcome of the discord served as a milestone in the history of the lower classes:

> Pahti, a foreigner, seized me. He took me to Ipip at the time when Amenhotpe, who was first prophet of Amun, had been under attack for six months. I returned nine whole months later, after the aggression suffered by Amenhotpe, who was first prophet of Amun.[94]

Though the expression used here is somewhat imprecise, the verb *th* means "to attack," and it is clear that Amenhotpe was deposed from office for a time, as he himself acknowledges in an inscription from Karnak:

> [Panehsy] seized it (= my office); he exercised it for eight whole months, while I was in extreme distress from the fact (or, "from his deed").[95]

Amenhotpe complained not only to Amun, in accordance with the ideology of the times, but also to Pharaoh,[96] in the hope of getting a practical result. The king apparently ordered a general named Piankh to defend the pontiff and to punish his attacker. This happened at the price of a civil war about which we know almost nothing, except that the conflict even spread to Lower Egypt and that it brought its share of death and destruction. The funerary temple of Ramesses III, which was the administrative center of the west of Thebes, was taken by foreign troops, evidently Nubians from Panehsy's army. Panehsy, apparently wishing to pose as an honest administrator and a zealous defender of morality, arrested and punished some tomb robbers, thus pursuing a new policy of law and

A "King's Son of Kush" (here, Huy) is rewarded by his sovereign. Drawing by N. de Garis Davies.

order that had already been put in place, perhaps at the instigation of Amenhotpe himself.[97]

Having become a public enemy, and branded as such by a special hieroglyph in the writing of his name,[98] Panehsy was definitively defeated. Amenhotpe expressed his gratitude to Amun as follows: "He (i.e., Amun) attacked the one who had attacked me."[99]

But although Amenhotpe was restored to office, it was undoubtedly only for a short while—he was no longer a young man. In any event, the triumph of law and order—that is to say, of the interests of the temple of Amun—was not treated as merely a return to normal after a period of disorder, but as the advent of a new era, which was called the "Repeating of Births."[100] This era served as a reference point in official chronology, with its year 1 falling within year 19 of the reign of Ramesses XI. Although this new form of reckoning time scarcely exceeded year 10, after which it was replaced by the traditional count of the regnal years of the reigning pharaoh, its importance cannot be underestimated. Its intent was to stress a veritable modernization in the doctrine of power. Previously, Egyptians had believed that the creator god had delegated to Pharaoh, his earthly representative, the task of administering this world below, contenting himself with brief, sporadic interventions. Now, however, there was a doctrine of theocracy; from this time on, the god would rule

Here the Nubians are bringing tribute, but they were also formidable mercenaries in the pay of their governor. Drawing by N. de Garis Davies.

on earth directly, through the medium of oracles that had to be obeyed by Pharaoh, right down to his political program (see chapter 6).[101] Adherents of this ideological novelty sought practical ways to manifest it, even if that only meant restoring that which had been destroyed:

> The portable shrine had been taken and set on fire. When order was restored, the governor of the west of Thebes, the scribe of the white house, Pasmennakht, and the scribe of the army, Qashuty,[102] said, "Let us collect the pieces of wood, so that the people of the storehouses will not set fire to them!" The remainder was returned; it was caused that a seal be affixed to it, and it is intact today.[103]

Widespread Pillage

In general, as often happens, the restoration of civil order was accompanied by good resolutions, however ephemeral they might have been. Thus, efforts to mark the new era as a sort of moral renaissance touched off a major wave of proceedings against the pillagers of western Thebes in years 1 and 2 of the Repeating of Births, though the effort had begun half-heartedly at an earlier date (see note 97). Typical of the times, the reports regarding the preliminary investigation that led to the trials were presented to Pharaoh and his vizier by the governor of the west of Thebes, Pawero, the very man who, in the reign of Ramesses XI, had skillfully tried to cover up the extent of the robberies. Evidently, the moral spirit of the Repeating of Births had inspired him so deeply that he became the initiator of a crusade against theft! In any event, the commission appointed to conduct the proceedings consisted of the following high officials:

- the overseer of the city and vizier, Nebmaatrenahkt;
- the overseer of the white house of Pharaoh, l.p.h., and overseer of the two granaries, Menmaatrenakht;
- the steward and royal cupbearer, Yenes, the fan bearer of Pharaoh, l.p.h.;
- the steward and royal cupbearer, Pameryamun, the scribe of Pharaoh, l.p.h.[104]

Five administrative documents contain reports on the interrogations and lists of the persons who were implicated. Unfortunately, they are far from clear, for some of them alternate, and sometimes even interweave, depositions relating to different gangs.[105] Nevertheless, they enable us to evaluate the extent of the pillage.

First, the extent of time: the practices incriminated in years 1 and 2 (of the era) of Repeating of Births had been going on for a long time, in some cases even before the civil war. Several witnesses called to answer for the activities of their fathers, who were deceased or who had fled, stressed that they were children at the time. Here are examples:

> The pure priest Nesamun, son of Paybaki, was brought because of his father. . . . He was told, "Tell how your father set out with the men who were with him." He said, "My father was truly there, when I was a young child. I have no knowledge of how he acted."[106]

> The weaver of the house, Unnekh, son of Tatay, was brought. . . . He was told, "Tell how your father set out and seized the portable shrine with his accomplices!" He said, "I was (still) a child when my father was killed."[107]

Even if these witnesses had every interest in exaggerating their youth so as to exonerate themselves,[108] it is clear that the events transpired long before the inquiry. The punishment inflicted on those of the robbers from the time of Ramesses IX whom the authorities were pleased to punish,[109] along with the increased vigilance of officials whose awareness was heightened by the scandal, must have led only to a brief interruption of the pillaging,[110] however. In fact, the evidence indicates that the proceedings conducted in the new era merely settled some very old scores.

The geographical extent of the pillaging also appears to have been wide-ranging: certain clever thieves occasionally preferred to "delocalize" their field of activity, passing from Thebes, where they undoubtedly felt there was too much competition, to the larger area around the city:

> I was in the west of Iuemiteru[111] with Nesamun, who was chief of the
> Medjay. I was also in the west of Thebes with him. I was in the west of
> Hefau[112] with all the foreigners of Hefau.[113]

Moreover, as is necessary to the growth of any business, some
were able to introduce diversification into the thievery. In fact, the
proceedings revealed that the accused had various objectives. First,
there were the tombs of private individuals. These were often designated by the vague term "funerary monuments,"[114] and only exceptionally by the names of their owners.[115]

Second, there were the tombs in the Valley of the Queens. We have
seen how one thief, the shepherd Bukhaaf, entered the tomb of
Queen Isis (Ta-)Heberdjet, which had already been damaged in the
reign of Ramesses IX (see p. 14). Further, the indefatigable Bukhaaf
confessed to having added the tombs of two other queens to his list
of achievements:[116]

> He said, "I opened the tomb of the royal wife Nesimut." He said, "It is
> I who opened the tomb of the royal wife of King Menmaatre, l.p.h.,
> Bake(t)-werel."[117]

Queen Nesimut is not known from elsewhere. As for Bake(t)werel,
she is presented in this document as the wife of King Menmaatre—
that is, Ramesses XI.[118] A queen named Bake(t)werel had a chamber
made for herself in the tomb of King Amenmesse,[119] which was in
the Valley of the Kings.[120] Some scholars have thus made her the
wife or the mother of this pharaoh,[121] but in fact, she might postdate
him; however, this chamber could well have been reused,[122] which
makes her identification as the wife of Ramesses XI plausible. In this
case, the tomb violation would have occurred in the Valley of the
Kings, and in a tomb belonging to the wife of the reigning pharaoh.
Though this idea has been asserted, some Egyptologists[123] hold that
the Bake(t)werel, wife of Ramesses XI, mentioned in the report of the
interrogation of Bukhaaf is to be distinguished from the Bake(t)werel
of the Valley of the Kings, and that she would have had her tomb in
the Valley of the Queens.

Third, there was the Valley of the Kings. The robbers attacked not
only the tombs of queens, but also those of their august husbands.
Thus, robbers succeeded in penetrating into the tomb of Ramesses
VI after digging for four days.[124] The records of the proceedings that
have come down to us seem to fall short of reality, however. Such
records may reflect the usual hazards of documentation or a desire
to ameliorate the scandal at the point when it would have been the

most lively.[125] Or perhaps the pillage in the Valley of the Kings simply did not become extensive until after these proceedings.

Fourth, there was pillage in the funerary temples, to which we shall now turn.

Too Tempting Temples

Let us once again recall that the west bank of Thebes included not only tombs but also sanctuaries,[126] and in particular, funerary temples whose attraction lay not only in their cult furnishings but also in their decoration. In fact, however well preserved these temples may be, the modern visitor cannot fully appreciate the extraordinary richness of their original decoration. This is because a major component of the decoration has disappeared: the sheathing of precious metals—gold, silver, and copper—that covered many of the architectural elements, including columns, obelisks, and door frames.[127]

Such materials were certainly a stimulus to avarice. In fact, we have partial records of investigations and proceedings undertaken against persons who committed theft in the funerary temples of the west of Thebes. The main targets were evidently the two largest funerary temples, that of Ramesses II, today called the Ramesseum, and that of Ramesses III at the site of present-day Medinet Habu. Certain people treated these temples as reserves of precious metals to which they helped themselves according to the needs of the moment, somewhat like a modern ATM—except that they were not debiting their personal accounts! Here is an instructive example:

> Receipt of the deposition of the pure priest and gardener of the House,[128] Keri. Hearing his deposition. He was told, "Tell how you set out and took gold from the door frames,[129] along with your companions." He said, "The scribe of the temple Sedy set out with the pure priest and goldsmith Tuty for the frames; they removed one *deben* and three and a half *qite* of gold, which they took for the chief of the gang Pameniu. We did it again; we set out for the frames, and we took three *qite* of gold, when we were with the scribe of the temple Sedy, the pure priest Tetuy, and the pure priest Paysen, a total of four persons. We did it again; we set out for the frames with the scribe of the temple Sedy and the pure priest Nesamun, we took five *qite,* and we divided it up. We did it again; we set out for the frames with the pure priest Hori, son of Pakhar, the scribe of the temple Sedy, the pure priest Nesamun, for the frames once again. We took five *qite* of gold; we exchanged it for barley at Thebes, and we divided it up. After some days, the scribe of the temple Sedy came bringing three men who were with

him. They set out for the frames, they took four *qite* of gold, and we shared it with him. . . . Some days later, the pure priest Hori and the pure priest Tutuy left by night. They entered the house of gold and took a (piece) of gold from the frames. We got hold of it, and we delivered it to the scribe Sedy. He seized it, he had it melted, and he gave it to Pameniu."

He said, "The pure priest Tutuy and the pure priest Nesamun went to the double doorway of the sky. They saw the gleaming. They collected the gold. They took it with the scribe Sedy."

He said, "We went one more time to the frames; we went together, we three. We took three *qite* of gold, and we shared it, we three. Some days later, the scribe Sedy set out for the frames with the goldsmith Tutuy; they removed three *qite* of gold, and they carried it off."[130]

This simple game took a little patience, but it did not cost much—just a few scissor snips—and paid off handsomely. The reports on the investigation sometimes yield substantial figures. In the funerary temple of Ramesses III, robbers who dedicated themselves solely to the copper sheathing on the doors accumulated, from door leaf to door leaf, 1,100, 150, 222, and 1,200 *deben,* making a total of more than 535 pounds[131]—at that time, the equivalent of 2,915 bushels of barley.[132] A pure priest named Amenkhau removed 300 *deben* of silver (just over 60 pounds) and 89 *deben* of gold (about 17½ pounds), which amounted to the cost of 31,289 bushels of barley.[133]

The furnishings of the funerary temples proved no less rewarding. The robbers had a definite predilection for the naoi, the shrines that sheltered divine statues, and which, because of the sanctity of their content, were luxuriously wrought, being sheathed with gold or some other metal and framed with precious wood, a rare commodity in Egypt. The thieves also valued the variety of the portable naoi, which were designed to carry the divine statues during processions outside the temple during the many festivals that punctuated the calendar:

The sacristan[134] of the House of King Usermaatre-meryamun, l.p.h., in the domain of Amun, Ahautynefer, was brought in. He was told, "You are the doorkeeper of this place. Name every man you have seen entering this place after they appropriated the *ipt* of this portable naos." He said, "Bring in the carpenter Penpahut, so that he may tell you everything that happened to this portable naos of Ramessesnakht, who had been first prophet of Amun. As for those who did that, they were those who committed depredations on this portable naos of King Usermaatre-setepenre, l.p.h., the great god, and in the storehouse of King Menmaatre-Sethos, l.p.h."; thus he spoke. The carpenter Penpahut was brought in. He was made to swear by the Lord, l.p.h., under pain of being mutilated, not to lie. Hearing his deposition. He said, "The door-keeper Panefer sent the weaver Tatiy to me with this message: 'Come!' I set out for the place where he was, and he said to me, 'Do you want to go with Tatiy and take copper from the reliquary of Ramessesnakht, who had been first prophet of Amun?' I left with him. I met the weaver Tutuy, the weaver [. . .] his brother, the guardian of the barge Pataena-mun, the acolyte Wenenamun, son of Userhat, the scribe Djehutimose, son of Userhet, the scribe Hori, son of Seny, the chief of the gardeners Ptahemheb, the coppersmith Paysen, son of Amenher—he is dead—the scribe Paybaki, the deputy of the House Nesamun, and the pure priest Tata-the-younger, son of the divine father Hori, the total of the robbers being ten persons, eleven including me (lit., "I complete eleven"). They took some large stones and set to breaking the ends of the shafts of the portable naos of this first prophet of Amun."[135]

These portable naoi were in fact provided with long shafts from which much could be taken: not only the ringed reinforcements and the copper tips,[136] but also the wood itself:

> They took some large stones and set to breaking the ends of the shafts of the portable naos of this first prophet of Amun.[137] I said to them, "Don't ignore the wood," for they had cut the two ends of the middle shaft, the one in front, the other in the back. They broke the four other ends, six in all. It was the scribe Paybaki and the pure priest Tata-the-younger who stole the two copper rings of the shafts.[138]

Besides this portable naos dedicated by the high priest of Amun, two similar objects suffered this rapacious vandalism: one belonging to Ramesses II and the other to Sethos I.

Of course, temples offered many other delectable objects to these men of taste, and the investigations established, step by step, the depredations they committed on statues, vases, door frames and their complex door bolts,[139] trellises, vases, and even a throne.[140] The metal was melted down, and the wood was sometimes deliv-ered in the form of objects to be cut up. Getting wood was no com-plicated matter; one could simply send for it, as in this case of a "mail-order" sale:

> The scribe Aneru wrote to him again in these terms: "Have a naos of fir delivered to me." The scribe Sedy gave him a naos of fir that was two cubits high.[141]

Stolen from tombs, gold was melted down before being divided among the plunderers. Drawing by N. de Garis Davies.

Most often, the thieves salvaged boards with which a skilled artisan could make objects of the utmost necessity:

Report concerning the four boards of fir from the "silver floor"[142] of King Usermaatre-setepenre,[143] l.p.h., the great god, which the scribe Sedy gave to the citizeness Taherer, the wife of the divine father Hori. He gave them to the carpenter of the house of Huy, Ahuty, and he made her a sarcophagus out of them.[144]

We are struck by the apparent impudence with which the robbers acted. At best, the most cautious of them resorted to ruses that have always been used by servants everywhere, such as replacing the purloined valuable material with something that restored its original appearance:

The affair of the unguent vase of eighty-six *deben* of silver . . . It was the scribe of the treasury Sutekhmose, who was overseer of fields, who came. He took the unguent vase from the vizier's butlery that was in the House; he removed from it [. . .] *deben* of silver, and he carried them off. The divine fathers, the pure priests, and the lector priests of the House came back again, and they again seized the unguent vase. They removed [. . .] *deben* of silver from it; total, five *deben,* and thirty-six *deben* were left. It was given to the caretaker Pasero, and the unguent vase was repaired;[145] it was inscribed with the name of Pharaoh, l.p.h., and it was put back in place.[146]

Ineffective Measures

Under the last Ramessides, the cult equipment of the temples was disappearing on a daily basis. And, as the preceding example indicates, not only did the royal personnel show little concern; they were often the culprits! The reports of the investigations and trials from the reign of Ramesses XI give the impression of a nearly systematic sack of whatever could be fenced from the objects or precious materials in the west of Thebes, while the authorities remained passive, if they themselves were not participants. Yet, when trials were conducted, it was because certain persons had done their duty:

> This day of interrogating the thieves of the portable naos of the King of Upper and Lower Egypt Usermaatre-setepenre, l.p.h., the great god, and of the reliquary (?)[147] of King Menmaatre-Sethos, which had been placed in the white house[148] of the House of the King of Upper and Lower Egypt Usermaatre-meryamun, and about which the chief of the Medjay Nesamun had made a report, making a list of them. It was he who opposed the thieves there when they laid their hands on the portable naos. . . . The chief of the Medjay Nesamun was brought in. It was said to him, "How did you encounter these men?" He said, "I had heard that the men had gone to take the portable naos. I left, and I found the very six men whom the thief Pakamen had mentioned. I shall have to testify about them today."[149]

We would sing the praises of this Nesamun with more conviction, were we assured that his ethics had never been compromised. In fact, there are indications that his rigor sometimes changed to complaisance, if not complicity, with regard to thieves.[150] In any event, although the thefts took place during an extended period, this was not because the perpetrators were careful to keep the crimes hidden, but rather because the top authorities took their time in acting on the incriminating information that they could not have failed to receive. It took a political development, the beginning of the era of Repeating of Births, for the sporadic attempts at law enforcement to become systematic. From then on, investigations were carried out on a large scale, and with a certain care. This much is shown, for example, by lists of the accused, grouped not only according to the activities in which they were involved—tomb robbery or theft of portable naoi—but also according to their degree of involvement—recognized perpetrators, those accused of being accomplices, receivers of stolen goods—and according to their lot—discharged, fled, or already executed. There is even a special list of women who were imprisoned.[151]

In the last analysis, however, all this admirable zeal had little deterrent effect, for in year 6 of the Repeating of Births, four years after these trials, the royal mummies of Sethos I and Ramesses II were moved and put into the shelter of the famous cache[152] at Deir el-Bahari, which means that their tombs had been violated. Other mummies would follow them at the beginning of Dynasty 21.

The Sack of the West of Thebes: A Social Phenomenon

The Social Class of the Thieves

We cannot overestimate the scope of these thefts, which deserve to be called affairs of state. But their quasipolitical or quasihistorical dimensions should not obscure the light they shed on the society within which the events transpired. The colorful world of the thieves emerges from the archives that these affairs produced.

A basic question: just who were these robbers? The bureaucratic minutiae of the pharaonic state permit an answer, for lists of robbers were drawn up and reproduced many times in the official documents, with changes that were imposed by the development of the inquiry. Here, we shall analyze three such lists, which supply a highly representative sample of the information at our disposal.

The first list enumerates "the eight thieves who had been in the pyramid," that is, of Sebekemzaf, in the theft from the reign of Ramesses IX:

> Amenpanefer, son of Inhernakht, quarryman of the domain of Amun-Re, king of the gods, under the authority of the first prophet of Amun-Re, king of the gods, Amenhotpe.
>
> Hapywer, son of Merneptah, quarryman of the House of Usermaatre-meryamun, l.p.h., in the domain of Amun, under the authority of this second prophet of Amun-Re, king of the gods and *setem*-priest of the said House, Nesamun.
>
> The carpenter of the House of Usermaatre-meryamun, l.p.h., in the domain of Amun, Sethnakht, son of Penanukis, under the authority of the second prophet of Amun-Re, king of the gods, and *setem*-priest of this House in the domain of Amun, Nesamun.
>
> The fashioner of precious metals, Hapyo, of the domain of Amun-Re, king of the gods, son of [. . .], under the authority of this first prophet of Amun.

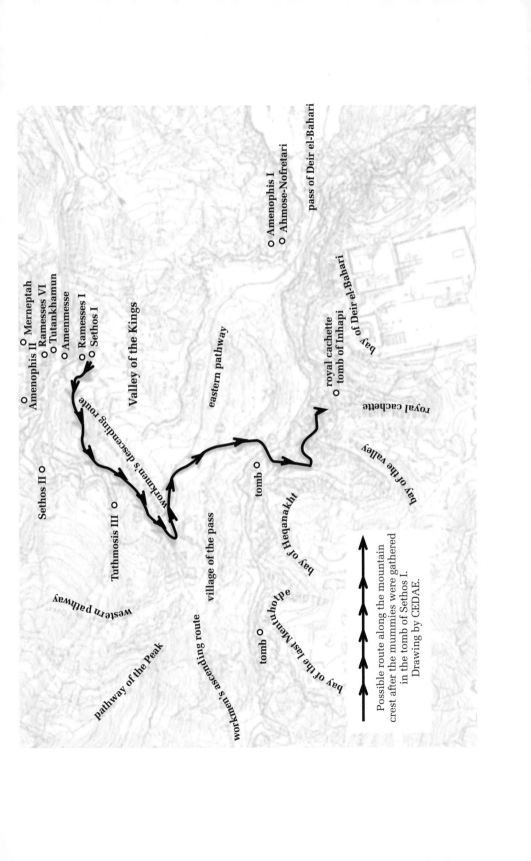

Amenophis I
Ahmose-Nofretari

pass of Deir el-Bahari

Merneptah
Ramesses VI
Tutankhamun
Amenophis II
Amenmesse
Ramesses I
Sethos I

royal cachette
tomb of Inhapi

bay of Deir el-Bahari

Valley of the Kings

royal cachette

Sethos II

eastern pathway

bay of the valley

workmen's descending route

tomb

Tuthmosis III

bay of Heqanakht

western pathway

village of the pass

tomb

pathway of the Peak

workmen's ascending route

bay of the last Menkhotpe

Possible route along the mountain
crest after the mummies were gathered
in the tomb of Sethos I.
Drawing by CEDAE.

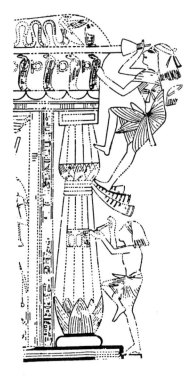

Two of the plunderers of the tomb of Sebekemzaf were carpenters. Drawing by N.
de Garis Davies.

The carpenter of the overseer of hunters of the domain of Amun-Re,
king of the gods, Nesamun, Iirienimen.

The cultivator of the domain of Amenemope, Amenemheb,[153] who
is assigned to the isle of Amenemope, under the authority of this first
prophet of Amun.

The choachyte of the palanquin of King Menkheprure, l.p.h.,[154]
Khaemwese, under the authority [. . .]

Ahanefer, son of Nekhemmut, who had been entrusted to the Nubian slave[155] of this first prophet of Amun, Telimen.[156]

As could have been expected, these robbers were from Thebes and
worked on either the east or the west bank, or even on an island that
was probably situated between the two locales. Most of them
worked for top-ranking institutions, the domain of Amun and the funerary temple of Ramesses III; only one of them was attached to a
lower-ranking funerary temple, that of Tuthmosis IV,[157] in the position of choachyte, a servant whose job was to pour libations.[158]
Thus, with the exception of this robber and Ahanefer, who seems to
have been a simple laborer assigned to a servant, they were all artisans possessing skills that were highly useful in their "second job."

They included two "quarrymen,"[159] and official reports state that certain tombs had been violated specifically by quarrying. By the same token, the skills of a carpenter or of a fashioner of precious materials,[160] or even a cultivator's basic ability to ply a hoe would have been useful for the job of plundering the rock-cut tombs.

The second list names "robbers of the necropolis"[161] who were tried during the reign of Ramesses XI and the era of Repeating of Births:

> List of the men who denounced[162] the shepherd (of the domain of Amun) Bukhaaf, saying that they were in his gang of thieves.
>
> The workman Pawerkhetef, son of Hor-Min.
>
> The scribe of divine writing, Nesamun.
>
> The acolyte (of the domain of Amun), Shedsukhons.
>
> The acolyte (of the domain of Amun), Nesamun, surnamed Tjyby.
>
> Amenkhau, son of the singer of the altar, Hori.
>
> The acolyte Ankhefenkhons.
>
> The young slave Amenkhau, son of Mutemheb (songstress of the domain of Mut).[163]
>
> The foreigner Userhat(nakht), under the authority of the overseer of hunters of Amun. He is in the disposition of the governor of Thebes.
>
> The sailor of the domain of Amun, Pawero.
>
> The surveyor of the domain of Amun, Pawero, son of Qaqa.
>
> The surveyor Paaemtaumet.
>
> The trumpet player (of the domain of Amun) Perpatjau(emope).
>
> Total: thirteen men.[164]

For the most part, the members of this gang were recruited from the minor personnel of the domain of Amun. Some of them were probably united by family ties. The gang consisted not only of persons employed in agricultural activities, but also of technicians occupied with subsidiary cult activities: acolytes, trumpet player, and especially, scribe of divine writing, a literate person specializing in religious texts. We note with interest the presence of Pawerkhetef, a workman—that is, one of the workers engaged in preparing the tomb of the reigning pharaoh. These workmen devoted their efforts to the tombs of the queens and kings, and he used his knowledge of the terrain in suggesting and planning the break-ins. Bukhaaf swore, "It was Pawer, a man of the gang of (the institution of) the Tomb, who showed us the tomb of the royal wife (Ta-)Heberdjet."[165] We have every reason to believe that the name Pawer is here an abbreviation of Pawerkhetef.[166] He acted exactly like the workman Panefer, a member of another gang at that time: " 'It is I who showed you the tomb'; so said the son of[167] Panefer, this workman, to the shepherd Ihymeh."[168]

The third list is taken from the deposition of a thief implicated in the depredations of the portable naos of Ramesses II and the receptacle (?)[169] of Sethos I, which were stored in the treasury of the Ramesseum:

> The foreigner Pakamen, under the authority of the overseer of the cattle of Amun, was brought in. He was made to swear an oath by the Lord, l.p.h., not to speak falsely. It was said to him, "In what way did you set out with the men who were with you, and did you take the portable naoi of the kings, which had been placed in the white house of the House of King Usermaatre-meryamun, l.p.h.?" He said, "I went with the pure priest Tata-the-younger, son of the divine father of the House, Hori, (with) Pabaki of this same domain, son of Nesamun, (with) the foreigner of the domain of Montu lord of Hermonthis, Nesumontu, (with) the foreigner Panehsy, son of Tjat, who had been divine father of Sobek of Perankh,[170] (with) Tety, a man belonging to Panehsy, son of Tjat, who had been divine father of Sobek of Perankh, six (persons) in all."[171]

This was a more heterogeneous band, for along with persons working at Thebes, we encounter two men[172] from Hermonthis, a city near Thebes whose god was Montu, as well as a "foreigner" who worked in a small provincial town in Upper Egypt. The presence of employees of the funerary temple of Ramesses III was to be expected, for the band was prosecuted for having rampaged in this edifice.

Study of the social status of the robbers, not only in these three lists, but also in all of the information at our disposal, reveals an extremely important fact: these thieves were employed, if only in subordinate positions, by the institutions, departments, and domains that constituted the "pharaonic state." Some of them were servants. More belonged to the lower and middle clergy—pure priests, divine fathers, *setem*-priest, scribe of the divine book—or to the temple administration. More exceptionally, they were employees of government departments, such as a scribe of the army or a scribe of the white house, or an overseer of fields.[173] Among those who participated directly in the robberies, few were high officials; nevertheless, the leader of one of the gangs that pillaged the royal tombs was Iufenamun, a prophet of Montu, "the personnel of Montu being under his control," as one of the accused specified.[174] The thieves included a number of "foreigners,"[175] but these foreigners were entirely integrated into Egyptian society, often bearing Egyptian names and working in the institutions of pharaonic Egypt. One of them was even "divine father" in a temple of Sobek.

On the whole, the robbers were recruited from the middle and lower classes. They were mostly ordinary people, to be sure, but not unemployed, nor were they marginal individuals or outcasts, and they were certainly not brigands by trade.[176]

The Robbers' Motives

Why did these people take the risk of being cruelly punished?[177] In some instances, it was simply a desire for gain, so as to assure a comfortable life. Such was the case with Bukhaaf, the head of a gang of plunderers; a humble shepherd, he bought himself some luxury fabric, two cows, and a few acres of land.[178] The no less humble brewer of the domain of Re on the terrace of Amun, Nespare,[179] suddenly bought himself some land and a maidservant; these purchases, which were a bit too ostentatious, did not fail to attract the attention of the investigators:

> Tell us the story of the *deben* of gold that you gave to the prophet of Montu in exchange for this land, and of the four *deben* of silver that you gave in exchange for this servant.[180]

He pretended that he had acquired the silver from the Libyan Meshwesh who were marauding in the region from time to time. Evidently, he reckoned that no one was going to seek confirmation from the Meshwesh!

Indiscreet purchases were also made by the servants of Panehsy, the former divine father of Sobek, and by the gardener Kel. Their wives were much embarrassed when they were interrogated regarding the origin of these signs of wealth. One of these women chose to evade the judges' questions:

> The citizeness Irynefer, wife of the foreigner Panehsy, son of Tjat was brought in. . . . It was said to her, "What do you have to say about the silver that Panehsy, your husband, brought to you?" She said, "I did not see (it)." The vizier said to her, "How did you and he acquire the servants?" She said, "I did not see silver. It was when he was taking one of his trips that he acquired them."[181]

The wife of another man offered an explanation so unconvincing that it seems incredible she imagined the judges would believe her:

The profaners of the royal tombs could be ordinary gardeners. Drawing by N. de Garis Davies.

> The scribe Djehutimose said to her, "How did you acquire the slaves[182] whom you acquired?" She said, "If I acquired them, it was in exchange for produce from my garden."[183]

She was in fact not believed, and the vizier summoned her slave to confute her testimony.

For others, their loot enabled them to enjoy one of those pleasurable moments that life can bring:

> I heard, when I was imprisoned with the warehouseman Iufenamen, that the silver had been given to Nespare in exchange for beer.[184]
>
> The thief Amenkhau gave one *deben* and five *qite* of silver to the acolyte Paenimentet in exchange for a measure of honey; the incense preparer Paenimentet said that he gave him (= Amenkhau) another measure of honey, and Amenkhau, the thief, gave him in exchange one *deben* and five *qite* of silver.[185] Total: three *deben* of silver.[186]
>
> The thief, the young slave Amenkhau son of Mutemheb, gave five *qite* of silver to the scribe of the overseer of the domain of Amun Aasheftemwese in exchange for a [. . .] of wine; we took it to the house of the overseer of peasants; we added two *hin* of honey to it and we drank it.[187]

That much said, the motives were often more basic. We have already stressed the economic problems of the time and the inability of the institutions[188] of the pharaonic state to pay their employees on a regular basis. Starvation occurred, and one witness evoked "the year of the hyena, when one was hungry."[189] Another witness recounted, "I remained seated, starving, under the sycamores."[190]

Market scene. Not having coinage as a means of exchange, the Egyptians practiced barter. Drawing by N. de Garis Davies.

Moreover, during their interrogation, some of the accused justified their misdeeds by attributing them to necessity:

> This sarcophagus is ours; it belonged to our great men. We were hungry; we set out and brought it back.[191] As for me, I am a cultivator of the domain of Amun. The citizeness (Nesmut) came to the place where I was. She said to me, "Some men have found something that permits the purchase of some bread. Come, let us share the profits with them"; so she said to me.[192] They said to me, "Go. Leave with us to search for this piece of cake,[193] so as to profit from it."[194]

Bellies were in fact so empty that the thieves often hastened to exchange the fruit of their larceny for grains, which were the basic food staple:

> They brought me two rings of copper. They gave them to me and to Qer. I gave him a sack and a quarter of emmer wheat and an eighth of a sack of *iky*-grain in exchange. I saw (nothing) more.[195]

> I gave some three sacks of barley to the carpenter of (the institution of) the Tomb, Panefer. He gave me two *qite* of silver.[196]

> I gave a little barley to the workman Panefer. He gave me two *qite* of silver.

> I took my husband's share and I put it in my storehouse. I took a *deben* of silver from it, and I purchased *ss*-grain with it.[197]

Theft was thus the ultimate recourse in the face of arrears in wages from the state, when the latter was unable to provide sustenance to those whom it employed. Theft was also the ultimate recourse against the repressive powers of the authorities, when the latter threatened those who were denouncing those arrears a bit too energetically.[198]

The Modus Operandi of the Thieves

The thieves were organized into bands of roughly a dozen members, centered on men who were united by family[199] or professional ties. They often acted on suggestions from a member who was in a position to find good places to pillage. Their *modus operandi* evidently differed according to their target, for stealing furnishings and architectural sheathing from temples required different techniques from those employed to pillage rock-cut tombs. The former case has been illustrated in detail on pages 25–27. But the information from the judicial inquiries regarding the *modus operandi* of the robbers who ravaged the cemeteries deserves further examination, particularly because it enhances the information furnished by archaeology.[200]

Violating a rock-cut tomb was an extremely difficult job, for it required digging and clearing, whether the thieves were tunneling to reach the interior or clearing the entrance: "I spent four days clearing[201] while we five were there; we opened the tomb, and we entered it."[202]

Under such conditions, remaining inconspicuous was difficult. The west bank of Thebes was not a desert. People lived in houses built there, prayed in the innumerable sanctuaries and chapels, and worked in funerary temples and administrative centers that were veritable beehives humming with activity. A system of fortified guard posts[203] enabled the Medjay, the police, to assure surveillance: "I served as a Medjay of the west of Thebes, guarding the recesses of its great place."[204]

However isolated the Valley of the Kings and the Valley of the Queens might have been, people went there,[205] if only the workers of (the institution of) the Tomb, who labored on the rock-cut tombs of the reigning pharaoh and his wife. But these workers hardly constituted an impenetrable rampart; indeed, many of them were connected with the robbers, in differing degrees ranging from careful neutrality to total complicity. Security was further compromised by workers' reasons for not reporting for work at construction sites[206] and by the existence of radical means of getting rid of those who would prevent the pillaging:

> The foreigner Nesamun led us up, and he showed us the tomb of King Nebmaatre-meryamun, l.p.h., the great god. We said to him, "Where is the native of (the area of) the Tomb[207] who had been with you (lit., "him")?" He said to us, "[One] has (or, "[I] have") killed the native of (the area of) the Tomb, along with the little servant who had been with us, so he would not keep us out";[208] so he said to us.[209]

Let us suppose, then, that the troublemakers were done away with, and, because their depositions enable us to follow the plunderers at work, let us do so, though for the most part, we must resign ourselves to contemplating only deplorable results. By way of examples, here are two accounts of the violation of the tomb of King Sebekemzaf. We can profit by comparing them.

The Pillaging According to the Official Report

The first account reflects the official point of view, because it emanated from the authorities who made the official report:

> (The complex of) the pyramid of King Sekhemre-shedtawy, l.p.h., the son of Re Sebekemzaf, l.p.h. It was found that robbers had profaned it by a work of quarrying into the heart of his pyramid, beginning from the outside courtyard of the tomb of the overseer of the granaries of King Menkheperre,[210] l.p.h., Nebamun. The burial chamber of the king was found void of its owner, l.p.h., along with the burial chamber of the great royal wife Nubkhaes, l.p.h., because the robbers had laid their hands on them. The vizier, the dignitaries, and the cupbearers made an inquiry into this matter. The manner in which the robbers had laid their hands on them, on the king and his wife, was identified.[211]

The Pillaging According to One of the Robbers

The second account was made by a robber in the course of his interrogation:

I joined the [carpenter] of the House of Usermaatre-meryamun, l.p.h., in the domain of Amun,[212] Sethnakht, son of Penanukis, under the authority of the second prophet of Amun-Re, king of the gods, and the *setem*-priest of the House of Usermaatre-meryamun in the domain of Amun, Nesamun; the decorator of the domain of Amun, Hapyo; the cultivator of the domain of Amenemope, Amenemheb, under the authority of the first prophet of Amun-Re, king of the gods; the carpenter of the overseer of hunters of Amun, Iirymen; the choachyte of the palanquin of King Menkheprure, l.p.h., in Thebes, Kaemwese; the ferryman of the governor of Thebes, Ahay son of Tjery; total, eight men. We left to commit thefts in the funerary monuments in the manner to which we quite regularly conformed. We found that (the complex of) the pyramid of King Sekhemre-shedtawy, l.p.h., the son of Re Sebekemzaf, l.p.h., was not on the same model as (the complexes of) the pyramid and the funerary monuments of the dignitaries where we habitually went to commit thefts. We took our picks of copper and we broke into the pyramid of this king in search of its innermost part. We found its lower apartment; we took lit torches in our hands; we descended; we removed the backfill that we found at the entry to its niche. We found the god (= the dead pharaoh) lying in his grave. We found the grave of the royal wife Nubkhas, may she live, his royal wife, in the space beside him, protected and preserved in plaster and covered with backfill; we immediately removed it, and we found her there, reposing in the same manner. We opened their sarcophagi and their coffins, in which they were. We found the august mummy of this king provided with a scimitar, while a great number of amulets and gold jewels were on his neck, his mask on him, and that the venerable mummy of this king was entirely covered with gold, his coffins were accented with silver within and without and encrusted with every sort of august precious stone. We collected the gold that we found on this august mummy of this god, as well as the amulets and jewels which were on his neck and the coffins in which he rested. We found the royal wife in exactly the same condition; we also collected everything we found on her. We set fire to their coffins; we took their accessories, which we found with them and which consisted of utensils of silver and copper. We made a division among ourselves; we made eight shares of the gold we had found on these two gods, and on their mummies, amulets, jewels, and coffins, so that twenty *deben* of gold fell to each of the eight, which makes 160 *deben* of gold, not counting the smashed equipment. We crossed over toward Thebes.[213]

Of course, attempts have been made to find some trace of the robbers at the site itself. Unfortunately, the area had been disturbed by so many visitors, (dare we say) spiritual heirs of Amenpanefer, that no identification could be confirmed. We are not even sure that the pyramid of the complex of Sebekemzaf has been found![214] In any event, the thieves were so experienced that they were able to observe that the pharaoh's complex was not conceived on the usual model. Their experience also led them to divide the spoils immediately. Thus, there was no suspicion, no after-the-fact disputes.

A Tricky Moment: Dividing the Spoils

As we can easily imagine, the division of the loot was as tricky as the looting that preceded it. In principle, each participant had a right to an equal amount, but the one who had suggested the target could legitimately (if we dare use that term) claim a double share:

> We opened the place. We removed a shroud of gold and one *deben* of silver. We tore it up; we placed it in a basket; we brought it down.[215] We divided it up; we made six shares. We gave two shares to Amenkhau, son of the singer of the altar Hori, because he said, "It is I who suggested the job (lit., "who stretched out your hands")." That left us four shares for the four of us as well.[216]

Dividing the loot could, of course, occasion disputes:

> The shepherd Ihymeh came out. They made me go into a storehouse. I lent an ear to what they said,[217] as they quarreled over a sum of money[218] in these terms: "You have wronged me!" said one of them to his companion.[219]

A cross-checking indicates that the quarrel had to do with the fact that the man who had suggested the target felt he had been insufficiently rewarded:

> They stood looking at one another, speaking in these terms: "I have been wronged about the money," said one of them, addressing one of his companions, "for it is I who showed you the necropolis."[220]

Since these people were not exactly scrupulous, each of them had an interest in keeping a careful watch over the division his accomplices were making. Disputes occurred frequently:

> "The division you have made with me is not good, given that you are taking three shares and giving me only one";[221] so I said to him. We made an estimate of the silver we found; it was three *deben* of silver.

He gave me one *deben* and five *qite,* and he took one *deben* and five *qite;* total, [three *deben*] of silver.[222]

In addition to the problems inherent in human nature, the thieves confronted a more technical one. The loot often consisted of objects and fragments of metal and precious materials. If it was a small amount, it could be immediately exchanged for an easily divisible product such as grain: "We took five *qite* of gold; we exchanged it for barley at Thebes, and we shared it."[223]

Circumstances did not always permit so quick an outcome. When possible, whatever constituted the loot was divided into equal shares:

> They divided a "sum of money";[224] they made it into four parts, ten *deben* of silver, two *deben* of gold, two rings falling to each of them. I took my husband's share, and I put it in my storehouse.[225]

But often the booty could not be divided in the form in which it existed. Its value then had to be assessed; the unit of reckoning was the *deben* (about 3.21 ounces) of silver. This was not a coin, however, and the assessment was thus not represented by standardized material objects; the division entailed a hypothetical aspect. While waiting for the loot, which was hidden in a safe place,[226] to be melted down or exchanged, each member of the gang thought not in terms of a concrete portion, but rather of an abstract share of the whole, whose volume, valued in *deben* of silver, was represented by a stone "weight"[227] that was placed in the care of a trustworthy individual:

> He left us four shares for us four, also. Their stone weight is here today, left in the possession of the citizeness Nesmut, the concubine of the trumpet player Perpatjau. When the sister of Mutemwia, the wife of Perpatjau, went to the place where Bukhaaf was, she said to him, "They left to look for the money." The shepherd Bukhaaf came with the scribe of the divine book, Nesamun; the measurer Pauo; the sailor Pawero; the surveyor Paaemtawemet, son of Qaqa; and Amenkhau, son of Mutemheb; total, six men. They went to seek the stone weight in the possession of the citizeness Nesmut, the wife of the trumpet player Perpatjau. They received their four shares. They took them.[228]

This stone weight did not represent an algebraic share of a standard unit, but rather the result of a specific act of weighing that was carried out under a precise set of circumstances. That is to say, there were many possible fluctuations with regard to its nominal value.

Such fluctuations could be exploited, if only to reduce the bribes that certain persons demanded as the price for their silence:

> One gave to the scribe Tata-the-younger and to the chief of porters Pakauempaweba, and if we gave to them, it was a little weight of stone with which we gave to them, it was not the large stone with which we made the division.[229]

Thus, by determining the value with a stone weight that was smaller than the one used for dividing the spoils, the robbers robbed those who were robbing them.[230]

Troublemakers and Profiteers

Thievery was no easy task; constant care was needed, for the robbers had to evade the vigilance of authorities in order to ransack temples and tombs. Much more to be feared, however, was the greed of acquaintances, colleagues, and superiors who intended to profit from the goods so dishonestly acquired after hours of sordid labor. Here is a typical precaution of a workman from Deir el-Medina claiming his share:

> Come outside, I'm going to give you this stash (lit., "this bread"), and you'll take my due out of it, but don't give me more than is coming to me, so that my colleagues, employees of (the institution of) the Tomb, won't ask me questions.[231]

He had good reason to distrust those around him. In fact, it was distrust that caused certain prudent robbers to take the initiative and to buy the silence of witnesses at the outset:

> When my father made the crossing to the island of Amenemope, he found a coffin in the possession of the pure priest of the palanquin of King Menkheprure, l.p.h., Hapy, and of the pure priest of this same domain, Kaemwese. They said to him, "The coffin is ours; it belonged to our great men. We were hungry; we set out and we brought it back. Keep silent! We'll give you a kilt"; so they said to him. They gave him a kilt.[232] My mother said to him, "You're an old fool! What you have done is committing robbery": so she said to him.

Here, the robbers bribed the innocent old man who ferried them across, and his wife berated him because she was either honest or simply afraid. More often, the robbers were blackmailed by those who learned of their misdeeds by chance or by reason of their professional activities:

> Then, some days later, the foreigner Pais set out for the home of the foreigner Nesamun. He found the objects there on the floor, and he seized them. The foreigner Nesamun wrote to me, saying, "Come!" for the foreigner Pais was living with me (lit., "him").[233] The foreigner Pais said to him, "As for the silver objects you found, if you don't give me some of them, I'll go and tell it to the governor of the west and to the caretakers"; so he said to us. We cajoled him, saying, "We'll take you to the place where [we] found [it], and you will take for yourself, as well"; so we said to him.[234]

> It was said to him, "What do you have to say about the pieces of copper that you took from the upper door of the stone massif of Elephantine?"
> He said, "The followers [of the overseer] of cattle came to us. We set out for the gate; we took 40.5 *deben* of copper from it. Then, while we were there dividing it up, the follower Nakhtamenwese arrived; he took seven *deben* of copper; the foreigner Ptahkhau arrived; he took four *deben* of copper; and the apprentice pure priest Paher seized half (a *deben*) of copper. Twenty-nine *deben* were left to us; we divided it among us."[235]

As always, the more highly placed the racketeers, the more costly and imperious were the demands to which the thieves had to submit:

> Some days later, Pameniu, our superior, took us aside, saying, "You never give me anything!" We set out for the frames;[236] we took five *qite* of gold from them; we exchanged them for an ox.[237] We gave it to Pameniu. The scribe of the royal book, Sethmose, learned of it, and he took us aside, saying, "I am going to make a report to the first prophet." We took three *qite* of gold. We gave them to the scribe of the royal book, Sethmose. We pulled another job. We set out, and we gave him a *qite* and a half of gold. Total of the gold that was given to the scribe of the royal book, Sethmose: four and a half *qite* of gold.[238]

Learning that their immediate supervisor had blackmailed the robbers, a dignitary decided that he, too, would practice extortion on them. But there was a difference between the two: the second man contented himself with a share of the gold taken from the door frames, while the first had demanded that his share of the gold be realized in the form of an ox, or on another occasion, that it be melted

Gold and cattle were an essential part of wealth. Drawing by N. de Garis Davies.

down,[239] which was undoubtedly less compromising in case of an inquiry.[240]

Besides the greed of their superiors, the robbers also had to fear their own accomplices once the spoils were divided:

Some days later, Amenkhau, son of Mutemheb, came with the scribe of the divine book Nesamun. They said to me, "Give (us) this money." He was with Amenkhau, my own brother. They said, "Give (us) this money." I confidently said to them, "My brother will not cause me to be the object of reproaches";[241] so said I. Amenkhau hit me on the shoulder with a lance, and I fell down. I got up and went into my storehouse. I went to look for the money. I gave it to him, along with the two *deben* of gold and the two rings, one of genuine lapis-lazuli and the other of turquoise, and which amounted to a quantity of six *qite* of fine gold in the settings and the bezels.[242]

Taking advantage of the absence or death of one of their own, the thieves would not hesitate to rough up his wife in order to recoup his share. Here, we have a blatant example of the violent behavior that crops up sporadically in the depositions.[243] In the dog-eat-dog world of the thieves, it was important to be on one's guard so as to earn interest on one's cash before spending it.

Spending the Loot

Spending the loot was in no way as easy as we might think, at the very least because there were people who were honest—or careful people who chose to cancel a transaction if there was reason to doubt the origin of the payment. The following anecdote is evidence of this phenomenon; we have two versions, which we cite here one after the other:

> I gave a little barley to the workman Panefer. He gave me two *qite* of silver. I noted that they were suspect, and I set out to return them to him.[244]

> I gave some three sacks of barley to the carpenter of (the institution of) the Tomb, Panefer. He gave me two *qite* of silver. I disputed them with him, saying, "This is bad!" I did not come to an agreement[245] with him (?).[246]

What the witness disputed was of course not the physical quality of the metal, but rather its origin.

Fortunately for the robbers, such reactions were the exception, and we have a long list of those who accepted what the thieves had to exchange without quibbling over what they had to offer, undoubtedly on advantageous terms.[247] By a paradox of Egyptology, we have rich documentation on this topic, about which sources otherwise tend to be silent. This is because the judicial authorities used bastinados, thrashings, and other tortures to force the thieves to indicate precisely where the goods they stole had ended up.[248] Special reports[249] often included detailed notations that recapitulated what had already been found in the possession of the guilty parties and inventoried what they had spent and to whom they had given it. Here is an example referring to a thief whom we have already noted:

> Acquaintances[250] to whom Bukhaaf's share of the valuable goods[251] was paid:
> He said:
> "The servant of the domain of Amun, Pakenny: two *deben* of silver.
> "The overseer of fields of the domain of Amun, Akhmenu: one *deben* of silver and two *qite* of gold in exchange for land.
> "What was given to him by the hand of Amenkhau, son of Mutemheb: two *deben* of silver.
> "What was given to him by the hand of the shepherd Bukhaaf: two oxen.

The bastinado was a frequent punishment. Drawing by N. de Garis Davies.

"The scribe of the domain of Amun, Amenhotpe, surnamed Seret: two *deben* of silver in exchange for land; forty *deben* of copper; ten sacks of barley.

"The servant Shedpabag, in exchange for the slave Dega: two *deben* of silver; sixty *deben* of copper, thirty sacks of emmer wheat—it was in exchange for silver that I had obtained them; sixteen [. . .] shawls of fine fabric of Upper Egypt, eight cubits wide by four cubits; two smooth kilts.

"The groom Khonsmose, son of Tairy: five *qite* of silver.

"The goldsmith who lived in the *sr:* five *qite* of gold.

"The servant of Pabakbin, Nesamun: five *qite* of gold.

"Nesmut, the wife of Panehsy: five *deben* of gold."[252]

Study of all these documents reveals that the robbers evidently turned mostly to nearby acquaintances living or working in the west of Thebes or on the east bank. Still, one point merits comment. In the enumerations of the people whom the thieves paid with their booty, we are struck by the large number of individuals designated as *shuty* (*šwty*), "brokers," who were often attached to persons or institutions far from Thebes: the domain of Sobek-Shedty in the Faiyum,[253] the domain of Ptah at Memphis,[254] the chief of the Tuher of the office of Mermeshaf at Herakleopolis,[255] Merwer (Kom Medinet Ghurab) at the entrance to the Faiyum,[256] and the domain of Khnum, lord of Elephantine.[257] In fact, a special rubric is devoted to them in one document:

Total of the gold and silver recovered from the brokers after the robbers of the necropolis gave them to them.[258]

This title "broker," which Egyptologists have conventionally translated as "merchant," which is a serious misrendering, does not refer
to independent shopkeepers, but rather to employees whose role
was to negotiate in-kind exchanges of products or materials, or even
of slaves.[259] This role was all the more important in that, for lack of
coinage, the balance of deficits and surpluses had to be effected by
means of barter.[260] For this reason, these "brokers" made excellent
go-betweens.

Apparently, the fact of having accepted goods stemming from the
results of the robberies was not considered to be an act of wrongdoing when it was a matter of transactions:

> The overseer of peasants Akhmenu was brought in. It was said to him,
> "What do you have to say about the 'money' that Bukhaaf said he gave
> you?" He said, "I received five *qite* of gold, one *deben* of silver, and
> two oxen from Bukhaaf. I received two *deben* of silver from the hands
> of Amenkhau son of Mutemheb." Total in his hands: five *qite* of gold,
> three *deben* of silver, and two oxen. He was set free. The vizier said,
> "Return this 'money' to us." He said, "I shall return it."[261]

The records show that this deposition tallies with the inventory of
the booty spent by Bukhaaf and that Akhmenu was set free with the
sole obligation of returning what had come from the theft, the "dirty
money," as it were. But those who had received this dirty money in
the role of passive accomplices, rather than as receivers of stolen
goods, were placed in a particular category in the enumeration of
persons incriminated:

> Men who received amounts of silver when people took to theft.
> (But) they did not go (to the places where the thefts took place):
> The scribe Tata-the-younger, son of Khaemwese.
> The singer of the altar, Pakaempaweba.
> Total: two men.[262]

Theft as Recycling of Assets

From thieves to passive accomplices and specialized inter-
mediaries to unknowing receivers of stolen goods, the chain of theft
contained many links. Thus, the eight thieves from the Valley of the
Queens enumerated no fewer than a hundred receivers of stolen
goods, in the broad sense of the term, in their depositions, which

were set down in year 17 of Ramesses IX; again, this was a matter solely of persons to whom they had given only a part of the copper from their loot.[263] In other words, this example, along with other convergent data, suggests a wide distribution of stolen objects and materials. On a more general level, the plunder of the west of Thebes appears to have been a veritable factor bearing on what we may call, *mutatis mutandis,* the "economy." These riches, which had been accumulated by the imperialism of the New Kingdom and which religious beliefs had doomed to remain immobilized in consecrated temples and tombs, were put back into circulation by the theft. Of course, a part of the loot was recovered by the forces of law and order when they decided to strike, and undoubtedly it ended by being reused in temples and tombs after a long bureaucratic odyssey.[264] But even if it was ephemeral or episodic, this availability of precious goods did not fail to bring new life to exchanges that were often weakened by the dysfunction of the institutions that constituted the state. In a way, the sack of the west of 'Thebes permitted the recycling into daily life of assets that ideology had confiscated, so to speak, in its hieratic realizations.

2

The Strikes

The Institution of the Tomb

From antiquity to the present, pharaonic Egypt often has been hailed as the archetype of civilization, the land where human culture had its beginnings. Although much of that reputation is well deserved, such an image also is vulnerable to hyperbole. In any case, an exhaustive inventory has yet to be made of the aspects of our modern world that originated or at least already existed in the shadow of the pyramids. The present chapter makes a modest contribution to such an inventory by showing that in addition to the charming practices that brightened their daily life, the Egyptians set the stage for another modern endeavor: they knew how to go out on strike.

Again, the scene is New Kingdom Thebes, its west bank, and the royal necropolis. In this period, there were no royal pyramids. The pharaohs[1] had established a topographical separation of the two basic elements of their funerary monuments, the actual burial place, where the mummy rested, and the funerary temple, where rituals were carried out to maintain them. The latter was erected in the plain, along the strikingly abrupt line that separates the arable fields and the *gebel* (the uncultivated area); the former was placed in a depression that extends into the western plateau, the Valley of the Kings. Preparing the funerary monuments was no small matter. Every pharaoh began the job as soon as he ascended the throne. An appropriate site had to be chosen with care, after which came the digging of a descending corridor, sometimes more than a hundred

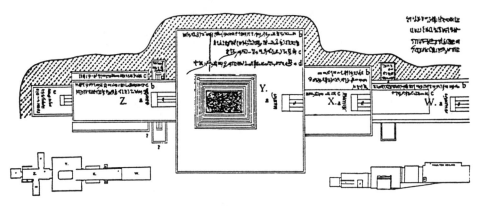

Plan of the tomb of Ramesses IV, as preserved on a papyrus in Turin. Drawing by E. Hornung.

yards in length,[2] that was punctuated or adjoined by a number of rooms and pits. Then, appropriate inscriptions and representations had to be placed on the walls and the pillars. Consider, for example, the amount of work and technical mastery needed to create the exquisite painted bas-reliefs for which the tomb of Sethos I is justly famous; it was the first tomb intended to be decorated in its entirety, from its entrance to its sarcophagus chamber.[3]

To create his tomb in the Valley of the Kings, as well as those of his family members in the Valley of the Queens, the pharaoh made use of a specialized department, the institution of the Tomb, the generic term "tomb" becoming a physical reality during the reign of each sovereign. This institution[4] included a group of workers who were specialists in the three areas of needed competence, "quarrymen,"[5] sculptors, and painters/designers.[6] Their number varied; they averaged forty to sixty, divided into two groups of equal number, the "right side" and the "left side," each commanded by a foreman who was assisted by a deputy. Along with a scribe, these two foremen constituted the "three captains." Subordinate personnel, including doorkeepers, physicians, fishermen, gardeners, woodcutters, water carriers, launderers, and carpenters, were attached to the institution of the Tomb and saw to the basic needs of the workmen. Security was assured by assigning the institution a squad of policemen called "Medjay," after the name of a Nubian people from whom they had originally been recruited. Supervision of the Tomb also fell within the competence of the two "administrators ($\jmath tw$) of the west of Thebes."[7]

The workmen of the Tomb lived in a village whose remains are still to be seen in the valley called Deir el-Medina, where we can

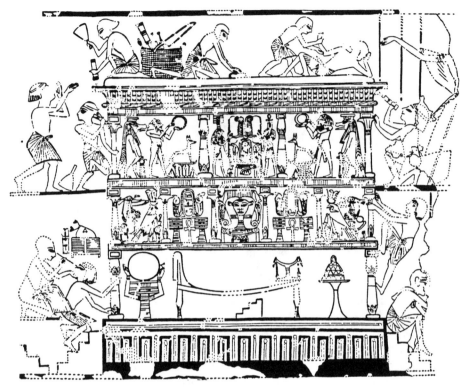

In addition to the workmen of the Tomb, other artisans prepared the furniture for the eternal life of the sovereigns. Drawing by N. de Garis Davies.

gaze upon the sixty-eight houses of the final phase of the village's history. The workmen's tombs were constructed on the adjacent hillsides. Two pathways led to the Valley of the Kings and the Valley of the Queens, where they worked. These locales were dominated by a pyramid-shaped mountain called "the Peak," which was believed to be haunted by a cobra goddess named Meretseger.

By good luck, we have rich archaeological and philological documentation regarding this community, with information on its lifestyle and its history in detail rarely attained in other areas of Egyptology. Apparently these workmen were far from being the least fortunate of Egyptians.[8] To be sure, the work itself was difficult for those who carved or painted in the stifling semidarkness of the rock-cut royal tombs, in the flickering light and the acrid smoke of their oil lamps. And the work was arduous for the quarrymen, who plied their picks and carried baskets filled with debris until they were out of breath.[9] But all in all, the manner in which the workers were orga-

Along with bread, beer was a staple in the Egyptian diet. Drawing by N. de Garis Davies.

nized was relatively liberal, and their many official leave days were complemented by an easygoing complaisance with regard to absenteeism.[10] What the workmen received from the pharaonic state, their employer, seems quite comfortable compared with compensation systems of other ancient, or even modern, civilizations. The foundation of their wages[11] was grain. The workmen received, on average, four "sacks" a month—that is, eight and a half bushels—of emmer wheat, enough to bake eleven pounds of bread per day. Of course, the ranking members of the institution of the Tomb were entitled to more abundant rations. Additionally, ready-made loaves of bread and

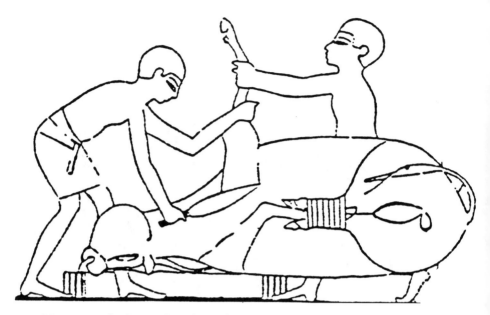

Meat appeared infrequently in the workmen's diet. Drawing by N. de Garis Davies.

cakes were furnished episodically. Each man also received another grain, barley—on average, one and a half sacks, or just over three and a quarter bushels, per month—which was used to make beer. In addition to this beer, there was an average monthly allotment of six jugs of just over two and a half quarts, undoubtedly coming from the offerings consecrated to deities.[12] Though beer played an important role in their diet, it was as much for its nutritional value as for the enchanting virtues of its alcoholic content. Besides these grains, the workers received nearly ten pounds of fish per day, which furnished them a considerable amount of protein,[13] along with vegetables, fruits, milk, oil, and fat. Meat was distributed only on the occasion of festivals and exceptional events. The workers also received firewood, pottery, clothing, and—something crucial in a desert locale such as Deir el-Medina—water, which was brought by specialized carriers. In short, these workmen had the means to live well.

The Financial Shortages of the Administration

Though workers received various forms of compensation in theory, actually getting paid was another matter. The final years of the reign of Ramesses III were marked by serious political and economic difficulties. The complex machinery of the pharaonic state began grinding to a halt, and finding the means to provision those who were dependent on it became difficult.[14] For example, here is an appeal for help that was probably written at the beginning of year 29[15] to the vizier To[16] by the scribe Neferhotep,[17] who worked on the preparation of the tombs of the royal children:

> Another communication to my master: I am working in the tombs of the royal children, which my master ordered me to prepare. I am working quite well and efficiently, with a perfect manner of acting and an efficient manner of acting. My master need have no care with regard to them. Assuredly, I am working excellently, I do not let myself go in the slightest.
>
> Another communication to my master. We are in extreme destitution. We are left lacking in every staple that comes from the white house, that comes from the storeroom, and that comes from the reserves. A load of stone is not light! Also, six *oipe*[18] of barley have been taken from us in order to return them in the form of six *oipe* of soil! My master must procure means of subsistence for us. For truly, we are already dying, we are no (longer) alive. It (i.e., subsistence) is no longer being assured to us in any way at all.[19]

Though the writing employs conventional excess,[20] can we doubt the seriousness of the situation for the workmen? Was Neferhotep's cry of distress heard? Probably not. At best, the plea would have prompted temporary, insufficient measures, for in the second month of the winter season, the workmen, who had exhausted all legal recourse, decided to employ more effective means of action to win their cause.

The Initial Demands

The workers' response is related principally in a papyrus written by the scribe Amennakht;[21] Egyptologists have dubbed it the Turin Strike Papyrus, because it is in the Museo Egizio in Turin and because it speaks of the strike, though that is not its only topic.[22] The information from this papyrus is complemented, and to a certain extent repeated, by various journals and documents that were in the possession of those who administered the institution of the Tomb.[23]

One of these evokes what seems to have been the first skirmish in the lengthy social conflict that would rock the twenty-ninth year of the reign of Ramesses III:

> Year 29, month 2 of the inundation season, day 21; on this day, receipt by the scribe Amennakht of the gang's complaint: "Twenty days

have gone by in the month without our rations having been given to us."[24] They went to the temple of Djeserkhepru-meryamun, life, prosperity, health, in the domain of Amun. One went in search of forty-six sacks of emmer wheat. It was given to them in month 2 of the inundation season, day 23.

The vizier To was named vizier of Upper and Lower Egypt.[25]

The year apparently began badly: from the second month on, the workmen complained about nonpayment of rations. Following a procedure that would often be used, they displayed their discontent by going to a funerary temple, in this instance that of King Haremhab (mentioned under another of his names, Djeserkhepru-meryamun), which lay next to that of Ramesses III, the reigning pharaoh.[26] The latter temple probably was their actual objective, since it constituted the administrative center of the west of Thebes, but apparently unable to reach it, they satisfied themselves with the other one. The records also indicate that the vizier To was appointed vizier of the entire land on the very day that witnessed the beginning of a conflict that would bring him many challenges, as we shall see. This was only a first warning, and although the authorities were able to find something with which to calm the anger of the workmen this time, they would have many other occasions to scrape the bottom of the barrel—or more precisely, of the granary.

In fact, the same problems resurfaced three months later. Here are the different versions of the events:

[Year 29, month 2 of winter, day 10]; they went past the redoubt because of their rations, near the causeway [of King Mentuhotpe (?)[27]].[28]

Year 29, month 2 of winter, day 10; the very day that the gang went past the redoubt because of their rations.[29]

Year 29, month 2 of winter, day 10, passing the five redoubts of (the institution of) the Tomb by the entire gang. Arrival at the back[30] of the House of Pharaoh [. . . . Coming] by the three captains, the [two] deputies, and the two administrators, l.p.h. It was noted that they (i.e., the workmen) were in back of the House of Menkheperre, in the road outside.[31]

Year 29, month 2 of winter, day 10; this day of passing the five redoubts of (the territory of) the Tomb by the gang with the following declaration: "We are hungry, for eighteen days have passed by in the month."[32] They installed themselves behind the House of Menkheperre. Coming by the scribe of (the institution of) the reserved (?) Tomb, the two foremen of the gang, the [two] deputies, and the two administrators. They called out to them (i.e., the workers) in these terms: "Go inside!"[33] They (i.e., the workers) made a solemn statement in these terms: "Please go back! We have a matter relating to Pharaoh, l.p.h." Spending the day in this same place. Spending the night in (the territory of) the Tomb.[34]

The sequence of events can be reconstructed by comparing these four versions. The workers' wages were unpaid, and to show their discontent, the workers left their village, which belonged to the territory of the institution of the Tomb. Sauntering across the plain, they arrived at the back of the House of Pharaoh—that is, the funerary temple of Ramesses III—and then, after having been excluded from this strategic spot, they occupied the rear of the House of Menkheperre—that is, the temple of Tuthmosis III[35]—which was well to the north. Their response to the entreaties of their immediate supervisors was that the matter did not fall within the supervisors' purview, but rather needed to be submitted to Pharaoh himself. After spending the day outside the territory of the institution of the Tomb,[36] they returned there to spend the night. Thus, the act by which the workmen displayed their demands was less the cessation of actual work—especially given that day 10 was the end of a ten-day "week" and thus in principle a day of rest[37]—than their emergence from the zone where they were administratively stationed. This emergence was marked by their "passing the five redoubts," which, with its variants "passing the redoubt" and "passing the redoubts," essentially meant "going on strike." Though the figurative meaning of the expression is beyond doubt, the topographical reality covered by its literal meaning has yet to be entirely explained. The term "redoubt" (*inbt*) designates a small fortification of stone or brick in which policemen were stationed to control the road[38] leading down from the village housing the workmen of the Tomb, which was in the valley known by the modern name of Deir el-Medina. This valley had two access routes to the plain, not counting the trails that led south to the Valley of the Queens and north to the Valley of the Kings:

- an access route to the southwest with a path leading toward the plain and ending north of the temple of Ramesses III, and
- an access route to the northeast with a path leading to the plain south of the Ramesseum.

The five redoubts lined one of these routes, but which route cannot easily be determined. Still, the arguments in favor of the southern path leading to the Ramesseum[39] might be more cogent than those in favor of the other one.[40] In any case, it is likely that whichever of the two routes was not defended by these five redoubts was protected by an analogous system of guard posts.

Whether the five redoubts lay along the northern or the southern route, for the workmen of the institution of the Tomb to pass by them meant leaving the area to which they were administratively assigned and thus signaling a break with the normal course of events. In fact, in the French language, the expression "to go on strike" (*faire grève*) has an analogous origin: in Paris, it was once the custom for unemployed workers to gather in Grève Square.

Of course, this blatant assault on bureaucratic order and the tranquillity of long-standing routine could not have failed to disturb, and even terrify, the administrators. For the workmen, it was an opportunity to express their grievances and make their demands.

Armed with these details, we can better appreciate the development of the conflict. Despite their spectacular action, the workers did not win their cause, and they would have to be stubborn and try again. In fact, on the next day, the eleventh day of the month, a similar scenario ensued:

> Year 29, month 2 of winter, day 11. They passed by (the redoubts) again. Arrival at the doorway on the southern side of the House of Usermaatre-setepenre.[41]

The workmen thus went to the Ramesseum to make their demonstration. Terrified, the administrators attempted to appease them by distributing whatever they could find:

> Year 29, month 2 of winter, day 11. What was brought by the scribe of (the institution of) the Tomb, Pentaweret:
> 28 *sab*-cakes
> 27 *sab*-cakes
> Total: 55 cakes.[42]

As we can easily imagine, the distribution of fifty-five cakes—undoubtedly scarcely more than one cake per person[43]—would not induce the embattled workmen to give up their legitimate demands. It is thus no surprise that they continued their protest the next day:

> Year 29, month 2 of winter, day 12; they passed by; they arrived at the rear of the House of Usermaatre-setepenre [. . .] to the gang: "Finish your affairs and let's go out."[44]

> Year 29, month 2 of winter, day 12. Arrival at the House of Usermaatre-setepenre. Spending the night [upset (?)] before their ar-

rival. Entering there. The scribe Pentaweret, the two chiefs of the Medjay, the two porters of the fortress of (the institution of) the Tomb [. . .
] of the chief of the Medjay, Montmose, saying: "I must go and look for
the governor of Thebes." [. . .] I said to him, "The people of (the institution of) the Tomb are in the House of Usermaatre-setepenre!" He
said to me [. . .] The scribe of the mat Hednakht and the divine fathers of this sacred enclosure heard their declaration. They (i.e., the
workers) said to them: "If we arrived there, it is because of hunger, because of thirst. There is no clothing, no unguent, no fish, no vegetables. Write to Pharaoh, l.p.h., our goodly Lord, l.p.h., and write to the
vizier, our superior, to procure us means of subsistence." They were
granted the rations of the first month of winter on this day.[45]

To be sure, one version is quite concise, while the other contains
several lacunae. What is clear is that the workmen's initiative had
reached a new level. No longer content with noisy demonstrations
near the funerary temple, they decided to enter it, undoubtedly
when the doors were opened. There, they presented their grievances
to the staff, hoping their display of solidarity would find some echo
with the pharaoh and his vizier. This was a step forward for the
workmen and a step backward for the authorities, who on this occasion granted them not cakes, but rations—though the rations were
for the preceding month. The struggle was beginning to pay off.

New Developments in the Conflict

The matter was not over, however, for the wages of the current month were still pending:

Year 29, month 2 of winter, day 13, in the enclosure of (the institution
of) the Tomb.[46] What [the chief of the Medjay], Montmose, said: "See,
I am telling you my reaction:[47] go up and gather your tools, close your
doors, and bring your wives[48] and children. I'll walk ahead of you to
the House of Menmaatre, l.p.h., and I'll get you there as soon as possible."[49]

This was a new phase in the conflict and a fresh escalation in tactics. From this time on, the workmen would involve their families in
their struggle, deserting their village and taking their wives, children, and equipment to the new front, the "House of Menmaatre,"
which was the funerary temple of Sethos I at Qurna, the southern-
most of the series of temples. Undoubtedly, the authorities had
placed a strict guard on the funerary temples the workmen had already used to stage their demands. In any case, as often happens, a

leader emerged during the course of a social conflict. In this case, it was Montmose, the chief of the Medjay, who assumed command of the movement for reasons that escape us. In any case, the workmen continued their movement for another four days, rejecting the dilatory or deceptive tactics of the administrators,[50] and continued putting pressure on the high officials:

> The overseer of troops of the House of the King of Upper and Lower Egypt Usermaatre-meryamun, [l.p.h.] came before the gang. He listened to their declaration, saying, "[Tell me what] I should write regarding this matter to Pharaoh, l.p.h."[51]

Finally, the rations were delivered, as the following account testifies:

> Year 29, month 2 of winter, day 17. Delivery of the rations of the second month.[52]

In fact, the delivery continued into the next day, undoubtedly because it had been started at a late hour. In all, the workmen succeeded in getting their demands met because they had asked only for what was due them.

Unfortunately for them, they were not at the end of their travail. In the following month, they had to go on strike again:

> Year 29, month 3 of winter, (blank). Passing the redoubts by the gang. Standing in the Enclosure of[53] the Tomb. The three captains set out in search of them. The man of the gang Mose, son of Aanakht, said, "As Amun endures, and as the sovereign, l.p.h., endures, whose wrath is worse than death, if I am taken from here to up there today, I (lit., "he") shall spend the night only after undertaking to profane a tomb,[54] and if I do not do it, because I swore on this subject in the name of Pharaoh, l.p.h., may punishment be inflicted on me (lit., "him").[55]

To demonstrate their discontent, which again was due to delay in the payment of their wages, according to another document,[56] the workmen apparently chose, after passing the redoubts, not to occupy the funerary temples, but to remain in the Enclosure of the institution of the Tomb, the administrative center and meeting place of that institution.[57] A new weapon was launched against the authorities: the threat of tomb violation. The dispute became particularly critical on the twenty-eighth day of the same month, probably because it was payday[58]—or the day on which the process of payment was set in motion[59]—and the administration did not have the means to make up the delay.

The Vizier's Half-Measures

The workers' resolve made recourse to force useless for the authorities, who decided that persuasion was the only means left. Alerted to the seriousness of the situation, the vizier To decided to confront it with dialogue. He chose to have this willingness to dialogue announced to the angry workmen by a chief of the Medjay, so as not to have to face them directly.

> Year 29, month 4 of winter, day 28. The vizier To went north, having taken the gods[60] of the southern region for the jubilee.[61] Arrival of the chief of the Medjay, Nebsumenu son of Panehsy, to tell the three captains and the gang while they were in the Enclosure of (the institution of) the Tomb, "Here is what the vizier said: 'If I have not come to you, was it without a serious reason (lit., "for a trifle")? If I did not come to you, was it not because there was nothing to bring you?' As for what you said, 'Do not take away our ration,' is it I, the vizier, who gives only to take away,[62] and would I not wish to give that which the one who occupied the same position as I did? (But) it happens that there is nothing in the granaries themselves. I shall (thus) have to give you what I have found."[63]

This is obviously captious rhetoric. One sentence contains no fewer than four negative elements that successively modify one another.[64] The style was intended to confuse the workmen to whom this message was addressed, just as it has confused the unfortunate Egyptologists who have attempted to translate it. The vizier's somewhat paternalistic protestations of good will were evidently intended to mitigate the negative impact of his final admission: he was unable to deliver the rations because the granaries of the state were empty. In fact, he took the half measure of delivering half the rations:

> The scribe of (the institution of) the Tomb Hori said to them, "You will be given half the rations, and I shall distribute it to you myself."
> Year 29, month 1 of summer, Amenkhau and Userhet gave two "sacks"[65] of emmer wheat to the gang as the ration of month 1 of summer. The foreman of the gang Khons said, "Lo, I say to you, take the rations and go down toward the riverbank,[66] to the Enclosure. And let the vizier's informers[67] tell him about it!" And when the scribe Amennakht finished giving them the rations, he directed them toward the riverbank,

After the harvest, the grain was stored in granaries and could be used to pay the work-men. Drawing by N. de Garis Davies.

as he had said to them. Then they passed by a redoubt. The scribe Amennakht went and said to them, "Do not pass by (the redoubts to go) to the riverbank. For truly, I have just given you two 'sacks' of emmer wheat. And if you leave, I shall have you found in the wrong in any tri-bunal before which you go. I[68] shall bring them up again."[69]

The administration thus found itself unable to pay the wages in their entirety; in fact, a contemporary ledger confirms the unavail-ability of sufficient grain.[70] Incited by one of their foremen, the workers were quite upset that they had been given only half of what was owed to them—and this a whole four days after this half measure had been announced. It took all the persuasive powers of the scribe Amennakht to lead them back to the "straight and narrow"—from the point of view of the administration, of course—and he was so proud of his accomplishment that in his account of the facts, he dropped his mask, switching suddenly from the impersonal bureaucratic style with which he attempted to clothe his document, under pretext of objectivity, to a narrative statement in the first person.[71] But the payment was only partial, and his zealousness had only a limited effect.

In fact, on day 13 of the same month, the workers displayed fresh discontent, unable to resign themselves to the fact that only a half ration had been allotted to each man:

> Year 29, month 1 of summer, day 13. Passing the redoubts by the gang, saying, "We are hungry!" Standing behind the House of Baenre-meryamun, l.p.h. They called out to the governor of Thebes, who was passing by; he had the gardener of the overseer of cattle, Meniunefer, come to them to say, "Look, I have given you these 50 sacks of emmer wheat to serve as a means of subsistence until Pharaoh, l.p.h., gives you the rations."[72]

Having made the blunder of passing near the workmen gathered behind the funerary temple of Merneptah (called Baenre-meryamun, another of his names), the governor of Thebes was taken to task and then spoke up. Displaying the same courage as the vizier To, he chose to respond through an intermediary. He must not have had a clear conscience. In fact, several days later, the workmen registered a complaint that he had misappropriated one of their special allocations:

> Year 29, month 1 of summer, day 25, departure[73] by the gang for the House of Usermaatre-setepenre, life, prosperity, health, the great god. Meeting with me[74] there. He[75] said to them, "I must go to Thebes to make a complaint before the first prophet of Amun regarding the governor of Thebes. He has not given them the loaves of the divine offering of Usermaatre-setepenre, l.p.h. It is a serious misdeed that he has committed.[76]

This passage illustrates a basic practice, the "reversion of offerings." It was based on the fact that once consecrated, an offering remained available and could thus be reconsecrated to one or more further cults and/or placed at the disposition of private individuals.[77] Among other advantages, the workmen of the institution of the

Tomb had a right—statutorily or exceptionally—to loaves that had been dedicated to the cult of Ramesses II[78] but which the governor of Thebes had misappropriated. This fact suggests that the interruptions in the workmen's compensation were due not only to the economic crisis, but also to corruption and breach of trust.[79]

Sporadic Strikes at the Beginning of Dynasty 20

The trouble persisted through the end of the reign of Ramesses III and into the beginning of that of his successor, Ramesses IV. During this period, we find scattered mentions of strikes, using such expressions as "pass by a redoubt"[80] or "pass outside,"[81] nonpayment of rations being the alleged motive for these demonstrations:

> . . . after the men of the gang passed outside, for they were hungry, saying, "If we have passed outside, it is because we are hungry, because there is no wood, vegetables, or fish." The opinion of the magistrates of the tribunal was sought; they said, "[The men of the gang of (the institution of) the Tomb][82] are in the right."[83]

Here, the workmen's protests led to a judicial hearing, and a tribunal arbitrated this conflict between the administration and its dependents.[84] We do not know who composed the tribunal or tribunals, but high officials were members; later, we shall see that the first prophet of Amun could participate in the deliberations of a high tribunal presiding at Thebes.

The arrears in the payment of the workmen of Deir el-Medina were just one example of the general impoverishment of the state. During the same period, in year 3 of Ramesses IV, an official complained that payments were being demanded, but that nothing was being delivered to the temples to assure the offerings, thus penalizing those to whom they were given after being consecrated:

> And although it was said to me, "Give them (= the payments)," no loaves were delivered to the temples where I am; rations have not been delivered, nor have offerings been delivered to me.[85]

Renewed Unrest under Ramesses IX

Unless the silence of the sources is purely fortuitous, this series of strikes seems to have ended between the reign of Ramesses IV and that of Ramesses IX, when the workmen once again made de-

Fish were often a part of the diet, and they could be carried to offering tables. Drawing by N. de Garis Davies.

mands, beginning in year 9 and continuing sporadically until the reign of Ramesses XI.[86] As always, nonpayment of wages sparked these protests:

> This day of going up to the Great Field,[87] which was done by the vizier, the first prophet of Amun, the royal cupbearer and overseer of the white house Nesamun, and the scribe of Pharaoh, l.p.h., to receive what had been commanded in the great and august Tomb of millions of years of Pharaoh, l.p.h.[88] The gang of (the institution of) the Tomb complained to them in these terms: "We are destitute; we are hungry; we are not being given the dues that Pharaoh, l.p.h., has accorded us." The vizier, the first prophet, and the royal cupbearer and overseer of the white house of Pharaoh, l.p.h., said, "The men of the gang of (the institution of) the Tomb are in the right!"[89]

Here, the workers seized the opportunity afforded by an official visit by high officials to present a demand that was immediately recognized as legitimate. The first prophet of Amun was a member of the commission, along with the vizier and Pharaoh's secretary. In fact, during this period, the first prophet was often mentioned during disputes over wages, undoubtedly because a part of these wages was the responsibility of the domain of Amun:

> They passed by four (!) redoubts. They spent the day in the Enclosure of the Tomb, but no attention was paid to them. . . . They began again; they went down toward the riverbank in year 9, month 4 of summer,

A vizier, dressed in the distinctive costume of his office. Drawing by N. de Garis Davies.

day 26 [. . .] the Enclosure of the Tomb. They appealed to the first prophet [of Amun]. He came before (?)[90] them, (to) the Enclosure of the Tomb.[91]

Note that on this occasion, the authorities, who were undoubtedly a bit blasé, chose a new tactic, indifference. It must have had a certain effectiveness, for the workers in their turn were obliged to change tactics and to call directly on the first prophet, who consented to hear them. When he did not prove to be very accommodating, they took the legal route of submitting their grievance to the great tribunal of Thebes to force him to listen to their demands:

> Month 2 of summer, day 28 . . .
> Crossing over to Thebes by the gang; spending the night (there).
> Month 2 of summer, day 29.
> Absence of the gang. Appearing before the high officials and the first prophet of Amun. He said to us,[92] "I will not give you the rations." We went back up and we spent the night at his[93] place. When month 2 of summer, the last day[94] arrived, they appeared before the high officials. They said, "Let the scribe of the vizier, Amenkhau, be brought."[95] He was brought before the high dignitaries of Thebes. They said to the scribe of the vizier, Amenkhau, and to the deputy of the granary of Pharaoh, l.p.h., "Look at the grain of the vizier and take some of it to give rations to the men of (the institution of) the Tomb." . . . We were given rations that day. We gave two coffers to the two fanbearers, along with a box[96] for manuscripts.[97]

Evidently, persistence paid off, and in the face of the first prophet of Amun's refusal to pay the rations, the great tribunal was able to find a solution by calling on the scribe of the vizier. This would be an example, rare in this period, of sound justice, attentive to the pleas of ordinary people crushed by the arrogance of high officials. Still, the situation was not idyllic; the workmen were obliged to provide generous compensation[98] to the two fan bearers,[99] who probably intervened to facilitate their access to the great tribunal.

Strikes to Safeguard Public Morality

Up to this point, we have described strikes that were provoked by demands for payment of wages. But the workmen also knew how to use this formidable means of putting on pressure to draw the attention of the authorities to scandalous situations that the latter pretended not to know of. Such incidents are reported in the Turin Strike Papyrus, which was devoted to the demands of the workers of (the institution of) the Tomb in year 29 of Ramesses III (see p. 55):

> The gang set out to pass by the redoubts behind the village after the three captains raised their voice to them at the gateway[100] of the village. The scribe of (the institution of) the reserved (?) Tomb sent the two administrators and the two deputies to search for them. Return of the administrator Reshpeteref to tell us,[101] "This is what Qenna son of Rut and Hay son of Huy told us: 'We will not go back, you will tell it to your superiors.'—they were standing before their comrades—'Truly, it is not because of hunger that we have passed (the redoubts); we have an accusation too serious to state. Truly, a misdeed has been perpetrated[102] in this place of Pharaoh, l.p.h.'; so they said. When we went to hear their statement, they (each) said to us, 'I have said it truly.' "[103]

Unfortunately, the scribe Amennakht, the author of the document, maintains a prudent silence regarding this serious accusation,[104] leaving us famished in our own way. Still, he is a bit more explicit regarding a scandal that might have had some connection with this accusation, especially given that several persons were implicated in both cases:

> Year 29, month 1 of summer, day 16. What the man of the gang Penanukis said to the scribe Amennakht and the foreman of the gang Khons: "You are our superiors and you are the controllers of the institution of the Tomb. Pharaoh, l.p.h., our goodly Lord, has caused me to undertake to respect the following resolution:[105] 'There is no question

that I learned of an affair or that I gave an account of a wrong in the deep Great Places[106] and that I concealed it.'[107] Lo, Userhet, along with Pentaweret, has carried off a stone from the superstructure of the tomb of the Osiris, King Usermaatre-setepenre, l.p.h., the great god. Moreover, he carried off an ox that was marked with the brand of the House of Usermaatre-setepenre; it is in his cowshed. Furthermore, he has fornicated[108] with women who are married, the citizeness Menat, when she was with Qenna, the citizeness Tayuenes, when she was with Nakhtamun, and the citizeness Tawerethetepti, when she was with Pentaweret. You have seen the attitude of the vizier Hori regarding the problem of theft of stones.[109] He was told, 'The foreman Paneb, my father, told a man to take stones from it . . . quite exactly.' And Qenna son of Rut acted in exactly the same manner with regard to the superstructure of the tomb of the royal children of the king, the Osiris Usermaatre-setepenre, l.p.h., the god. Have what you should do to them examined, or I shall make a complaint for Pharaoh, l.p.h., my Lord, l.p.h., and to the vizier, my superior."[110]

Here, the object of the scandal is explicitly stated: the misconduct of two workmen in different domains, and in particular, the damage they had inflicted on a royal tomb, that of Ramesses II. This was not a violation by intrusion, but rather the removal of stones from the superstructure. But a much more serious violation was imputed to Userhet in an indictment added later to the end of the preceding column of text:

He said, "Userhet undertook his excavation; he did it in the necropolis (or, "the tomb")[111] of the royal wives."[112]

Two interpretations are possible. "His excavation" might be Userhet's own tomb,[113] in which case his fault was to locate it in the zone reserved for the royal wives. Alternatively, the expression designates a hole[114] by means of which he intended to enter a queen's tomb in order to rob it.

Curiously, Qenna son of Rut, one of the accused, was himself the accuser in an earlier episode. In the name of his comrades, he denounced an affair so serious that he did not dare to explain it. We shall doubtless never know the truth of the matter, but it smacks of a settling of scores, as though Qenna, Userhet, and Pentaweret, on the one hand, and on the other, Penanukis, were involved in one of those interminable feuds that so often spring up within communities isolated from the outside world.[115] Though we do not know the events that followed this denunciation, it is colored by the fact that Penanukis, the man who made it, seems to have been the son of

Paneb,[116] who was such an incorrigible scoundrel that he has merited an entire chapter in the present work (chapter 3). Some scholars have even suggested that Penanukis's accusations were intended to discredit the members of the institution who had taken his father's place.[117]

In any case, the strikes show that the deterioration of the economic situation not only induced the workmen to transgress the law to make their demands known, but also provoked an increase in fraudulent practices and exactions due to tension and distress. The atmosphere of the final years of the reign of Ramesses III was certainly a pernicious one. In these conditions, it is hardly surprising that a plot was hatched against the king, one that probably led to his death.[118]

3

Paneb

The Perfect Picture of a Rogue

In the previous chapter, we saw that the protest movements that often stirred up the workmen laboring in the tomb of the reigning pharaoh originated not only in the malfunctioning of an administration incapable of paying its employees on a regular basis but also in serious misdeeds that were frequently perpetrated in their tight-knit community. In one of the documents we have read, the name of Paneb was associated with some of these misdeeds, but only via an allusion to a judicial precedent. To leave the matter there would be to mistreat someone who so badly treated his contemporaries; it would not do justice to someone who defied justice so frequently; it would treat dishonestly a very dishonest man. But since "an eye for an eye" is not the law of the historian, the transgressions of this grand villain demand an examination proportionate to their magnitude.

Paneb perpetrated his crimes at the earliest[1] during the reign of Sethos II (c. 1204–1198 B.C.E.) and that of his lackluster successor, Siptah (c. 1198–1192 B.C.E.). This was a troubled period, during which the last pharaohs of Dynasty 19 found themselves obliged to defend their legitimacy from usurpers. In other words, Paneb's misdeeds took root in a rich compost. We have a detailed list of them, for a workman of (the institution of) the Tomb, the scribe Amennakht, inventoried them in a denunciation that he set down in a document (Papyrus Salt 124) that is in the British Museum.[2]

A Disputed Succession

Though Amennakht wrote the document (or had it written),[3] he was not inspired purely by love of virtue and a correlative abhorrence of vice; rather, he was impelled to do so by a frustration that he did not conceal in the introduction:

[What the man of the gang A]mennakht [declared]: "I am the son of the foreman of the gang, Nebnefer. My father died . . . Neferhotep, my brother, [was appointed] in his place. The enemy killed Neferhotep [. . . h]is brother. Paneb gave five servants of my father to Pareemheb,[4] who was vizier [. . . m]y father, though it was not an office that was his due."[5]

These lines call for a detailed explanation. Nebnefer, Amennakht's father, held the prestigious position of foreman of (the institution of) the Tomb; that is, he supervised half the workmen who resided at Deir el-Medina.[6] Upon his death, his position fell to Neferhotep, his older son and Amennakht's brother. But Neferhotep was murdered under dramatic circumstances[7] that elude us; the text mentions "the enemy," behind whom some have seen the incursions of foreigners,[8] while others have seen an allusion to a civil war that many have thought was provoked by the usurper Amenmesse.[9] In any event, since Neferhotep had no son, his brother Amennakht stood at the forefront of the candidates for his office, according to Egyptian custom.[10] But this custom did not have the force of law, and the central power was free to confirm or deny him. In this case, his hopes were dashed: the unworthy Paneb was appointed instead, in return for a bribe he paid to the vizier[11] by giving him five servants who had belonged to Neferhotep—the height of cynicism. Moreover, Paneb took to hounding Amennakht and the family of Nebnefer:

Memorandum[12] concerning the fact that he made me make a solemn[13] renunciation regarding the chapel[14] of my mother and my father, in these terms: "I shall not enter it," and that he had the man of the gang Pashed come, and that he began to cry out (in) the village: "Do not let any member of the family of the foreman of the gang Nebnefer be seen going to make offerings to Amun, their god"; so said he. And when the members went to make offerings on the [. . .] side, they were afraid of him, and he began to throw stones at the servants of the village."[15]

Paneb did have grounds for being a contender for the position, however. First, he had been a member of the gang since at least year 66 of Ramesses II (c. 1213 B.C.E.), when he and his wife testified in a judicial proceeding,[16] and he was the son and grandson of men of the gang, "those who heed the call (of the Lord of the Two Lands) in the Place of Truth,"[17] Nefersenet and Kes. Furthermore, as even Amennakht conceded, he had been raised by the foreman Nefer-hotep. The latter, who was childless, had turned the frustrated ardor of his paternal feelings on two protégés on whom he lavished all his care, Paneb and Hessunebef (of whom we shall speak later, p. 76),[18] who were probably orphaned at an early age. Undeniably, in the case of Paneb, he had nurtured a viper, as we shall see (p. 75). But the fact remains that Paneb could assert the rights of an adoptive son against those of Neferhotep's brother, Amennakht. The bribe he paid the vizier could thus be considered more as an encouragement to choose one of the two legitimate alternatives than as something tantamount to a denial of justice. Even so, it was a case of bribery pure and simple.

A Certified Expert in Bribery

Paneb in fact mastered bribery with great panache. This is how, for a consideration, he obtained the protection of a person who was influential in the world of (the institution of) the Tomb:

> [Memorandum concerning the fact that . . .] Paneb gave "something" to the [scribe] Qenherkhopshef, and that he (i.e., the scribe) got him (i.e., Paneb) out of trouble.[19]

The writer of this complaint used the term *nkt,* "something" (p. 152), a discreet term for a payment made (or extorted)[20] as *bak-shish* (an Arabic word whose meanings include both "tip" and "bribe"). In return for this "something," Qenherkhopshef had used his authority to extricate Paneb from the tight squeeze in which one of his villainies had landed him, as he also did for the workman Re-hotpe,[21] whose misdeeds he covered up. Likewise, the scribe Khaemope twice had obtained the release of a tomb robber in exchange for a share of his loot.[22] We are right to postulate Qenherk-hopshef's purchased indulgence in another anecdote[23] reported in the denunciation:

> [Memorandum concerning the fact that Paneb . . .] in the temple of Hathor,[24] and that the scribe Qenherkhopshef registered[25] what he had done in the temple of Ptah.[26]

Though the passage contains lacunae, we cannot help but suspect that Paneb had made an offering of stolen foodstuffs, and that the

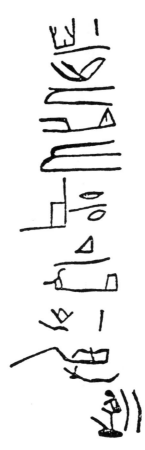

This graffito that Qenherkhopshef left in the Theban mountain resembles the graffiti left by a number of his colleagues. Facsimile by J. Černý.

scribe had duly registered this offering while closing his eyes to its origin, like a banker laundering dirty money. The scribe Qenherkhopshef was a colorful individual,[27] known not only for having abused his position, as Paneb did, but also for having endowed Egyptologists with many examples of his horrible—sometimes indecipherable—handwriting.[28] Evidently, his conceit was the equal of his dishonesty; in the Valley of the Kings, he appropriated a projection on the side of a cliff that he deemed particularly suitable for his august person, using the following graffito: "The place where the scribe Qenherkhopshef sits."[29] Chance has preserved to us the phylactery that he wore on his neck. It has a fragment of papyrus bearing a text intended to invoke magic to protect him, not from justice in this world, as we might have expected considering his conduct, but from the genie Sehaqeq, who supposedly had the power to cause headaches.[30] Qenherkhopshef no doubt believed that his efforts at intellection entailed the risk of hurting his head.

In any event, his protection proved capable of covering up some of Paneb's misdeeds. But the latter had committed so many others that ten scribes as influential and as corrupt as Qenherkhopshef would scarcely have sufficed to conceal them. We shall attempt to present them by grouping them into categories.

A Penchant for Brutality

Paneb had a complex character that was inclined to angry outbursts and led him down regrettable avenues of action:

> Memorandum concerning the fact that he constantly attacked the men during a nighttime gathering, and that he took to walking on the top of the walls, throwing stones at the men.[31]

> (Memorandum concerning the fact) that he attacked nine men during the night, and that the foreman Neferhotep denounced him to the vizier Amenmose,[32] and that he (i.e., the vizier) punished him (i.e., Paneb), and that he (i.e., Paneb) denounced the vizier to Mesy, and that he (i.e., Paneb) caused him (i.e., the vizier) to be dismissed from office, accusing him of having hit him.[33]

There is one quality we cannot deny Paneb: his robust constitution, which enabled him to take on no fewer than nine men in a single night, like a veritable force of nature. We must even accord him another: a talent for lying that made it possible for him to depose a vizier, who was the head of the administration, a sort of prime minister, *mutatis mutandis*.[34] When he employed this artifice, it was no doubt because Amenmose was immune to bribes, or at least more difficult to purchase than his predecessor Pareemheb had been. Since the pharaoh was the only authority higher than the vizier, it is a near certainty that the name Mesy designates the reigning sovereign. From the lengthy debates that have been devoted to him, his identification with Amenmesse—a usurper, which explains why his name is written with a determinative indicating an enemy[35]—has emerged as probable.[36] Amenmesse evidently seized power during the reign of Sethos II.[37] He was deceived by Paneb, who succeeded in getting the vizier punished for what he himself was guilty of, namely, battery.

Here, the denunciation does not furnish the precise motives for these acts of violence, which do not appear to have been exceptional in this period.[38] Were they solely for the pleasure of wrongdoing? In any case, Paneb was otherwise rather careful in his selection of victims: they were those who could get in his way, beginning with his colleagues:

> Memorandum concerning the fact that he said to the foreman of the gang Hay, "I'll attack you on the mountain, and I'll kill you."[39]

Let us recall that there were two foremen, each in charge of half the workmen. Such a dichotomy offered much potential for conflict, all the more so in that Paneb loved to make a show of his authority. Thus, on the occasion of a legal proceeding, he managed to stand out from the rest of the tribunal on which he was sitting to the extent that the official report mentions that he led the interrogation, which was exceptional:[40]

> The tribunal said to them, "Tell what you heard." They went back on their declaration to the point of quarreling. The foreman Paneb said to them, "Tell us what you heard."[41]

Could we imagine that Paneb, who was driven by such a need to assert himself, could rub shoulders daily with someone whose position put him in the first rank of the little world of Deir el-Medina without conflict? It is thus no surprise that prior to threatening his colleague Hay, he had attacked his predecessor, Neferhotep:

> Memorandum concerning the fact that he ran in pursuit of the foreman Neferhotep, my brother, though it was he who had raised him, that he (Neferhotep) closed his doors before him and that he (i.e., Paneb) took a stone and smashed his (i.e., Neferhotep's) doors, and that persons were set to watch over Neferhotep, because he (i.e., Paneb) had said, "I'll kill him during the night."[42]

To be sure, Neferhotep was a foreman of the gang, like Hay, and this was evidently reason enough to arouse the hatred of Paneb.[43] But he was also Paneb's adoptive father. Paneb could hardly have forgotten that. Yet from Hay to Neferhotep, the persecutions escalated, progressing from the threat of murder to qualified attempts.

Paneb's Amorous Excesses

Paneb knew how to adapt the exuberance of his character for the ladies, as signaled in the denunciation:

Memorandum concerning this: his son ran before him to the place of the doorkeepers, and he pronounced[44] an oath by the Lord, l.p.h., in these terms: "I no (longer) wish to put up with him," and he said: "Paneb fornicated with the citizeness Tuy when she was the wife of the man of the gang Qenna; he fornicated with the citizeness Hel when she was with Pendua, he fornicated with the citizeness Hel when she was with Hessunebef,"[45] so said he, his son. And when he fornicated with Hel, he fornicated with Ubekhet, her daughter,[46] while Aapehty, his son, also fornicated with Ubekhet.[47]

Thus, while a unilaterally conflictual relationship existed between Paneb and Neferhotep, who were adoptive son and father, an even more complex relationship existed between Paneb and Aapehty, who were biological father and son. And, in a public place, the station of the doorkeepers, who were the *de facto* subordinate authority for maintaining order,[48] Aapehty denounced the sexual excesses of his father. Though Aapehty claimed to be infuriated about those excesses, according to his own statement, he was in part associated with them. In the accusations that were hurled in denunciations of misconduct, such excesses were often added to other sorts of misdeeds—theft, embezzlement, bribery—as in the cases of Userhet[49] and Penanukis.[50] These incidents must be characterized accurately: were they cases of adultery, or of rape?[51] In all these cases, the Egyptian texts employ the verb *n(i)k*, which even French people can understand. This word, which has deep roots in the Afroasiatic family of languages,[52] is still alive in Arabic, and like many other words, it has entered into French slang via the Maghrebi dialects.[53] In ancient Egyptian, the verb *n(i)k* does not necessarily imply mutual consent; thus, threats against transgressors are formulated in the following manner: "A donkey will fornicate with him, a donkey will fornicate with his wife, and his wife will fornicate with his children."[54] We can genuinely doubt that all the protagonists involved in this formulation were entirely consenting participants! Still, the use of the term does not always imply that the sex act was imposed by force, as we can see from this disillusioned admission by a humble laborer whose wife was unfaithful to him while he was straining under the weight of some baskets: "I carried (or, "would carry") the basket and another man fornicated (or, "would fornicate")."[55] Thus, Paneb is not, strictly speaking, being accused of rape here—though he would also commit this crime—but rather of allowing his sex drive to lead him to seduce women who had husbands or partners. That situation evidently disturbed the peace of the households of Deir el-Medina, and with that, the peace of the village. Let us note

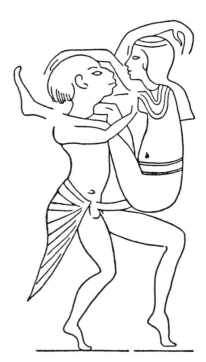

Little inclined to depict their sexual excesses, the Egyptians left us only one erotic papyrus, which is now in Turin. Drawing by J. Omlin.

that Paneb knew how to take advantage of a situation. Not only did he have intercourse with Hel, but he also seduced her daughter Ubekhet and shared the latter's charms with his son Aapehty. And though he had been Paneb's accomplice, Aapehty was ungrateful enough to denounce his father.

In the effusion of his superabundant vitality, Paneb found a challenging way to increase his pleasure:

[Memorandum concerning the fact that he removed Iyem]wau's clothing, and that he threw her on top of a wall and took her by force.[56]

There are two observations to be made. One is that Paneb was not only a seducer but also an acrobat. The other is that he had a marked attraction to the tops of walls, for we saw earlier that he liked to perch on them to bombard his comrades with stones.

Misappropriation of Pharaoh's Property and Labor

Paneb's complex character did not express itself solely through physical violence or amorous excesses, or through both together. He also knew how to increase his well-being by taking dishonest advantage of opportunities.

And his position offered him many such opportunities. As a foreman, he had access to the materials loaned to the workmen. How, then, could he resist the temptation to help himself to the most valuable tools?

> Memorandum concerning the fact that he seized the large pick for breaking stone, and that when it was said, "It is not there,"[57] a whole month was spent[58] looking for it, and that he took it and threw it behind a large stone.
>
> Memorandum concerning the fact that he went in search of the large chisel of the construction site and that he broke it in his tomb.[59]

To appreciate these grievances fully, let us recall that in pharaonic Egypt, basic tools were mostly of stone. Metal tools, which in the New Kingdom were mostly of copper and bronze, were extremely valuable objects. They were only given out to the humble workmen in exchange for a weight that enabled verification that the tool had been returned after it was used[60] and that the man who used it had not profited by shaving off some of the metal portion.[61]

Paneb's position had other advantages. Supervising half the workmen of (the institution of) the Tomb, he had access to a good-sized workforce that he could use for his own benefit.

> Memorandum concerning the fact that he assigned the men of the gang to make the bed of straps[62] of the deputy of the domain of Amun, while their wives wove for him, and that he assigned Nebnefer son of Wadjmose to fatten his ox for two whole months.[63]

In the first case, the profit he realized was indirect: he had an object made for a third party, who reimbursed him for work done by workmen who were paid by the state. In the second case, he used one of these workmen to fatten his own ox. By happenstance, we are able to check the veracity of these two counts of indictment. For this period, we have fragments of the journals of (the institution of) the Tomb, administrative documents that contained all information deemed pertinent regarding the labor of the workmen or the reasons for their inactivity: festivals, illness, strikes, scorpion bites, and so forth. The following extracts are from years 1 and 2 of King Siptah,[64]

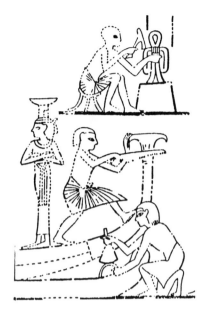

Paneb forced some of the staff of the royal workshops, such as these woodworkers, to labor for his own benefit. Drawing by N. de Garis Davies.

who succeeded Sethos II, probably after the interruption caused by Amenmesse's usurpation:

Year 1, month 3 of winter, day 28; Ipuy, Kes, and Khons were sawing wood for Paneb.

Month 4 of winter, day 5; Ipuy, Kes, and Khons again were sawing wood for Paneb.

Month 4 of winter, day 6; Ipuy, Kes, Khons and Nebnefer were sawing wood for Paneb.

Month 3 of winter, day 12, day 13, day 14, day 15, day [1]6 [. . .] wove a basket for Paneb.

Month 3 of winter, day 26, day 27; Ramery [and . . .] made the bed of straps for Paneb.[65]

Month 2 of inundation season, day 17, Ipuy and Khons worked for Paneb.

Month 2 of inundation season, day 18, Ipuy and Khons worked for Paneb.[66]

Month 4 of inundation season, [day . . .]; Nebnefer son of Wadjmose fed Paneb's ox.[67]

Year 1 [. . .] month 4 of inundation season, day 24; Neferhotep was absent with his superior, decorating the sarcophagus of Paneb.[68]

Month 1 of winter, day 17 . . . the designer Neferhotep was decorating the sarcophagus of Paneb.

[Month 1 of winter, day . . .] Neferhotep was absent, decorating the sarcophagus of Paneb [. . .].

Year 2, month 1 of winter, day 14, Kes son of Aapehty was working for Paneb on the platform.[69] . . . Nebnefer son of Wadjmose was feeding his ox.

Month 1 of winter, day 5; those who were absent with Paneb. Kes son of Aapehty was working [. . .] was making plaster for the tomb of Pa[neb].

Month 1 of winter, day 11; Harnefer and Khnummose were absent with Paneb [making pl]aster . . .

Month 1 of winter, day 17; Nebnefer was feeding the ox of Paneb.

[. . .] Month 1 of winter, day 27; Neb[nefer was feeding] the ox of Paneb.

Month 2 of winter, day 7; those who were absent with Paneb: Ramery was working in his tomb.[70]

These journals make for edifying reading. For the months for which extracts from the journal of (the institution of) the Tomb are preserved, we read a dismal litany of misappropriations of labor for Paneb's benefit.[71] Furthermore, not only do they repeat Amennakht's specific accusations regarding the bed of straps and the ox, but they reveal other instances as well: workmen sawing wood for Paneb, weaving a basket for him, decorating his sarcophagus,[72] and making plaster for his tomb. In his virtuosity at making employees of the state work for his own benefit, Paneb had an equal: the scribe Qenherkhopshef, who also excelled at taking personal advantage of the workforce he administered.[73] It is therefore not surprising that he connived with Paneb in covering up his activities, if only in return for a bribe; they had much in common.

Theft of Stones from Pharaoh's Tomb

Paneb was nothing if not realistic. Since he had a highly qualified workforce at his disposal, it made sense to take advantage of their skills, and since the workmen he supervised had been trained to prepare the tombs of pharaohs, he forced them to prepare his own.

Memorandum concerning the fact that he caused the men of the gang to break stones on the superstructure of the construction site of Sethos-merneptah, l.p.h., extracting some for his (i.e., Paneb's) funerary ensemble each day; and they erected four columns in his tomb with these stones. And he plundered the great place of Pharaoh, l.p.h. And it was when they were on top of the construction site of Pharaoh, l.p.h., that those who passed by on the hillside saw the quarrymen, and they heard voices. And he took the picks of Pharaoh, l.p.h., and the sledgehammer (?)[74] to work in his tomb.

List of quarrymen who worked for him:

Aapehty; Kes; Kes son of Ramose; Haremwia; Qenherkhopshef; Rom; Pashed son of Heh; Nebnakht; Nakhtmin; Nebsumenu; Haremwia son of Baki: Khonsnakht; Nakhtmin; Payom; Wennefer; Aanakht; total, 16 men.[75]

Thus, using Pharaoh's workmen and materials, Paneb was exploiting the very tomb of Pharaoh—in this case, Sethos II[76]—as a quarry. In Paneb's defense, it should be stressed that the practice of constructing monuments by exploiting those of predecessors was widespread in ancient Egypt, even among kings. Still, Paneb pushed the practice to the height of cynicism in using the very workmen charged with constructing Pharaoh's tomb to remove stone from it.[77] Paneb's tomb has been found; like the others, it was dug into a hillside of the valley of Deir el-Medina.[78] It seems to have been decorated when he was no longer foreman,[79] since he bears only the title "hearer of the call (of the Lord of the Two Lands) in the Place of Truth."[80] His use of the workmen under his authority and his exploitation of Pharaoh's tomb did not serve just to build a forecourt with pillars, which has today totally disappeared. The doorjambs are now in the Egyptian Museum in Turin; their very banality leads us to reflect on the nature of the documentation. Without the fortunate circumstance that preserved Papyrus Salt 124 to us, who would have suspected that these thoroughly stereotyped inscriptions, carved in the most unremarkable style of the period, preserve the name of someone who was so devoted to depravity?

Theft of Funerary Goods and Pillage of Tombs

Paneb was a clever rogue who knew how to take advantage of his situation. Given that he functioned where the dead were buried, how could he not profit from the products and goods that religious beliefs brought into play? In fact, he never ceased helping himself to a share when these products and goods came within immediate reach, as on the occasion of funerals:

Memorandum concerning the fact that he went to the funeral of Henutmire,[81] l.p.h., and that he took a goose,[82] and that he swore an oath by the Lord, l.p.h., in these terms: "It is not in my possession." (But) it is in his house that one will find it.[83]

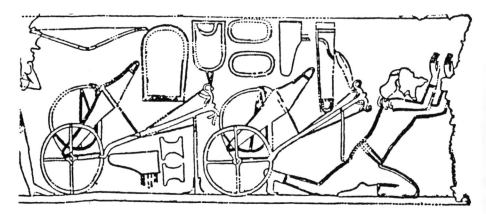

Sumptuous vehicles were often gilded: chariots were offered to the king by his courtiers and were included among the royal tomb furnishings. Drawing by N. de Garis Davies.

> Then the funeral of all the kings was carried out.[84] . . . [Memorandum concerning the fact] that Paneb stole goods of King Sethos-merneptah, l.p.h. List [. . .] storehouse of King Sethos-merneptah, l.p.h. It was in his possession that they were found[85] after the funeral [. . .] and that he took the covering of his chariot, after it was as a scribe [. . .] that profit was drawn[86] [. . .] after he took it during the funeral.[87]

Despite the lacunae that mar this passage, we learn that Sethos' funeral proved to be a godsend to Paneb, who managed to levy his tithe on the profusion of goods accumulated by Pharaoh. He even appropriated the covering of the chariot[88] that was supposed to be placed in the tomb.

Apart from these occasions when the hubbub and confusion of major ceremonies were favorable to surreptitious misappropriations, he found it necessary to go in search of the products and precious objects that had been placed in the depths of the vaults. And Paneb explored far and wide in the huge necropolis of Thebes, shamelessly entering the funerary chapels, which remained open for the cult that maintained the dead:

> [Memorandum concerning the fact that he] went to three tombs and walked around, although they did not belong to him, along with the man of the gang Qenna.[89]

On this point as well, chance permits us to verify Amennakht's accusations. A fragment of the journal of the Tomb notes the presence of Paneb and his son at Djeseret, a part of the necropolis now known by the name Deir el-Bahari (see the map on p. 2), which included not only many tombs, but also the imposing funerary temple of Queen Hatshepsut:

> Year 1, month 2 of inundation season, day 13, the day when Aapehty and Khons, the two children, came to Djeseret. They called Paneb. [He] set out for Djeseret when there was no work of Pharaoh, l.p.h.[90]

At the invitation of his son, Paneb went to Djeseret. The key element of the passage is the remark "when there was no work of Pharaoh, l.p.h.," which means there was nothing to do there—at least nothing honest. Paneb probably went there to evaluate the possibility of plundering a tomb in an area that his son had spotted.

When conditions were favorable, it was necessary only to dig a tunnel to gain access to the burial chamber and to lay hands on what it contained:

> [Memorandum concerning the fact . . .] and that he undertook the profaning of a tomb[91] west of the royal Necropolis, there being a stela allocated to it;[92] he descended into the tomb of the man of the gang Nakhtmin; he seized the bed that was under him; he went in search of the objects that are given to a dead person; he seized them.[93]

In all probability, the tomb robbed by Paneb was that of Nakhtmin, who lived at the end of Dynasty 18; the tomb was in the north of the western flank of the valley of Deir el-Medina[94] and thus could be considered by the Egyptians as being west of the Valley of the Kings. The stela that was set into the niche of the funerary chapel has been found, but the stela that was mentioned in the accusation might have been another one, outside the tomb.[95]

Further Violation of Pharaoh's Tomb

No doubt encouraged by his initial successes, Paneb set his sights higher still. Leaving behind the cemetery of Deir el-Medina, which after all contained only the tombs of people of his own status, he attacked the restricted sector of the royal necropolis:

> [Memorandum concerning the fact that . . .] and that he dug into[96] the floor that is forbidden in the place that is hidden[97] [. . . although he had undertaken] the commitment to respect the following resolution:[98] "I shall not overturn a stone in the area of the great place of Pharaoh, l.p.h."; so said he [. . .][99]

Tunneling into the vault, Paneb arrived at the site of the ultimate profanation, the tomb of Pharaoh Sethos II. We have seen that he had taken advantage of the occasion of his funeral to misappropriate certain items that were part of his grave goods. There was more:

> [Memorandum concerning the fact that . . . he stole jars] of inb-oil[100] of Pharaoh, l.p.h., and that he took his wine, and that he began sitting on [the sarcophagus of the king] after he had been buried.[101]

Thus, while rummaging in the profusion of objects heaped up for the postmortem benefit of the deceased pharaoh, Paneb helped himself to some amphorae of wine[102] and began to drink their contents while sitting on the sarcophagus—"while he (i.e., the pharaoh) was in the bier," adds the accuser. Of the august sarcophagus that Paneb so disrespectfully used, only some fragments of the lid were found in the actual tomb of Sethos II.[103] The bottom portion had been transferred to the tomb of Amenophis II,[104] where pious priests had assembled the remains of the burials of some of the pharaohs to protect them from the pillaging that marked the end of Dynasty 20.[105] In his own period, Paneb was thus avant-garde; he was a pioneer of sorts in the exploration of the rock-cut tombs of the Valley of the Kings!

Sacrilege against Pharaoh's own person, albeit dead and buried, was thus added to a list of notorious accomplishments that was already long enough to constitute an impressive dossier.

Paneb's Punishment

A question immediately comes to mind: did Paneb commit his many atrocities with total impunity? We have seen how a vizier was removed from office for having dared to punish him. Another tried to muzzle him by getting him and his son to promise to calm down:

> Memorandum concerning the fact that he swore an oath by the Lord, l.p.h., in these terms: "(. . .)[106] if I [cause] that the vizier hears my name again, I (lit., "he") will be removed from my (lit., "his") office, and I will be made a quarryman"; so said he. And his son did the same in these terms: "(If I cause that the vizier hears my name again), I (lit., "he") will be dragged out and I will not remain in (the institution of) the Tomb." See, he could not stop his clamor."[107]

From what Amennakht had to say, the vizier's formal notice did not have much effect, and that is why he addressed the highly de-

Jars of wine were placed in tombs. Paneb took advantage of them, but his imbibing was anything but mystical! Drawing by N. de Garis Davies.

tailed complaint that reveals the affair to us. The complaint concludes as follows:

> He is thus not worthy of this position. For truly, he seems well, (but) he is like a crazy person.[108] And he kills people to prevent them from carrying out a mission of Pharaoh, l.p.h. See, I wish to convey knowledge of his condition to the vizier.[109]

But did his complaint get results? Did his vehement closing argument, which ends with a rhetorical flourish, achieve its goal? Though there is no irrefutable proof, certain indications suggest a positive answer. For one thing, Paneb's case was cited as a well-known judicial precedent with regard to an affair involving theft of stones.[110] For another, after an indeterminate lapse of time following the complaint,[111] a new foreman, Aanakht, replaced Paneb, who makes no further appearance in the documentation at our disposal. This abrupt silence could lead us to think that Paneb was not only dismissed from his position, but also harshly punished.[112] As for his son Aapehty, he did not succeed his father, though he was appointed deputy of (the institution of) the Tomb in the interval. In any case, he does not seem to have been ostracized by the community of workmen, for he is attested again in year 5 of Ramesses III.[113]

Paneb's punishment scarcely proved to be a deterrent, in that others repeated his crimes. In particular, we have seen how the reigns of the last Ramessides were marked by mammoth scandals involving not only workmen of the institution of the Tomb and some people even more humble than they, but also some high officials.

Still, even among so many acts of turpitude, Paneb's crimes stand out. As they review these crimes, readers, like a judge, can decide among the following three proposals: was Paneb an incorrigible scoundrel, an inveterate knave, or an exceptional crook?

The stern and commanding Peak of the Theban mountain did not discourage the plunderers who ravaged the necropolis at the end of the New Kingdom. Photo by I. Franco.

The workmen of the necropolis lived in the village of Deir el-Medina, which was nestled between two valleys in the Theban mountain; the workers' tombs were located nearby. To the north was a temple dedicated to Hathor, the patron goddess of the necropolis. Photo by I. Franco.

Between their village and the Valley of the Queens, the workmen built a sanctuary dedicated to Ptah and to Meretseger, the patron goddess of the sacred Peak. Photo by I. Franco.

The Valley of the Queens was not spared by the pillagers. Photo by I. Franco.

When the necropolis was inspected, the tomb of the Great King's Wife Isis was found to have been profaned. Photo by C. Desroches Noblecourt.

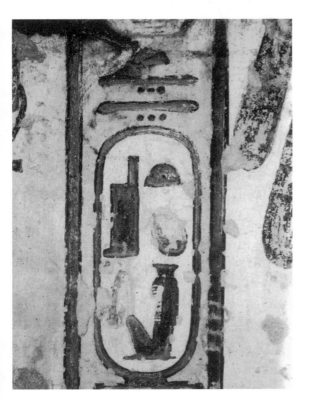

The cartouche of Queen Isis. Photo by C. Desroches Noblecourt.

The entrance to the tomb of Isis: the blocks of stone that had once obstructed it were smashed by the plunderers. Photo by A. Ward.

On a number of occasions, Medjay played a role in the affairs that rocked Thebes during the Ramesside Period. Photo by D. R.

The Mansion of Millions of Years of Ramesses III at Medinet Habu became the administrative center of the necropolis—and an object of greed for those in search of
wealth and power. Photo by I. Franco.

Pasturing their cattle at the edge of the cultivated fields, herdsmen were able to observe the plunder of the temples and even to denounce the pillagers, as Bukhaaf did.
Photo by D. R.

Periods of famine and unrest were associated with the negative image of the hyena. Photo by Chuzeville.

When famine raged, the riches of the Ramesseum were a temptation. Photo by I. Franco.

The granaries of the royal temples (here, those of the Ramesseum) stored food that could be used for the workmen's rations. Photo by I. Franco.

Paneb did not hesitate to make grave threats against Hay, a foreman of the gang.
Photo by D. R.

Papyrus Salt 124 records the various accusations leveled against Paneb. Photo by
British Museum.

Paneb directed his activities not only against royal foundations. He also plundered private tombs, such as that of Nakhtmin, located at Deir el-Bahari. Photo by I. Franco.

The charming site of Elephantine island has retained all of its attractiveness. Photo by I. Franco.

4

A Provincial Scandal
Crimes at Elephantine

An Enchanting and Enchanted Site

The villainies we are about to describe were unworthy of the enchanting setting in which they unfolded, the area where the river crosses the rocky barrier that traditionally marked the boundary between Egypt and Nubia. Even today, we cannot escape the charm of this enchanting landscape, which despite all efforts has yet to be entirely spoiled by the encroachment of urban sprawl. In antiquity, the site must have been more grandiose still, with its reddish rocks rising up from the foaming water, and the craggy cliffs of the western mountain leading down to the golden-yellow sands of the desert. As early as prehistoric times, the Egyptians had sensed divine presences here, and here was where theology located the caves from which the annual flood surged forth. The town of Elephantine,[1] capital of the first nome of Upper Egypt, had been founded at an extremely early date on a granite island at the entrance to the First Cataract. Its Egyptian name Abu (*3bw*), which means "elephant" and is echoed by the Greek name Elephantine, derived from the trade in ivory that came from Nubia.[2] The notion of trade is even more explicit in the Egyptian name given to the settlement located on the east bank opposite Elephantine, Sunet (*swnt*), which means "trade." This name is preserved in the modern Arabic name Aswan, via the Greek form Syene. The ram god Khnum was the principal deity, and the goddesses Satis and Anukis[3] were associated with him to form the local triad. It was in the temple of Khnum that scandalous activities would multiply during the reigns of Ramesses IV (c. 1156–1150 B.C.E.) and Ramesses V (c. 1150–1147 B.C.E.).

95

Qakhepesh's Denunciations

The denunciations made by Qakhepesh are known to us from a papyrus now in the Egyptian Museum of Turin and known to Egyptologists as the "Turin Indictment Papyrus."[4] Written on this papyrus, probably in its original version,[5] is a denunciation worded similarly to the one drawn up against Paneb, though in this case, the many lacunae obscure its interpretation. The document is entitled "The memoranda[6] that are against the pure priest (a priestly title) of the temple of Khnum, Penanukis surnamed Sed."

As we shall see, Penanukis was not its only target. As for the author of this complaint, he could well have been the god's father (another priestly title) Qakhepesh, to judge from a passage in which, abruptly freeing himself from the impersonal formulations required by administrative style, he switches from the third person to the first person:[7]

> Memorandum concerning the fact that the vizier Neferrenpet[8] sent the attendant Pakhar-the-younger and the attendant Patjauemdikhons with these words: "Go look for the god's father Qakhepesh. [. . .]" The attendants found me when I was in the monthly service of the first phyle.[9] The servants let me go, saying, "You may not be seized, because you are in your monthly service"; so they said [to] me. This pure priest gave them kilts of Upper Egyptian cloth, a folding chair,[10] two pairs of sandals, two ivory tusks,[11] a bunch of vegetables, a thousand *dom* nuts, and gutted fish, as well as bread and beer. He said to them, "Do not release him."[12]

Notwithstanding the lacunae, it seems clear that the vizier Neferrenpet dispatched his attendants—that is, his hired hands—to fetch Qakhepesh for an interrogation, likely following a denunciation by the pure priest Penanukis. The latter generously greased their palms to get them to take Qakhepesh into custody, even though he enjoyed temporary immunity because he was on duty. The size of the bribe shows how keen Penanukis was to rid himself of this troublesome Qakhepesh. We understand why, when we read the complaint he drew up once he extricated himself from his difficulty. The accusations he lists are impressive in their variety and their gravity, as well as in the rank of the persons involved and in the length of the time during which they were running amok. We shall group them by category.

From Boorishness to Barbarity

The scandal at Elephantine displays the association, already noted in the cases of the strikes and the Paneb affair, [13] of sexual misdeeds with barbaric acts of all sorts:

Memorandum concerning the fact that he fornicated with the citizeness Mutnemeh, daughter of Pasekhet, when she was the wife of the fisherman Djehutyemheb, son of Pentaweret.

Memorandum concerning the fact that he fornicated with Tabes, daughter of Shuy, when she was the wife of Aahuty.[14]

Though these were simple cases of adultery, they were especially reprehensible because of the disorder they could arouse in the community. But they also show that Penanukis was as dominated by his drives as Paneb had been. When the consequences of these drives seemed likely to bring him an increase in responsibility that he had no desire to assume, he did not hesitate to resort to radical means: "Memorandum concerning the fact that he aborted[15] the citizeness Tarepyt."[16]

In pharaonic Egypt, abortion is attested principally as an accident that magic or medicine sought to prevent.[17] To be sure, there were prescriptions for "delivering an infant in the womb of a woman," such as the following:

Salt of Lower Egypt: 1 (measure); white emmer wheat: 1 (measure); female reed (?):[18] 1; bandage the lower abdomen with that.[19]

But such prescriptions were principally intended to facilitate labor or the expulsion of physiological substances, rather than to interrupt pregnancy.[20] Deliberate abortion is mentioned only exceptionally.[21] If it is a count of indictment in this complaint, it is evidently because the practice was condemned.[22]

In any event, to avoid any inconvenience that his amorous excesses might cause him, Penanukis resorted to more brutal measures:

Memorandum concerning the fact that the man set fire to the house of the servant [. . .] Mutnofret. [She came] to tell him. He blinded [her], and he also blinded Baksetjyt, her daughter. They remain blind today.[23]

Thus, to intimidate a troublesome woman, probably an unfaithful or cumbersome mistress, Penanukis first burned her house. When she came to complain to him, he then blinded her and, for good measure, did the same to her daughter.[24]

Penanukis was also strict and quick to punish anyone he thought blameworthy:

Memorandum concerning the fact that this pure priest cut off the ear of Sekhatuemnefer, son of Baksetjyt, without the knowledge of Pharaoh, l.p.h.[25]

Cutting off the nose and/or the ears was a punishment that was often used during the New Kingdom.[26]

What the complaint denounces is less the mutilation itself than the fact that it had been inflicted without informing Pharaoh, who would normally have decided on it.[27] Penanukis had quite simply arrogated to himself a royal prerogative. Under these circumstances, we should not be surprised that he shamelessly helped himself to the contents of the storerooms of the temple, doubtless convinced he had the right to assume ownership of the goods accumulated for the service of the gods.

Theft of Temple Property

Let us recall that divine temples, like the royal funerary temples (see p. 25), were not only cult places but also veritable economic units[28] crammed with all sorts of products, materials, and precious objects that were used in religious services and in maintaining personnel and equipment. Such opulence continually whetted the appetites and often kindled the rapacity of the priests by exposing them to strong temptations. Penanukis, like his colleagues, was not a man who could resist.

They devoted themselves to a multitude of thefts, passing quickly from an amulet representing an *udjat*-eye—that is, the Eye of Horus—to a herd of cows:

> Memorandum concerning the fact that an *udjat*-eye in the temple of Khnum was stolen; he used it, along with the one who had stolen it.[29]

> Memorandum concerning the fact that they stole a *ma*-piece of copper belonging to the barque of Khnum; they used it.[30]

> [Memorandum concerning the fact that . . .] clothes of the god's fathers and the prophets with wh[om they car]ried the god. They were found in their possession.[31]

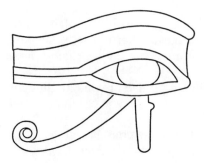

Symbol of wholeness and plenitude, the *udjat*-eye was an amulet often made of the most precious materials. Drawing by E. Hornung.

The divine barque used in processions was decorated with precious ornaments—such temptations for plunderers! Drawing by C. F. Nims.

> Memorandum concerning the fact that twenty cows were handed over to this pure priest in year 1 of Heqamaatre-setepenamun,[32] the great god; cows were seized in his possession. [. . .] He led them up.[33]

This last case concerned theft by Penanukis of ordinary cows belonging to the domain of the temple of Khnum. But in the matter of cattle, he was also capable of setting his sights higher:

> Memorandum concerning the black cow that was in his possession after she had given birth to five images of Mnevis. He led them out and he disposed of them[34] in the countryside; he profited from them;[35] he took them south and he delivered them as payment[36] to the pure priests.
> Memorandum concerning the great image of Mnevis that is in his possession. He drew profit from it;[37] he gave it to some Medjay of the fortress of Senmut; he received payment for it from them.[38]

This instance was no ordinary larceny, but rather sacrilege, for the cow and five calves that Penanukis laid his hands on, no doubt during a stay in the region of Heliopolis, had been recognized as hypostases, or "images," of the local sacred bull, who was called Mnevis. Like the sacred animal of Apis at Memphis, the sacred animal of Mnevis had a right not only to a cult, but also to a grandiose funeral and to a burial that was provided with all the furnishings necessary for survival. In fact, we know of two Mnevis tombs dating respectively to Ramesses II and Ramesses VII,[39] and thus, in the latter case, to a period of time close to that in which Penanukis lived. How can we not be indignant at this mention of the sad fate of these living images of the god? One of them was sold to the Medjay of the fortress of Senmut, the present-day Biga Island facing the former island of Philae. These Medjay, who were crude Nubian policemen, surely did not display the respect to which the august young bull was due. It is even probable that they ate it.

To be sure, these repeated thefts, sometimes aggravated by sacrilege, did not fail to alert the authorities, who reacted differently according to the levels at which they operated. The administrator of the temple, the prophet,[40] admitted he was powerless:

> [Memorandum concerning the fact that they opened the . . . of the temple of Khnum. They sto]le . . . shawls. The prophet found them in their possession; he took them (back) without being able to do anything against them.[41]

We may suspect that if the prophet was obliged to content himself with recovering the shawls without punishing Penanukis and his accomplices, it was because they had support in high places, just like Paneb, who got out of a tight squeeze thanks to the remunerated protection of the scribe Qenherkhopshef (see p. 72).

Montuherkhopshef's Lies

In any event, when an inquiry was conducted at the highest level of the local hierarchy, that of the governor, the perpetrators were able to buy the man who held that office:

> [M]emorandum concerning the fact that [five pieces of cloth] and ten shawls[42] [of smooth cloth] were stolen, a total of fifteen, in the temple of Anukis, mistress of Syene. The scribe of the white house Montuherkhopshef, who was exercising the office of governor of Elephantine, made an inquiry concerning them. He determined that they had been in their possession and that they had given them to Imenrekh,[43] a carpenter of the Place of Truth,[44] and that they had received payment for them. This governor received their *bakshish* from them, and he released them.[45]

Before being promoted to governor, the scribe Montuherkhopshef had already dealt with Penanukis, compelling him to swear to the prophet of Khnum that he would not enter the temple in a state of impurity, a prohibition that Penanukis in no way respected (see p. 104). Thereafter, knowing the species of the beast, so to speak, he preferred to exact bribes from him rather than to condemn him to a punishment that, in the unlikely event that it was actually carried out, would scarcely have mended his ways. Montuherkhopshef resigned himself to this attitude easily. His own morality was in no way strict, and with regard to Penanukis, he must have felt some affinity. In fact, the hazards of the preservation of documentation, once again benevolent, have handed down to us a papyrus in which this Montuherkhopshef was caught cheating in flagrante delicto:

> Khay of the domain of Harakhty gre[ets the governor] of Elephantine [Montuherkhopshef,[46] in life, prosperity], health, in the favor of Amun-Re, king of the gods. I say to Amun-Re, to Har[akhty] when he rises and sets, to Harakhty and his ennead, that they make[47] you well, that they make you live, that they make you be in the favor of Harakhty, your lord who watches over you.
>
> I opened the jars of honey that you brought for the god. I removed ten *hin*[48] of honey for the divine offering. I noted that they were all filled with bars of unguent. I closed them again. I had them taken south. If it is someone else who gave them to you, make him answer for it, and see if you find a good (honey), and have it brought to me.[49]

Honey intended for the divine offering and sent by the governor Montuherkhopshef had thus evidently been replaced with unguent.[50] The writer of the letter, obviously careful, avoids directly accusing the governor of the substitution and even leaves him an honorable way out by suggesting that someone else might have given the honey to the governor. But Khay's clever formulation, courageous but not foolhardy, cannot dissipate the suspicion that weighs on the governor. Would an official so corrupt as to set thieves free in return for a bribe have hesitated to appropriate the god's honey, replacing this valuable foodstuff with crude unguent? Finally, the inertia of the local hierarchy alerted the central power, which decided to carry out, in the "white house" of the domain of Khnum, one of those inventories that were periodically conducted in the temples:[51]

> Memorandum concerning the fact that Pharaoh, l.p.h., dispatched the overseer of the "white house" Khaemtyr[52] to make an inventory of the "white house" of the domain of Khnum. This pure priest stole sixty kilts in the "white house" of the domain of Khnum. And when one came in search of them, thirty-four were found in his possession, given that he had disposed of the others.[53]

Since the minimal average price of a "kilt"[54] fluctuated between 11 and 20 *deben* (of copper), the stolen objects were worth between 660 and 1200 *deben;* to give an idea of their value, these sums were enough to purchase 6,659 to 13,100 bushels of barley, which would represent the total amount of barley allotted to a workman of (the institution of) the Tomb during a period of seventeen to thirty-three years (see pp. 53–54).

Theft of Grain from the Temple

A temple offered many other resources, if only because it disposed of large quantities of grain that came from its own domains, from statutory revenues, or from privileges. Qakhepesh's denunciation evokes several methods of stealing it.

The most unsophisticated method was simply to break into the granaries or the storerooms:

> [Memorandum concerning] the fact that they opened a storeroom[55] of the domain of Khnum, which was under the seal of the controllers of the granary who control[56] for Amun; they stole eighty sacks of barley from it.[57]

This was a case of a highly villainous forced entry and theft from a storehouse, even though it was sealed. But there was a more subtle technique. Again, it was necessary to be in a favorable situation—for example, one entailing the transport of grain. In fact, in the New Kingdom, transport was an area in which responsibilities were not clearly defined, which produced all the more difficulties in that the resources of an institution often came from places quite distant from its administrative center. One text indicates that, because different parties denied responsibility, the conveying of the "dues" of (the institution of) the Tomb posed such a problem for one official that he ordered a consultation of the archives to search for some old regulation that would enable a decision.[58] Of course, such administrative uncertainties opened up fertile prospects for those who were astute. Such was the case with Khnumnakht, a "broker"[59] who, it seems, was appointed "barge captain (of the domain of Khnum)" by Merihu, the prophet of the domain, in year 28 of Ramesses III, at the death of the preceding holder of that responsibility. After some virtuous years to establish his position, Khnumnakht seized the opportunity to carry out large-scale misappropriations of barley, which Qakhepesh's denunciation details with bureaucratic meticulousness:

As for his debiting from the barley, it is not in the granary of Khnum, given that [he] had taken it for himself.

Year 1 of King Heqamaatre-setepenamun,[60] l.p.h., the great god [. . .] toward Elephantine by the intermediary of the barge captain [. . .] 100 sacks; remainder due:[61] 600.

Year 2 of King Heqamaatre-setepenamun, l.p.h., the great god. 130 sacks; remainder due: 550.

Year 3 of King Heqamaatre-setepenamun, l.p.h., the great god. 700 sacks. He brought none of it to the granary.

Year 4 of King Heqamaatre-setepenamun, l.p.h., the great god. 700 sacks. Arrived in the boat of the Staff[62] through the intermediary of the sailor Nekhte: 30 sacks; remainder due: 680.

Year 5 of King Heqamaatre-setepenamun, l.p.h., the great god. 700 sacks. Arrived at the divine offering of the Staffs of Khnum: 20 sacks; remainder due: 680.

Year 6 of King Heqamaatre-setepenamun, l.p.h., the great god. 700 sacks. He did not bring them.

Year 1 of Pharaoh,[63] l.p.h. 700 sacks. He did not bring them.

Year 2 of Pharaoh, l.p.h. 700 sacks. Arrived by the intermediary of the barge captain Khnumnakht: 186 sacks; remainder due: 514 sacks.

Year 3 of Pharaoh, l.p.h. 700 sacks. Arrived by the intermediary of the barge captain: 120 sacks; remainder due: 580 sacks.

Total. Barley of the domain of Khnum, lord of Elephantine, to make the debits about which the barge captain made an agreement with the scribes, the controllers,[64] and the cultivators of the domain of Khnum, by disposing of it in their own circles of acquaintances:[65] 5,004 sacks.[66]

To interpret this account, we must understand that the temple had a fixed revenue of 700 sacks of barley from a domain situated in the north of the land. For nine years, the barge captain managed regularly to subtract a large part of these 700 sacks, and often all of them, with the explicitly denounced complicity of a good part of the personnel of the domain of Khnum, from the cultivators to the scribes. The total of 5,004 sacks is impressive. It is less than reality, though, because of some bad readings and an omission: in fact, the correct figure is 5,724. But even the figure of 5,004 sacks represents 10,926 bushels of barley, or 1,214 bushels per year and 3.3 bushels per day. Khnumnakht was obviously dissatisfied with the proceeds from these misappropriations, for he secured a complementary profit through the following procedure:

Memorandum concerning the fact that this barge captain had levied taxes[67] amounting to fifty sacks (on) Rome, son of Penanukis and amounting to fifty sacks (on) Paukhed, son of Patjauemabu. Total: two (persons), which makes 100 sacks from year 1 of King Heqamaatre-setepenamun, the great god, to year 4 of Pharaoh, l.p.h., which makes 1000 sacks. He disposed of it for his own use; he brought none of it to the granary of Khnum.[68]

Simply put, for ten years Khnumnakht had confiscated the proceeds of taxes that he was supposed to transport. For the temple of Khnum, 1,000 sacks, or 2,183 bushels, "went up in smoke," so to speak.

In another instance, a barge literally went up in smoke because of the clumsiness of this captain:

Memorandum concerning the fact that this barge captain of the domain of Khnum had set fire to a barge of the domain of Khnum, as well as to its mast and to its equipment. He gave his *bakshish* to the controllers[69] of the domain of Khnum; they did not make a report on this subject; there has been none to this day.[70]

We must note that although this captain set fire to the barge, he had not necessarily burned all his boats. He still had a way out: a bribe skillfully slipped to the controllers, and he went free.

Disrespect for the Sacred and Manipulation of the Oracle

The persons implicated in these scandals—Penanukis in particular—evinced a profound scorn for the sacred places to which their activities led them:

Memorandum concerning the fact that he (i.e., Penanukis) went inside the enclosure when he had spent only seven days drinking natron. The scribe Montuherkhopshef made the prophet of Khnum swear an oath by the Lord, l.p.h., in these terms: "I will not permit him to approach[71] the god before he completes his period (lit., "his days") of drinking natron." He did not comply. He approached the god when he (still) had three days to drink natron.[72]

As we can imagine, entering sanctuaries and approaching divine statues or emblems were subject to strict requirements of ritual purity. The entire body had to be purified, especially the hands, which made ritual gestures, and the mouth, which pronounced the required formulas.[73] Specifically, natron, a mixture of carbonate and bicarbonate of soda, was used to wash the mouth. Penanukis had thus transgressed the most basic rules by approaching the god prior to having completed his period of purification. But with things going so well, he could not curb his disrespect.

In the New Kingdom, the practice of consulting oracles was widespread.[74] People had recourse to oracles to shed light on problems that were quite personal: "Should I turn north and set off on my way?"[75] or "Should I not burn it?"[76] But oracles were also consulted to settle contentions, disputes, and questions of the sort we would call legal. In such cases, the oracle became a jurisdiction parallel to the secular jurisdictions, with which it entered into complex relationships of supplementation and complementarity.[77] In the Third Intermediate Period, the theocratic ideology made it the supreme authority, even in political matters. But even in the Ramesside Period, oracles were already a recognized authority at the local level, and because of that, they conferred power on those who controlled them—that is to say, the clergy in the broadest sense of the term.[78] The oracular decision of the god or the deified king was expressed by movements of the statue, which was set on a litter, the carrying-poles of which rested on the shoulders of the bearers.[79] In front of the writings submitted to it, a backward movement of the statue indicated, it would seem, a negative answer, while a forward dip might have indicated a positive response, or simply a choice between two written documents containing, respectively, a positive and a negative formulation of the same question. In any event, we can clearly see that these bearers in fact controlled the oracle's response, and that it was imperative that they be in agreement on the decision to be made. The following accusation alludes to this point:

> Memorandum concerning the fact that the vizier Neferrenpet appointed the pure priest Bekenkhons prophet of Khnum. This pure priest (i.e., Penanukis) said to the pure priest Nebwenenef,[80] "If[81] we had three other pure priests, we would throw out the son of this broker!"[82] He was interrogated: he confirmed that he had truly said it. He was made to swear an oath by the Lord, l.p.h., not to enter the temple. He gave his *bakshish* to this prophet, saying, "Let me approach the god!" This prophet accepted his *bakshish*. He let him approach the god.[83]

Penanukis had proclaimed his intention of winning the complicity of the bearers to manipulate the statue of the god, in this case Khnum, to make it give an oracle expelling a person who did not please him and whom he called the son of a broker. Alerted to his plans, the authorities imposed on him, by oath, an interdiction on

approaching the statue, a prohibition he got around by bribing the
prophet, who was decidedly obliging (see above, p. 105). It is possible that Penanukis's cynicism was even more massive than it
seems. In fact, considering that Nebwenenef was the son of a
prophet of Khnum named Pendjerty, it cannot be excluded that the
plot was directed against Bekenkhons, the prophet newly appointed
by the vizier, no doubt to the detriment of Nebwenenef, who had
been counting on succeeding his father.[84] In other words, the bribe
Bekenkhons received would have been a poisoned chalice, for in allowing Penanukis to approach the god, he would have brought about
his own downfall by enabling the machination that was supposed to
bring him down. Thus manipulated, the oracle would have disavowed the prior choice of the vizier.[85] Because of the ambiguity of
the text, this interpretation is not assured, but it is rendered plausible by the fact that Nebwenenef is indeed known as prophet of
Khnum.[86]

This was not the only oracular manipulation of which Penanukis
was guilty.[87] The denunciation mentions two others. One was apparently crowned with success:

> Memorandum concerning the fact that the prophet Bekenkhons took a
> chest to the temple. He (i.e., Penanukis?)[88] [. . .] opened it; he stole a
> [. . .] from it; he placed it before Khnum; he (i.e., the god) indicated
> his approbation[89] regarding it.[90]

Unfortunately, the interpretation of this passage is tricky because of
the lacunae. Our understanding is that Penanukis stole an object
contained in a chest.[91] He apparently succeeded in legitimizing his
right to this object by means of an oracle.

In the other case, Penanukis acted as an intermediary:

> Memorandum concerning the fact that he went to Thebes. He received
> some written documents from the one whom Pre did not permit to
> ever (again) exercise the office of controller.[92] He took them south to
> place[93] them before Khnum; he (i.e., the god) did not indicate his ap-
> probation regarding them.[94]

Apparently, Penanukis involved himself with a person whom the
document names only by means of a formula that implies he had
been expelled from office. This sort of magical punishment was directed at extremely serious crimes such as a plot against the person
of the king. A person who would commit such a crime was the sort
of person to whom Penanukis lent his dishonest services. In any

case, he seems to have failed on this occasion, for the oracle gave a negative decision.

Generally speaking, Penanukis's words and deeds betrayed his total disrespect for the oracular ceremonies in which he participated:

> Memorandum concerning the fact that this pure priest began to stand in front of this god. "If he (i.e., the god) must do something good for someone,[95] let him do it for you," so he said to him.[96] He stood [. . .][97]

Though it is incomplete, this passage clearly shows Penanukis's mocking, casual attitude and his insulting sacrilege. He placed himself at the front of the litter, evidently because that was the best position for guiding its movements, while making an ironic remark regarding the effectiveness of the oracle.

The Consequences of the Denunciation

As in the case of Paneb, once we learn of this implacable denunciation, we immediately wonder whether it had any effect. The inventory of wanton acts, misappropriations, and assorted crimes seems so overwhelming that it is difficult to imagine how the central administration could have remained indifferent. In fact, the inventory of the "white house" that it ordered carried out shows it was paying attention to the situation. Nevertheless, the documentation furnishes no clear indication that Penanukis and the other persons implicated in the scandals were punished. On the contrary, the few facts we have regarding the fate of these miscreants suggest that they emerged unscathed from the difficulty into which Qakhepesh's denunciation would have—or should have—put them. In fact, Nebwenenef, who participated in the manipulation of the oracle intended to remove Bekenkhons from the position of prophet, seems to have replaced him, suggesting that he, at least, was not punished. It is true that he had family ties with no fewer than two viziers and one first prophet of Amun.[98] In any event, the fact that certain misappropriations were spread out over a long period, more than ten years, without being interrupted by the change of pharaoh that occurred in the meanwhile allows us to gauge the weakness of the central authority.

5

The Harem Conspiracy under Ramesses III

The Shadow of Censorship

We can easily imagine that the little world of the royal court in Egypt offered a fertile field for ambition, intrigues, cabals, plots, and conspiracies. Such thoughts are undoubtedly correct, though the information at our disposal reveals little in this regard.[1] Does this situation stem from the hazards of the preservation of evidence? Probably, but not entirely. We must also bear in mind that the pharaonic sources tend to hide such subjects as though under the watchful eye of the conscious or unconscious censorship of the dominant ideology. In the exceptional instances in which the sources touch on them, they do so with omissions, circumlocutions, and euphemisms—in short, with devices that were indispensable when it was necessary to speak of what was, in principle, regarded as unspeakable. We see such devices in action especially in the documents that have come down to us from among those produced by the judicial proceedings against the persons who formed a conspiracy against Ramesses III—to the great consternation of the historian, we must admit, for they render even more obscure a documentation that is already partial, fragmentary, and sometimes known only from an amateur copy.[2]

The Judicial Papyrus of Turin

Our basic source for these proceedings is not lacking in style. Since it is a papyrus in the Egyptian Museum in Turin, it is known to Egyptological tradition as the Judicial Papyrus of Turin.[3]

108

Contrary to what this name suggests, it is less a transcript of a trial than a summary of the guilty parties and their punishments, presented by Ramesses III himself and intended to delimit his role in the matter:

> I entrusted[4] to the overseer of the white house Montuemtawy, to the overseer of the white house Payefru, to the fanbearer[5] Kel, to the cupbearer Pabes, to the cupbearer Qedenden, to the cupbearer Baalmaher,[6] to the cupbearer Pairsun, to the cupbearer Djehutyrekhnefer, to the royal herald Penrenut, to the scribe May, to the scribe of the bureau of archives Preemheb, and to the standard-bearer of the garrison Hori the following mission: "As for the words that men have spoken, I do not know them. Go and verify them!" They went, they inquired, they caused that those who had caused death die[7] by their own hand, without my knowing it. They inflicted punishment on others, without my knowing it and that[8] after [I gave them the] following [instructions]:[9] "Be conscientious and take care that [one] does not wrongly suffer a punishment [inflicted by a magistrate] who is not informed about his case"; so I said continually. As for everything that was done, it was they who did it. May everything they did be on their head, while I am protected and sheltered for eternity, and while I am in contact with the justified kings who are in the presence of Amun-Re, king of the gods, and before Osiris, ruler of eternity.[10]

With this preamble to the list of those who were punished, Ramesses III manifestly intended to distance himself from the cruel penalties that were inflicted on them.[11] To shed human blood, even that of criminals, was not an insignificant act in pharaonic Egypt. This repugnance, which was not always shared by other Near Eastern civilizations, doubtless reveals an embryonic humanism that was otherwise demonstrated by the magician Djedi when he refused to exercise his abilities on a human guinea pig, preferring a goose to a prisoner for his experiment in reconnecting a severed head:

> His majesty said, "Let a prisoner be brought to me who is in the prison and whose punishment has been fixed." Djedi said, "Not a man, o sovereign, l.p.h.! Lo, it has been ordained not to do such a thing to the noble cattle."[12]

Also at work was fear of the Judgment of the Dead, which was evidently evoked by the mentions of the "justified kings" and "Osiris, ruler of eternity."

The latter in fact clarify the situation. The primary intent of this text was to cleanse the king of the opprobrium inherent in any bloodshed. The basic rationale was quite simply the ancient concept of immanent and quasi-mechanical retribution for human actions (see p. 126). Those who were punished were the victims not of a vengeful despot, but of their own crimes: "Their misdeeds seized them" (see the next section).

The Principal Conspirators and Their Punishments

The text continues with an enumeration of the conspirators, who are divided into five lists according to the manner in which their punishments were inflicted. We shall begin by examining the first three, which deal with the principal agents; the last two contain some surprises, as we shall see:

Persons brought in because of the serious crimes they had committed and who were made to appear in the place of examination before the great magistrates of the place of examination so that they might be examined by the overseer of the white house Montuemtawy, the overseer of the white house Payefru, the fanbearer Kel, the cupbearer Pabes, the scribe of the bureau of archives May, and the standard-bearer Hori. They were examined. It was determined that they were guilty. Their punishments were caused to befall them; their misdeeds seized them.[13]

The great criminal Pabekkamen, who was chamberlain. He was brought in because of the fact that he had intrigued[14] with Teye and the women of the harem; he associated himself with them. He began taking out their messages to their mothers and their brothers, namely, "Gather people, conduct a war to make rebellion against your (lit., "their") Lord!" He was made to appear before the great magistrates of the place of examination. His misdeeds were examined. It was determined that he had committed them. His misdeeds seized him. The magistrates who had examined him caused his punishment to befall him.

The great criminal Mesedsure, who was a cupbearer. He was brought in because of the fact that he had intrigued with Pabekkamen, who was chamberlain, and with the women to assemble (what was needed to conduct) a war to make a rebellion against their Lord. He was made to appear before the great magistrates of the place of examination. His misdeeds were examined. It was determined that he was guilty. His punishment was caused to befall him.

The great criminal Panik, who was overseer of the king's chamber of the itinerant harem. He was brought in because of the fact that he had intrigued with Pabekkamen and Mesedsure to make rebellion against their Lord. He was made to appear before the great magistrates of the place of examination. His misdeeds were examined. It was determined that he was guilty. His punishment was caused to befall him.

The great criminal Penduau, who was scribe of the royal chamber of the itinerant harem. He was brought in because of the fact that he had intrigued with Pabekkamen, Mesedsure, the other great enemy who was overseer of the chamber, and the women of the harem to form a conspiracy with them to make rebellion against their Lord. He was made to appear before the great magistrates of the place of examination. His misdeeds were examined. It was determined that he was guilty. His punishment was caused to befall him.

The great enemy Patjauemdiamun, who was a controller of the itinerant harem. He was brought in because of the fact that he had knowledge of plans (lit., "words") that the conspirators had made with the women of the harem but did not reveal them.[15] He was made to appear before the great magistrates of the place of examination. His misdeeds were examined. It was determined that he was guilty. His punishment was caused to befall him.

The great enemy Karpus,[16] who was a controller of the itinerant harem. He was brought in because of plans of which he had knowledge, but he hid them.[17] He was made to appear before the magistrates of the place of examination. It was determined that he was guilty. His punishment was caused to befall him.

The great enemy Khaemope, who was a controller of the itinerant harem. He was brought in because of plans of which he had knowledge, but he hid them. He was made to appear before the magistrates of the place of examination. It was determined that he was guilty. His punishment was caused to befall him.

The great enemy Khaemmal, who was a controller of the itinerant harem. He was brought in because of plans of which he had knowledge, but he hid them. He was made to appear before the magistrates of the place of examination. It was determined that he was guilty. His punishment was caused to befall him.

The great enemy Setiemperdjehuty, who was controller of the itinerant harem. He was brought in because of plans of which he had knowledge, but he hid them. He was made to appear before the magistrates of the place of examination. It was determined that he was guilty. His punishment was caused to befall him.

The great enemy Setiemperamun, who was cupbearer. He was brought in because of plans of which he had knowledge, but he hid them. He was made to appear before the magistrates of the place of examination. It was determined that he was guilty. His punishment was caused to befall him.

The great enemy Welen,[18] who was cupbearer. He was brought in because of the fact that he had knowledge of the projects through the chamberlain,[19] to whom he had been close, but he hid them and did not make a report concerning them. He was made to appear before the magistrates of the place of examination. It was determined that he was guilty. His punishment was caused to befall him.

The great enemy Aahebsed, who was the assistant of Pabekkamen. He was brought in because of the fact that he had knowledge of plans through Pabekkamen, with whom he had conspired. He did not make a report concerning them. He was made to appear before the magistrates of the place of examination. It was determined that he was guilty. His punishment was caused to befall him.

The great enemy Palik,[20] who was cupbearer and scribe of the white house. He was brought in because of the fact that he had intrigued with Pabekkamen; he had knowledge of plans through him. He did not make a report concerning them. He was made to appear before the magistrates of the place of examination. It was determined that he was guilty. His punishment was caused to befall him.

The great enemy, the Libyan Yenen,[21] who was cupbearer. He was brought in because of the fact that he had intrigued with Pabekkamen; he had knowledge of plans through him. He did not make a report concerning them. He was made to appear before the magistrates of the place of examination. It was determined that he was guilty. His punishment was caused to befall him.

Wives of the men of the harem gate who had joined the persons who had hatched the plans. Brought before the magistrates of the place of examination. It was determined that they were guilty. Their punishment was caused to befall them: 6 women.

The great enemy Pairy, son of Rum,[22] who was overseer of the white house. He was brought because of the fact that he had intrigued with the great enemy Penhuybin.[23] He associated with him to conduct a war to make rebellion against their Lord. He was made to appear before the magistrates of the place of examination. It was determined that he was guilty. His punishment was caused to befall him.

The great enemy Binemwaset, who was chief of the archers of Kush. He was brought in because of the fact that his sister, who was in the itinerant harem, had written him this: "Assemble men, take up arms (lit., "make a war") and come and make rebellion against your Lord!" He was made to appear before Qedenden, Baalmaher, Pairsun, and Djehutyrekhnefer. They examined him. They found him guilty. They caused his punishment to befall him.

Men who were brought in for their misdeeds because of the fact that they had intrigued with Pabekkamen, Pais, and Pentaweret. They were made to appear before the magistrates of the place of examination. It was determined that they were guilty. They were left to themselves in the place of examination. They took their own lives before violence was done to them.

The great enemy Pais, who was a general.

The great enemy Messui, who was a scribe of the House of Life.

The great enemy Prekamenef, who was a magician.[24]

The great enemy Iyry, who was overseer of the pure priests of Sakhmet.[25]

The great enemy Nebdjefau, who was a cupbearer.

The great enemy Shadmesdjer, who was a scribe of the House of Life.

Total: 6.

Persons who were brought in because of their misdeeds to the place of examination, before Qedenden, Baalmaher, Pairsun, Djehutyrekhnefer, and Merusyamun. One proceeded to examine their misdeeds. It was determined that they were guilty. They were left where they were. They took their own lives.

Pentaweret, he who had been given that other name.[26] He was brought in because he had intrigued with Teye, his mother, when she hatched plans with the women of the harem, making rebellion against his Lord. He was made to appear before the cupbearers for his examination. He was left where he was. He took his own life.

The great enemy Hentuenamun, who was cupbearer. He was brought in because of the misdeeds of the women of the harem, in whose midst he was, (misdeeds) of which he had knowledge, but about which[27] he did not make a report. He was made to appear before the cupbearers for his examination. It was determined that he was guilty. He was left where he was. He took his own life.

The great criminal Imenkhau, who was deputy of the itinerant harem. He was brought in because of the misdeeds of the women of the harem, in whose midst he was, (misdeeds) of which he had knowledge, but about which he did not make a report. He was made to appear before the cupbearers for his examination. It was determined that he was guilty. He was left where he was. He took his own life.

The great enemy Pairy, who was scribe of the king's chamber of the itinerant harem. He was brought in because of the misdeeds of the women of the harem, in whose midst he was, (misdeeds) of which he had knowledge, but about which he did not make a report. He was made to appear before the cupbearers for his examination. It was determined that he was guilty. He was left where he was. He took his own life.[28]

These three lists correspond to three procedures for inflicting punishment, which in all these cases was death. The first list enumerates those who were executed, which was evidently the most dishonorable method. In fact, it is indicated by a periphrasis[29]—"his punishment was caused to befall him"—because of the opprobrium attached to bloodshed, even when it was judicially justified. As for the condemned persons in the second list, they were compelled to commit suicide in the place where they had been judged, "the place of examination."

Suicide was also the lot for the condemned of the third list, but as far as we can tell, with a difference in the place where they were obliged to commit it: not in the place of examination, but "where they were." Is this to say that they were allowed to take their lives at home? Perhaps. In any case, from the logic of the text as a whole, it is clear that this change of place indicated a lesser degree of dishonor.

The Organization of the Conspiracy

Examination of the list furnishes some information regarding the conspiracy. It had a guiding spirit, Queen Teye,[30] who wanted to bring her son Pentaweret to the throne; it seems that the name under which he would rule had even been anticipated.[31] The conspiracy had a "project manager," the chamberlain Pabekkamen, who was assisted by the cupbearer Mesedsure; the overseer of the king's chamber of the itinerant harem, Panik; and the scribe of the royal chamber of the itinerant harem, Penduau.

The conspiracy comprised three major networks of persons. The first was the harem,[32] with the active participation of the women who resided in it, who speedily rallied relatives who lived on the outside to their cause, and who had the assistance of the wives of six guards. Some officials of this institution were passive accomplices but were nevertheless condemned to death: the scribe of the king's chamber of the itinerant harem, Pairy; the deputy of the itinerant harem, Imenkhau; and four controllers of the itinerant harem, Patjauemdiamun, Karpus, Khaemope, and Khaemmal. Among the passive accomplices were also cupbearers whose duties must have furnished them entry into the harem: Setiemperamun, Welen, the Libyan Yenen, Hentuenamun, and Palik, who was also scribe of the white house.

The latter was thus the link with the second network of persons, who lived outside the harem and who were expected to set themselves up as the armed contingent of the conspiracy. In fact, those who composed it were assigned the task of organizing an armed force and marching on the royal palace: "Gather men, take up arms (lit., "make war"), and come to make rebellion against your Lord!" Its members included the chief of the archers of Kush, Binemwaset; the brother of one of the schemers, Pairy, son of Rum; the overseer of the white house, who was associated with Penhuybin; an overseer of cattle, Pais, who was a general; and the cupbearer Nebdjefau.

The third network of persons was made up of a magician, Prekamenef; an overseer of pure priests of Sakhmet, Iyry; and two scribes of the House of Life, Messui and Shadmesdjer. What they had in common was their mastery of sorcery. The pure priests of Sakhmet, and *a fortiori* their overseers, were themselves redoubtable magicians.[33] In addition, the House of Life was the center of culture and sacred science (*sit venia verbo*), where, among other things, books of magic were preserved and studied.[34] Thus, with all these fearsome experts, the conspiracy had not only its armed wing, but also its magic wand, so to speak.

Sorcery in the Service of the Conspirators

The conspirators called upon the services of sorcery. In fact, two fragments of another document in the dossier, Papyrus Lee and Papyrus Rollin,[35] make it clear that the conspirators did not hesitate to use sorcery to achieve their ends:

He began to make magical writings in order to disorganize and spread confusion, making gods of wax and men to render human limbs weak, and to send them to Pabekkamen, whom Pre did not allow to be chamberlain, and to the other great enemies, with these words: "Take them in," and of course,[36] they took them in. And when he caused them to enter,[37] there were performed the bad deeds that he did, but which Pre did not permit to succeed. He was examined. One confirmed the reality of (lit., "that it was exact in") every bad misdeed that he (lit., "that his heart") had resolved to do, that they were indeed real (lit., "that there was exactitude in them"), and that they had done all of them, along with the other great enemies like him, and that what he had committed were grave misdeeds worthy (of the penalty) of death, great abominations of the land. And when he recounted the grave misdeeds, worthy (of the penalty) of death, that he had committed, he took his own life.[38]

"[. . .] by the Lord, l.p.h., to respect every commitment, sworn every year [. . . no part] of the place where I am for any man of the land."[39] And when Penhuybin, who was overseer of cattle, said to him, "Furnish me with a writing to give me something with which to inspire terror and fear," he gave him a document from the writing caskets[40] of Usermaatre-meryamun, l.p.h., the great god, his Lord. He began[41] to enter into contact[42] with the divine, making darkness for people (during sleep/unknown to people).[43] He came up beside the harem, and thus to the deep great place.[44] He began to make inscribed men of wax in order to have them taken inside by the intermediary of the controller Idrem,[45] spreading confusion in one gang, conjuring the others, causing certain messages to pass inside, and bringing others outside.[46] And when he was examined regarding them, one determined the reality of (lit., "that it was exact in") every bad misdeed that he had resolved to commit (lit., "that his heart had found to do"), that they were indeed real (lit., "that exactitude was in them"), and that he had committed all of them together with the other great enemies, the abomination of every god and every goddess, like him. Inflicted on him were heavy punishments entailing death, which the gods had said to inflict on him [. . . He was interrogated regarding] them, and one verified the reality of (lit., "that there was exactitude in") every bad misdeed that he had resolved to commit, that they were indeed real (lit., "that there was exactitude in them"), and that he had committed all of them along with the other great enemies, the abomination of every god and every goddess, like him, that they were grave misdeeds worthy (of the penalty) of death, [what he committed were] great abominations [of the land. And when he recounted the] grave [misdeeds] worthy (of the penalty of) death that he had committed, he took his own life. And when the magistrates who occupied themselves with him reported that he had taken his own life [along with the other great criminals, the great abominations of P]re, like him, (in conformity) with what[47] the writings of the divine words said: "Do it to him! [. . .]"[48]

Beyond the uncertainties of detail, it seems that certain conspirators took advantage of magical writings that they obtained from accomplices. In those writings, they found instructions in sorcery, with which they practiced execrations on wax figurines to neutralize the guards and to gain free access. Recourse to magic, far from being an original initiative on their part, was simply imposed by the very apparatus that surrounded Pharaoh's person. In fact, a whole system of magic, consisting of specific rituals, was perpetually at work to assure his protection.[49] Magic was therefore also necessary to counter its protective effects.

Was the magic effective? Apparently so, if we believe the lurid texts just cited. Did it enable the conspirators to put an end to Pharaoh? The answer is tricky, for unfortunately, we know little more regarding this conspiracy. We do not even know when it occurred, which would itself have furnished a good indication regarding its outcome. Many scholars maintain that it failed, for examination of the mummy of Ramesses III revealed no trace of wounds.[50] But is that enough to exclude the possibility of assassination?

The fact that Ramesses III reported that he appointed a commission to investigate the conspiracy cannot be invoked as an argument to prove that he survived it. The claim could be an example of apolo-

getics, like the fiction that had the same pharaoh draw up a report on
his reign in the celebrated Papyrus Harris, which was in fact written
under his successor, Ramesses IV.

In fact, the sources at our disposal yield no irrefutable indication
regarding the outcome of the conspiracy. They do, however, high-
light two facts that warrant special examination.

When the Unspeakable Must Be Spoken

We shall begin with the highly elaborate phraseological apparatus employed in writing the texts relating to the conspiracy. The
writing includes various omissions, periphrases, circumlocutions,
euphemisms—in short, various devices aimed at modifying what,
unadorned, was unacceptable to ideology.

Let us begin with the original names of certain criminals. In an article that has become a classic, G. Posener[51] showed that the names
given to some of the accused had a manifestly pejorative meaning:
Pabekkamen, "the blind servant"; Prekamenef, "Pre the blind";
Binemwaset, "the bad one in Thebes"; Mesedsure, "Re hates him";
Penhuybin, "Penhuy the bad"; Panik, "the demon." Scholars accept
that such names were not the original names of the conspirators. In a
civilization such as that of pharaonic Egypt, most names were dis-
cursive; that is, they had immediately accessible linguistic sense
and meaning. In addition, it was thought that a close link existed between a name and its bearer. Thus, these names were surely inflicted
on the conspirators in a new, defamatory baptism, a magical punishment that complemented their physical punishment.

Also magical were the formulations in which a displeasing fact
was retroactively erased by asserting that the creator had not ordained that it come about. Thus, just as the major criminals saw
their names modified in a pejorative manner, a formula invoking
Pre, the sun god, creator and master of his creation,[52] deprived them
of the benefit of having exercised an office of which they had shown
themselves to be unworthy.[53]

For example, while the Judicial Papyrus of Turin (4, 2) specifies
that the "great criminal Pabekkamen" was chamberlain, Papyrus
Rollin (2) states, "Pabekkamen, whom Pre did not allow to be chamberlain." Appearances notwithstanding, these two documents do not
contradict each other. In the second one, Pabekkamen is retrospectively denied a status that had nevertheless been his. There is an
analogous explanation for the following statement, which at first
seems disconcerting: "there were performed the bad deeds that he
did, but which Pre did not permit to succeed."[54] Here, allusion is

made to actions whose mention is particularly delicate, perhaps even the murder of the king. In any case, not only are the actions evoked with an evidently calculated imprecision, but no sooner are they mentioned than the distress inherent in noting them is in a sense exorcised by the proclamation that Pre, the solar creator god, had not allowed them to succeed, though they in fact had. When mention of such actions was unavoidable, the speaker had no choice but to take cover behind stereotypes. Thus, far from taking actual motives into account, the speaker pigeonholed the conduct of each conspirator as vile ingratitude, so that his crime appeared all the more odious and his punishment all the more deserved, while those who inflicted it bore less risk of being discredited or sullied. Here is an example that, however poorly established its literal meaning,[55] shows well to what caricaturing simplification—we might even say political cant—official discourse was subjected when it had to report on a plot hatched against Pharaoh, who was never even to be questioned:

The great enemy, deprived of his name, the cupbearer . . . [56] whom [Pre] did not [allow to be] a scribe of the House of Life,[57] insignificant and pathetic. [The many good deeds that] King Usermaatre-meryamun, the great god, his Lord, l.p.h., [did for him] when he was a scribe of the House of Life, insignificant and pathetic. He assured him subsistence, he did every (kind of) good deed in the world for him; one (i.e., Pharaoh) appointed him cupbearer. One (i.e., the conspirators) began to [repay] his (i.e., Pharaoh's) protection [with ingratitude (?)];[58] he (i.e., the cupbearer) proceeded to conspire in his (i.e., Pharaoh's) palace, l.p.h., though he (i.e., Pharaoh) had made him (i.e., the conspirator) more eminent than all the people who were conspiring.

What King Usermaatre-meryamun, the great god, his Lord, did for him. He nourished him with daily rations, [the one whom P]re did not allow to be cupbearer. The king went in search of him when his name was not known; he built him when he had[59] [. . . He did for him] every (kind of) good deed in the world, thanks to his efficiency. He (i.e., the conspirator) disregarded[60] the many good deeds [that King Usermaatre-meryamun, the great god, his Lord, l.p.h., had done for him. . . . He committed] bad deeds, great abominations of this land.

Need we enumerate the stereotyped expressions, the deliberately vague formulations, the euphemistic turns, and the omissions that punctuate this text? Speaking the unspeakable was assuredly no mean affair.

Notwithstanding this quasi-censure, the texts dealing with the harem conspiracy shed light on its seriousness and on the large number of people who were involved.

Judges Who Indulged in Debauchery and Fornication

The summary of the guilty parties reveals a huge surprise. We have already studied the first three lists of the Judicial Papyrus of Turin, the ones that enumerate those condemned to death. The fate reserved for those in the fourth list seems more enviable, if we might venture that formulation, for their lives were spared, though they lost some interesting elements of their visages:

> Persons on whom punishment was inflicted by cutting off their nose and ears[61] because of the fact that they had neglected the goodly instructions that I had formulated for them.
> The women went.[62] They found them there where they were. They had a fine party down there with them and with Pais. Their misdeeds seized them.
> The great enemy Pabes, who was cupbearer. He was punished by leaving him (to himself). He took his own life.
> The great enemy May, who was scribe of the bureau of the archives.
> The great enemy Taynakht, who was a soldier of the garrison.
> The great enemy Neney,[63] who was chief of the guards.[64]

Cutting off the nose and ears was a frequent punishment in the New Kingdom;[65] the information on this point is commonplace. What is less so is the presence, among the four people punished, of the cupbearer Pabes and the scribe of the bureau of archives May—two of the twelve members of the commission that Ramesses III charged with pursuing and judging the conspirators and their accomplices![66] Their crimes? Having succumbed to the attractions of comely young women, they shared their charms with Pais, a rogue general who participated in the strike force of the conspiracy.[67] It is possible that Pais in fact sent these women to seduce Pabes and May in order to compromise them. In any case, they paid for the sin of the flesh with pieces of their own flesh!

The final list consists of only one name:

> A man who had joined with them. He was reprimanded in very harsh terms; no proceedings were undertaken against him.
> The great enemy Hori, who was standard bearer of the garrison.[68]

This Hori was also one of the twelve judges. Though he shared in the lust of his colleagues, he received only a benign punishment. With unintended humor, the text states, "He was reprimanded in very harsh terms." But what was an admonition, even a severe one, compared with the mutilations that drove Pabes to suicide? There

could have been only one motive for such clemency: Hori had denounced his two colleagues, obtaining in exchange a mitigation of
his punishment. Such practices were well established. We may recall that in the matter of tomb robbery in the Valley of the Queens
under Ramesses IX, the coppersmith Pakhar received immunity for
agreeing to sway his testimony in the direction desired by the governor of the west of Thebes (see p. 16).

6

The Crisis of Values
in the New Kingdom

Behind the Stories: History

In the preceding chapters, the study of five affairs that marked the Ramesside Period, from the end of Dynasty 19 to the end of Dynasty 20, has conveyed its share of atrocities, brutalities, and crimes that were scandalous, often colorful, and sometimes revolting. Once past the initial reactions of amusement, indignation, and even horror, the Egyptologist is obliged to rise above the anecdotes, however spicy they might be, and inquire into their causes, and to rise above the stories, however juicy, so as to reveal history. For, although we must always take into consideration the hazards of the preservation and discovery of evidence, who would take it as purely accidental that all these scandals were concentrated in the New Kingdom, and specifically in the Ramesside Period?[1] Who could be satisfied with merely recounting the events? In fact, they were the symptoms and the catalysts of a profound moral crisis that shook pharaonic society and triggered a perceptible change in beliefs, leading to an ideological shift that was codified in political doctrine at the beginning of the first millennium.

Egypt's imperialism[2] reached its zenith in the New Kingdom, the period when this crisis occurred. Egypt expanded not only to the south, with the annexation of Nubia as far as the Fourth Cataract, but also into Asia, where a protectorate was established in Syria-Palestine and defended with varying degrees of success as Egyptian appetites came up against other imperialist powers. Beyond its successes and reversals, this expansion had two extremely important

121

consequences. One was an influx of people, technology, and new beliefs that caused pharaonic society to become more open to foreign
cultures. The other was an influx of raw materials and commodities,
and of finished products and luxury items that significantly contributed to the prosperity of those in a position to profit in one way
or another from their accumulation.

Evidently, these two facts conditioned, even if they do not mechanically explain them, the transformations and innovations experienced by Egyptian society in the New Kingdom, especially beginning
with the reigns of Amenophis II, Tuthmosis IV, and Amenophis III (c.
1426–1353 B.C.E.)—that is to say, the middle of Dynasty 18—and
which intensified considerably at the end of that dynasty and especially in the Ramesside Period (Dynasties 19 and 20, c. 1293–1069
B.C.E.).

That much said, this opening up to foreign cultures and this influx
of wealth assuredly affected the evolution of society, though not in
an even manner throughout the duration of the New Kingdom. Although the former phenomenon in no way diminished, the latter
quickly declined after the overlong reign of Ramesses II and the up-
heavals that marked the end of Dynasty 19 and ended in what we
must call, *mutatis mutandis,* an economic crisis. This crisis raged
endemically, with episodic aggravations, during Dynasty 20 after the
final years of Ramesses III (see pp. 5 and 54), when the fleeting up-
turn that characterized his reign came to an end. The crisis was experienced all the more severely in that the former prosperity had
created, in the various institutions that constituted the pharaonic
state, habits, needs, and demands that became ever more difficult to
satisfy.

What brought an end to this prosperity? As always, we cannot pre-
tend to draw up an exhaustive inventory of causal factors. General
factors include the climate changes that seem to have affected the
Near East at that time, but certainly not least was Egypt's loss of control over Syria-Palestine. Placed as they were under Egyptian influence or the Egyptian protectorate,[3] these regions had been obliged to
furnish tribute and taxes consisting of considerable amounts of
goods, especially metals and finished products,[4] that contributed to
the wealth of the land. Was it an accident that the last pharaoh under
whose reign, or at least for the greater part of it,[5] Egypt enjoyed an
evident prosperity was Ramesses III, who still had a solid foothold
in Canaan?[6] Be that as it may, just a short time later, the situation de-
teriorated to the point that famine drove the population to invade
cemeteries to survive (see chapter 1).

In a more general manner, the plunge in the standard of living[7] for all, impoverishment for many, and destitution for the least fortunate exacerbated proclivities toward corruption, prevarication, exploitation, and barbarities of every sort, proclivities that had already developed in the wealth and ease of the glory days. Impotent in the face of this multiplication of woes, institutions contributed to their own being put into question, a development that had already begun at the very moment of their acme. This development was a fleeting counterpoint to the triumphal hymns, all the more so in that the opening to other cultures and other models had facilitated critical distance.[8] Fed by both successes and setbacks, a crisis of values thus eroded New Kingdom Egypt to the point of inspiring a new ethic that changed the traditional relationships between individuals and the world they inhabited. To describe this development, we must first describe the older concept that the new ethic opposed.

The Original Concept

The concept that was replaced had been based on four essential points:

1. The creator god held himself aloof from his creation, according it a certain autonomy.
2. The social order, which was one of the elements of creation, possessed immanent principles of self-regulation that assured requital for human actions on earth or in the hereafter: punishment for those who transgressed it and recompense for those who respected it.
3. Sheltered, so to speak, behind this order that emanated from him, the creator god acted on human destiny only as the ultimate authority, whether in granting or refusing the individual knowledge of the laws of the social order, or in making direct, though sporadic and exceptional, interventions.
4. As a result, social success could be viewed as the just reward of the one who respected the laws of the established order and adhered to the social institutions through which they manifested themselves.

We shall examine each of these four points in detail.

The Relative Autonomy of Creation vis-à-vis Its Creator

Creation disposed of a certain autonomy, because it was ruled by a principle called *maat*. This term admits of no precise translation; according to context, it can be rendered as "proper order of things," "justice," "truth," or "equitableness."[9]

Maat, personification of triumphant universal order. Drawing by I. Franco.

Here is how Egyptian thought conceived the origin and role of *maat* (the word is feminine gender): the creator god made the world by causing being to emerge from the primordial waters, and he reigned directly over humanity. Then, in his old age, according to one myth, wearied from having had to suppress a revolt of humankind and feeling no enthusiasm for the prospect of other uprisings to put down, he abandoned his terrestrial kingdom for the comfortable routine of a daily circuit in the sky,[10] thus continuing to regulate the smooth functioning of the cosmos in the capacity of sun god. After an interlude presided over by demigods,[11] he entrusted the task of perpetuating his creation on earth to the Egyptians through the intermediary of Pharaoh, who was his representative before humanity and humanity's representative before him. Still, this new division of labor entailed no radical break. The functioning of human society under the care of Pharaoh and the functioning of the cosmos under that of the creator god were based on a common need: the maintenance of being, which was characterized specifically by order,[12] against the perpetual threat of nonbeing. Creation was in fact a sort of "entropic" system won from nondifferentiation,[13] incessantly tending toward self-annihilation. *Maat* had to be put into play to prevent a return to nondifferentiation. *Maat* was the active principle of cohesion between the various elements of the world, similar to the "negentropy" of physics, which worked on two levels. On one level, which we can call the "cosmological," that of creation in its totality, humanity—through the person of Pharaoh—assisted the gods and goddesses in continuing to function in the cosmic equilibrium by means of the cults devoted to the deities and the rituals that the cults entailed. Correlatively, these deities preserved the world in its original state, which was established so that humanity could live and thrive in it.

On the other level—the social level—*maat* sought to maintain harmonious relationships between the various ethnic and sociological groups that constituted humanity, so that they might fit in with one another and organize a way of life that was bearable. *Maat* furnished models and rules of conduct to which each individual strove to conform, and which were capable of preserving the cohesion that was necessary for the proper functioning of society. For example, while respect and obedience were imperatives regulating the relationships between inferiors and superiors, their corollary was the protection accorded to the weak against the strong, the vertical solidarity that justified the inequality inherent in social order. The creator god, who was the first to undertake this task, delegated it to Pharaoh. In his theodicy, one of the basic principles of social order on which the creator god claimed to have founded his terrestrial realm was "to shield the weak from the acts of the strong."[14] This principle was one of the governmental imperatives incumbent on Pharaoh as the creator god's successor: "Re has placed King So-and-so in the land of the living for all eternity to judge men,"[15] and "He (i.e., the creator god) made for them (i.e., humankind) predestined (lit., "in the egg")[16] sovereigns, sustainers devoted to come to the rescue (lit., "in the back") of the weak."[17]

Pharaoh thus repeated a deed done initially by the creator god when he set the world in place. Private individuals defined their ethical principles in similar terms, as shown by the autobiographical cliché in which we hear an echo of the formulae just cited: "I protected the weak from the strong."[18] The norms implied by *maat* regulated the complex organization of society, in which each person contributed, according to his position, to the smooth functioning of the whole and profited in return. *Maat* thus rested on reciprocity.

Immanent Retribution for Human Actions

An important consequence of this reciprocity was that retribution for human actions was immanent, in the very world in which they took place.[19] While measuring up to the normative values resulted in success, correlatively, acting badly resulted in ineluctable failure, for transgression more or less mechanically aroused punishment by way of return effect: "Wrong is given to the one who does it,[20] and *maat* (is given) to the one who comes with it."[21] This principle is formulated clearly in a famous wisdom text, the Instruction of Ptahhotpe, a work that beautifully illustrates this older concept:

Maat is powerful, lasting its pertinence,
It has not been disturbed since the time of Osiris.
He who transgresses the laws is punished.
This is what escapes the greedy one.
Baseness might seize riches,
but never has villainy brought its action to a safe harbor.[22]

According to a well-known study,[23] this text would seem to be ambiguous, in that the sanction entailed in the mechanisms of *maat* can take effect either during life on earth or in the afterlife, at the Judgment of the Dead. Conversely, observance of *maat* brings advantages only because of the mechanisms of retribution, whether on earth or in the realm of the dead. This pragmatic sentiment is often formulated, sometimes with so ostentatious a utilitarianism that we cannot tell where ingenuousness leaves off and cynicism begins:[24]

> If I rejoiced in saying *maat,* it was because I knew that it is useful for the one who does it on earth, from the beginning until the landing (i.e., death). . . .
> Do it, it will be useful to you; you will spend (your) existence happily until (you) rest in the beautiful West.[25]

Autobiographical and wisdom texts incessantly proclaim that he who models his conduct on *maat* serves his own interests: "How useful is good comportment for him who displays it," "Good comportment is more valuable to a man than that which a thousand acts bring," "It was my excellent comportment that advanced my position."[26]

With the social order thus established, and legitimated in that it was part of the creation set in place by the creator god, its justification was fostered by the principle of *maat*. It imposed itself, so to speak, by the force of things, for respecting it was both a necessary and a sufficient condition for success in this world and its continuation in the next one.

Thus, in action, ethics and effectiveness merged with one another. To be sure, it was not a matter of denying, as though through beatific innocence, the presence of evil in society. The distinction between that which was licit and that which was illicit and the respective consequences of observance and transgression were established in the very process of creation:[27]

> Distinction was made between that which is approved and that which is reproved, and since then, life has been given to the honest man,[28] and death to the criminal.[29]

In fact, there was evil in human hearts, though in his theodicy, the creator god denied having wished it so: "I did not command that they do evil. It was their wills that transgressed what I had said."[30]

Humans were thus fallible, and in fact, they continually sinned, if only because they were driven by necessity, as recognized by an eloquent peasant who was a herald of popular wisdom:

> The possessor of resources is easy-going,[31] while the desire to overcome is for the outlaw. Theft is natural for him who has nothing. If goods are stolen by an outlaw, the act seems reprehensible to the one who is not in need; yet he (i.e., the one who is not in need) should not reproach him (i.e., the outlaw), for it has to do with seeking his subsistence (lit., "for himself").[32]

An excuse is offered, or at least, it is admitted that the social order is transgressed by the very persons who are excluded from it; not only that, but there is scarcely any illusion regarding the officials charged with maintaining order. In fact, this same spokesman for morality who recognized a sociological justification for theft did not conceal his lack of faith in the honesty of judges:

> Watch out for the magistrates; they're a leaky bucket.[33] Judges, telling lies is their fodder; they do not weigh on their conscience.[34]

Under such conditions, justice was not invulnerable. Although wealth generally soothed characters, as we have seen, it could combine with lust for power to turn tribunals into instruments of theft:

> As for one who wishes to be impressive,[35] if he has wealth, it is in the manner of a crocodile that he robs in the court of justice.[36]

But the system was capable of correcting the lapses of certain of its members by means of self-regulating mechanisms, in particular the intervention of those who constituted its hierarchy. To be sure, even they could stray to the point of transgressing *maat*. But such cases were purely accidental, individual errors caused by a conjuncture of circumstances. The occasional dishonesty and partiality of a high functionary thus fell into the category of paradox, and it is precisely in terms of paradox that the eloquent peasant,[37] for instance, qualified the attitude of the dignitary who refused to give him justice after he was robbed:

He who administers according to the laws is commanding theft! Who then will repel evil? . . .
The guide is a man who has gone astray . . .
O you who make live, do not make die!
O provider, do not let someone find himself short!
Shadow, do not act like a blazing light![38]

The paradox was so flagrant that it was used in a *reductio ad absurdum:*

Does the balance tilt? Thoth,[39] is he lax?
(If so), you may do injustice.[40]

Assuredly, humans being what they were because of weaknesses or vices, the established order could be transgressed. But such occasional dysfunction would be temporary, because the effect of self-regulation would soon put the system back on the right track, or even eliminate those who disturbed it.

As for the creator god, he held himself aloof behind the order and the institutions he established, distancing himself from governing humankind after a somewhat inconvenient experience (see p. 124).

Occasional Interventions by the Creator God

This withdrawal did not mean, however, that the god had abandoned creation in general or humanity in particular to the point that it was ruled only by the inevitable play of principles that were immanent in its order. The older concept did not fall into a mechanical reductionism that would have signified that the world was entirely rational and predictable by anyone who knew and mastered its laws. In fact, the divine remained the ultimate authority over the course of events: "It is what the god has ordained that happens."[41]

This was so first of all because it was according to his own pleasure that the god accorded the ability to hear, which provided the sole access to this knowledge and mastery of the laws of the world, on which destiny depended:

> The one who hears is one whom the god loves, the one who does not hear is the one whom the god hates.[42]

Second, it was so because, when they deemed it fit, deities intervened directly in the lives of individuals.[43] Sinuhe bears witness to this phenomenon: he was induced to desert the expedition led by his lord, King Senwosret I, and to roam the lands of Asia by an irresistible impulse of divine inspiration; "it was the plan of a god," as he explained it.[44] Another example is Ankhtifi, whom Horus chose to restore order to a region wracked by dissension:

> Horus brought me to the nome of Edfu as possessor of life, prosperity, and health, to restore it to order in my name. Horus must have been fully desirous of restoring it to order, because he brought me there to restore it to order.[45]

Thus, although the creator god had withdrawn from his creation, far from having abandoned it to its own devices, he continued to control it, most often as a last resort, by means of sporadic interventions. But these interventions were unpredictable and unilateral; even when they were beneficent, the person who experienced them had not solicited them. Assuredly, then, the divine remained the first cause, but his effect on human society was exerted primarily through the order he had instituted and the principles of requital that were immanent in it—that is, punishment for the one who transgressed it and reward for the one who respected it.

Social Success as Reflection of Good Conduct

To the extent that it was viewed as legitimate, this postulated correlation between ethics and effectiveness resulted in the legitimation and exaltation of social success; just like a favorable verdict in the Judgment of the Dead, social success was viewed as a compensation for moral qualities:

> If you are of humble rank and in the service of someone who is successful,[46] whose situation is good with the god, (but) whom you learn to be of low origin,[47] do not be insolent toward him because of what

you have learned regarding him formerly. Respect him for what he
has become.[48] Fortune does not come on its own. It is their (i.e., the
gods') sanction for the one they approve . . . it is the god who causes
success.[49]

This is how a very early wisdom text advocates respect for a par-
venu, because good fortune, even if recent, far from being the result
of luck, is granted by the gods representing the principles of order as
a reward for observance of these principles. In the various periods of
Egyptian history, the yardstick by which this good conduct was measured could vary. In practice, good conduct manifested itself in a
sense of familial and regional solidarity in the so-called "intermediate" periods, when there was a withdrawal to the local level because
of divisions or weakness of the central power, or when invaders
were in power. Conversely, good conduct expressed itself through
loyalty to authority (pharaoh or deity)[50] when the political situation
favored it or demanded a show of submission to it. In either case, the
ultimate rationale remained respect for *maat.*

This concept justified ambition and careerism, and the central
power did not hesitate to encourage such impulses when it found
them to be in its interests. Thus, to recruit administrators from
among the sons of the middle class, who were often inclined to give
up the study of accounting and contracts for the splendor and glory
of a soldier's life, the central power held out the prospect of the
recognition, power, and ease that was promised to the competent
scribe:

> Be a scribe, that your limbs may become sleek and your hands soft,
> that you may go out dressed in white, finding yourself promoted to
> higher status, that courtiers might greet you.[51]
>
> Apply yourself to being a scribe, a good situation worthy of you. If
> you call one person, a thousand respond. You walk unhindered on the
> road. Far from being a lamb led to the slaughter, you are a leader of
> others.[52]

Or again, to assure the recruitment and loyalty of efficient battal-
ions, valiant warriors were heaped with land and slaves. These men,
such as Ahmose son of Ebana, inflicted those who visited their tomb
chapels with an ostentatious inventory of their rewards, with the
naive and blissful satisfaction of the nouveaux riches. These
homines novi (new men), whose type can be sketched from their autobiographical proclamations as well as from wisdom texts, were
right, after all, to declare themselves zealous followers of *maat,*[53] for

the concept according to which social destiny depended on moral comportment furnished a sort of alibi for the most unbridled ambition. It implied adherence to established order and respect for the institutions through which it manifested itself, even when this respect resulted more from calculated interest than from profound conviction.

Thus, the older concept elevated the order that ruled human society into a positive value; the concept did not deny society's imperfections, which were due to the principle of disorder inherent in society, but it credited society with the ability to overcome disorder. By adjusting their conduct to this value, individuals were assured of finding their reward, the cynical by way of the earthly success thus obtained and the faithful by way of the certitude of life after death.

The New Ethic

General Definition

Beginning with the New Kingdom, a new ethic competed with the old one in a lengthy crisis that shook the ideology of the ruling class. The crisis was characterized by a rejection of the established order as a positive value because of its inherent corruption, in favor of a personal relationship with a deity of choice.

Of course, this new concept did not suddenly emerge fully formed. It spread gradually in the ideology of the New Kingdom, coexisting with the traditional beliefs, which it sometimes partially eroded and sometimes entirely submerged.[54] Often it remained implicit and barely surfaced, while sometimes it blossomed robustly with the coherence of a reasoned doctrine. We thus find it expressed on two levels in ideologically weighted texts:

1. In normative texts such as the religious versions of royal decrees, and in wisdom texts and autobiographies that reflect their spirit, it manifests itself as a consideration of a serious defect in the established order—namely, the corruption of those who constitute the cogs of its machinery, from ordinary scribes on up to the vizier. In so doing, it casts doubt on the inherent merit of this order and its immanent capacity for self-regulation, which was the basis of the old ethic.
2. In erudite prayers collected into anthologies for schoolboys, or in certain innovative autobiographies, it is articulated in two theses that are linked by a cause-and-effect relationship:

a. far from being accidental, temporary, or superficial, the corruption of
the established order is viewed as lying at the heart of its normal functioning; and
b. since humans can find no hope in this world, nothing remains but to
seek salvation in a personal relationship with a deity in order to assure serenity here below and survival in the hereafter.

We shall now examine in detail each of these two ways in which the
new ethic manifested itself.

The New Ethic as a Questioning of the Established Order

At first, the new ethic asserted itself in the minor mode. In
the traditional text genres—autobiographies, wisdom texts, and
royal decrees—it took increasing account of the essential corrupt-
ibility of those persons who made up the machinery of the state by
virtue of their role in the institutions that composed it, from the
scribes in the administrative offices to the priests in the temples. In
this mode, this vice is denounced indirectly, through exhortations
not to succumb to it, through threats of legal sanctions against those
who succumbed, and through denials of ever having succumbed to
it. Its manifestations thus became a highly elaborate theme.

The Treatment of Embezzlement in the Ideology

The many proclamations of innocence that appear in autobiographies, beginning with the New Kingdom, evidently mean, *a
contrario,* that bribery and embezzlement were widespread and
imply a growing skepticism with regard to the effectiveness of institutions. Thus, in an autobiography from Dynasty 18, the governor
Pahery evokes possible illicit gains whose temptation he, as an honest official, was of course able to resist. The following passage has
more to do with falsifying accounts than with corruption in general:

> I reckoned the boundaries in writing, and the riverbanks, in the form
> of every sort of benefit for the king and every sort of goods of the royal
> domain, l.p.h., like the inundation extending to the Great Green;[55] my
> directives were firm in making arrangements for my Lord, and I was
> scrupulous regarding the amounts that were left. I was not negligent
> regarding equivalences. I did not obtain personal benefit from the sur-
> pluses.[56]

In a large section of Upper Egypt stretching from Dendara to El Kab,
Pahery's job was to estimate the revenues that could be realized, in

the form of taxes or tribute, for the benefit of King Tuthmosis III and the royal domain. His intent was to proclaim the integrity of his accounts,[57] which were alluded to by the terms "the amounts that were left," "equivalences," and "surpluses."[58]

Accounting was all the more complicated in that there was no currency in pharaonic Egypt, but rather standard units of value. There was thus a constant need to establish "equivalences" among the various staple products and the like, so as to exchange those of which there was a surplus for those of which there was a deficiency[59] and to enable conversions from one amount to another. Thus many opportunities existed to juggle figures, rounding off amounts so as to cause the disappearance of goods that in fact existed and were thus available. Our administrator boasts of not having drawn "personal benefit" from the surpluses, which leaves us to understand that others did so. Indeed, analysis of certain grain accounts from the Ramesside Period reveals an ongoing tendency of scribes to round totals down, neglecting fractions.[60] The quantities thus omitted seem small, to be sure, but constant repetition of this practice resulted in the diversion of a hefty amount of public property; small streams become great rivers.

Scribes deliberately falsified their accounts in various ways: omitting certain entries when reckoning the totals, employing deliberate "inattention" to consistent reading so as to reduce a figure by ten, and using other little tricks that we can only suspect without being able to pinpoint how they were employed.[61] Djehutimose,[62] scribe of (the institution of) the Tomb, was thus caught with his hand in the cookie jar. He functioned (or ran amok!) at the end of Dynasty 20, during the reign of Ramesses XI, and he was responsible for the transport of the grain intended to pay the artisans of Deir el-Medina, the men who often experienced irregularities in their provisioning, as we have seen,[63] for the pharaonic world was rather small. Though Djehutimose probably succeeded in duping his superiors, who were little inclined to initiate themselves into the arcana of bookkeeping, three millennia later, his dishonesty failed to escape the perspicacity of the great Egyptologist Sir Alan Gardiner, who concluded from a meticulous study of a document written by our scribe that he had "falsified his statement."

The Treatment of Extortion in the Ideology

The previously mentioned examples were cases of embezzlement, a sort of *bakshish* that an official would pay himself in the serenity of his office. In addition, some payments were extracted by threatening some balance of power. Such extortion must have been frequent in the New Kingdom, for it found explicit mention in normative texts, as witnessed by this decree of Sethos II:

> [Now],[64] the mind of his majesty led him to seek something useful to his father Amun-Re, king of the gods, to Mut the great, mistress of Asheru, Khons-in-Thebes-Neferhotep, and to all the gods and goddesses of Upper and Lower Egypt. . . . [65]
>
> [His majesty commanded] the organization of the corporation[66] of bearers of Amun, [Mut, and Khons-in-Thebes-Neferhotep, and all the gods and goddesses] of Upper [and Lower Egypt], and the god's-fathers and pure priests in order to prevent "something" from being exacted from them by any prophet who might arise in the time of [his majesty].
>
> As for any prophet who might be found[67] demanding something from them, he will be deprived of his position and made an agricultural worker.
>
> [As for any bearer, any god's-father, any pure priest, or any ritualist priest] of whom it is learned that he has given something to the prophet, [he shall be removed from] his position and be made an agricultural worker. Let [the law . . .] be applied.
>
> You will apply it (i.e., the decree) in very good condition (lit., "it being very, very good") and in its entirety, doing service in his (i.e., Pharaoh's) favor before the gods, saying to them, "Assure the health of Pharaoh, l.p.h., your perfect child, every day. Give him victory for his arm in every land . . . [foreign countries being under] his sandals forever and ever."[68]

Because of the corruption of morals, the prophets' extortion of the minor clergy and the bearers of the sacred barque became so widespread that a special decree forbidding it was issued by Sethos II, one of the pharaohs contemporary with Paneb. The measures were severe, for the guilty parties risked being removed from office and made "cultivators," an assuredly less enviable job.[69] And what is more, the "victims" were promised the same punishment! Without doubt, these victims were to some extent consenting, and the "something" (*nkt,* see p. 152) extorted by the prophet was in return for something.[70] The issuing of such a decree constituted an official recognition of the existence of these practices, all the more in that the text was displayed in hieroglyphs in the temple, after having been formulated with highly elaborate ideological pomp: formulation in the style of the "royal novel" (see n. 64), and thanksgiving for the pharaoh who decreed the measure.

Extortion could assume a more discreet form—for example, falsification of documents. Falsification and corruption are recurrent themes in the well-known Instruction of Amenemope, a work that illustrates the ethic that was born from the crisis of Egyptian ideology in the New Kingdom. In fact, Amenemope was particularly qualified to warn against these perversions, to judge from the titles and epithets heaped on him:

> Overseer of the seed of Egypt, overseer of grain, who guards the accuracy of the measure, who administers the grain for his Lord . . . who sets the markers on the borders of the fields, who protects the king with his registers, who holds the land-registers of Egypt, the scribe who determines the divine offering of all the gods.[71]

It is thus not surprising that he shows himself to be a zealous proponent of integrity in administrative and judicial conduct:

> Do not wrong a man with your pen on a scroll; it is the abomination of the god. Do not manufacture evidence out of false words or brush another aside with your tongue. Do not impose a fee on one who has nothing so as to falsify your pen (or, "if you impose a fee on one who has nothing, do not falsify your pen").[72]

This passage denounces abuses that could tempt a functionary because of his mastery of writing. Given that ninety-nine percent of the population was illiterate,[73] was it not easy to falsify an account, a delivery slip, or an administrative document?

In fact, we know of a private legal matter in which one of the parties seems to have been injured in this manner:

> I must complain in these terms: "It is a false register that has been made against me. For when my case was examined earlier, it was determined that I was on the register."[74]

During an interminable legal battle, Mes was astonished to learn that he was no longer in an administrative archive where he had previously seen his name.[75] In fact, such falsification was not exclusive to this period. In the Old Kingdom, three witnesses were required to authenticate a private legal document,[76] which implies a need for safeguards against forgeries. Still, in the case of Mes, it was official registers and not private legal documents that were altered. Moreover, only in the New Kingdom was falsification taken into account in a normative work such as the Instruction of Amenemope.

Questioning of the Judicial System

Fighting the good fight, Amenemope denounced *a contrario* the corruption of what we would call the "judicial system," though there was no exact equivalence in this regard between modern and pharaonic society:[77]

Do not disqualify a man in the tribunal,
do not reject the righteous one.
Do not let yourself be obsessed by a luxurious garment
only to reject it[78] when it is in rags.
Do not accept a "bonus" from a powerful man
in order to reject the case of a weak man in his favor.
Justice is a great gift of the god.
He gives it to whom he pleases.[79]

Such practices, which are denounced at length by Amenemope, were evidently occurring already in Dynasty 18.

From the reign of Tuthmosis III, the autobiography of Rekhmire, a vizier who was thus in charge of the justice system (see pp. 141–42), is highly instructive in this regard:

I judged the petitioner, (but) I was not unjust; I was not interested in "compensation."[80]

The term *ḏbꜣw*, "compensation," is clearly a euphemistic term for a bribe. "I in no way neglected the weak one, and[81] conversely, I did not accept anyone's bribe."[82] Here, the usual imperative of care for the weak is not invoked for its own sake, as it frequently is in the ancient texts, but rather as a synonym for incorruptibility: attention to the distress of the poor has its correlate in insensibility to the advantages of the rich.

In fact, corruption had become such a cancer on the judicial apparatus that Haremhab, who found himself obliged to restore order in an Egypt shaken by the heresy of Akhenaten,[83] had to formulate a veritable theory of the incorruptibility of a magistrate in a passage justifying a decree. It takes the form of an "instruction"—the term in Egyptian is also used to designate wisdom literature—addressed to those he had entrusted with the administration of justice:[84]

I have scrutinized men, [I have searched for] discreet [dignitaries] of good character, who know how to judge sentiments and who obey the words of the royal palace and the laws of the administration. I have appointed them to judge the Two Lands and satisfy the one who is in [the palace . . .] . . . I have placed them in the major cities of Upper and Lower Egypt, each man being at ease thanks to them, with no exception. I have given them rules that they have clearly in mind (lit., "before them") and laws that are in their reference books[85] [. . .]. I have inculcated in them a rule of conduct in order to guide them toward the just, my instruction being as follows: "Do not associate with those who are answerable (lit., 'others among men');[86] do not accept the 'bonus' of another. . . . It is in fact up to you to distinguish the guilty from the righteous."[87]

The word translated "gratification" (*fk3w*) literally means "recompense," but here it clearly refers to bribes given to judges, as in the hymns to Amun, "vizier of the poor," which we shall consider later. It is highly significant that Haremhab felt constrained to proclaim, via the solemn medium of a royal decree, that integrity, along with its corollary, rejection of corruption, constituted a norm of judicial ethics. The magistrates had no doubt failed to take note of them. In fact, the king decreed a fearsome warning to make the magistrates understand that above all, a judge was obligated to render justice:

As for any governor or prophet[88] of whom it is heard that he sits to render judgment in the tribunal[89] that was instituted to judge, that he treats a guilty party as innocent, it is as a grave crime worthy of (the penalty of) death that it will be imputed to him.[90]

If Haremhab felt justified in exhibiting such severity,[91] it was because he had abolished a tax to which the magistrates of the tribunals had evidently been subject and which had furnished them an excuse to take what they owed out of the hides of defendants.

Statements praising integrity and measures combating corruption appear only rarely in normative texts prior to the New Kingdom. At best, we can find sporadic and rather vague allusions in autobiographies.[92] But—and this is significant—the theme is not even mentioned in the long list of misdeeds that those aspiring to the realm of Osiris were obliged to deny having committed. This well-known list, known as the "negative confession," is part of the Book of the Dead, chapter 125 of the Late Period canon, and it was surely composed prior to the earliest known versions, which date to the New Kingdom.[93] Of course, no one would deduce from this fact that corruption or falsification of documents never occurred in earlier periods. It is simply that denunciation of these practices does not occur in instructions and normative texts prior to the New Kingdom. But why did this theme become frequent at that time? Surely because it was viewed as an issue that had assumed an importance not accorded to it earlier, either because it had in fact been more limited, or because ethics had excluded it from its preoccupations. If, from then on, ideology lent recognition to this phenomenon, it was apparently in the entirely sunlit arena of its moralistic combat. But in the shadows lurked an irrepressible implication: what are we to think of a society in which it was necessary to make incessant appeals to battle corruption? To remain half implicit, as in a Lacanian half statement, this implication was nonetheless real. Earlier, it had been believed that the established order in one way or another had means of self-regulation that corrected its imperfections. Would this concept continue to be maintained as a positive value, when earthly institutions and the people who assured their functioning proved to be corrupted? In a minor mode, then, the new ethics limited itself to discreet criticism formulated in a more or less indirect manner.

Divine Protection as Unique Recourse

The criticism not only grew stronger to the point of radical negation; it also aroused a positive correlate when the new concept was expressed in a major mode, particularly at the beginning of Dynasty 19, though we should not overestimate the influence of the Amarna heresy on this evolution.[94] If the established order was from then on rejected as an ethical value, the rejection was for the purpose of replacing it with seeking recourse in the divine.

The point of seeking the protective effectiveness of the divine was to make up for the failure of the judicial apparatus, which was decidedly the most vulnerable domain, or at least the one toward which criticism was the least restrained. In fact, the judges were the object of distrust and prejudice to the point that those governed denied that there was any justice beyond that rendered by a divine protector.

Radical Critique of the Judicial System

An example of this phenomenon is the following condemnation by an overseer of the cattle count of Amun, Simut, surnamed Kyky, in a composition that is a monument of the new ethic:[95]

> As for a despoiler, the one who stands up to him is under her (i.e., the goddess Mut, chosen as patron saint) jurisdiction. I say regarding the magistrate in the moment when he rages, "Powerful though he may be, he will not be able to cause prejudice, for the matter lies with

Sakhmet the Great.[96] One cannot measure the range of her action. No servant of hers can succumb to pettifogging, ever, ever."[97]

We have seen that in the older concept, what was reproached in a magistrate was his insatiable propensity to solicit bribes from pleaders—to be, as it were, a leaky bucket. But the highest authorities were counted on to correct the miscarriages of justice that this rapacity could provoke here and there. Now, discredit was heaped on all magistrates, whatever their ranks. Writers were no longer content to jeer at the mistakes of judges with a mocking smile; rather, they stigmatized the rapacious and generalized ferocity of the entire judicial system. There was no human parry for this ferocity; it could be opposed only by a divine ferocity, that of the goddess Sakhmet, a lion goddess who represented the aggressive drives to which every goddess was capable of abandoning herself when need arose. Otherwise put, in the new concept, the selective intervention of deities was substituted for the administrative and judicial institutions of pharaonic society, whose ineffectiveness was recognized, and whose patent failure was caused by their corruption.

Beyond these institutions, society as a whole, including its familial structures, no longer offered any protection. Simut, surnamed Kyky, expressed this situation candidly:

I did not acquire a protector among men, [I did not attach myself to . . .] among the powerful. It was not even my son.[98]

This radical skepticism regarding the system and its correlate, total abandonment to the divine, is particularly manifest in a frequent theme of personal piety that is illustrated by a number of hymns to Amun. In them, the god is invoked as the ultimate recourse for the "poor man" overcome by the injustice of human tribunals:[99]

Amun, lend an ear[100] to a man alone in the tribunal, and who is poor; he has no fortune (?), yet the tribunal exacts money from him for the "scribe of the mat,"[101] and clothing for the beadles. May it be determined that Amun has been transformed into the vizier, so that the poor man escapes! May it be determined that the poor man has been justified; may the poor man win over the rich man.[102]

Amun-Re, who comes to the aid of the poor man when he is in distress. He causes the tribunal to be unanimous when it passes justice on the poor man. The poor man is justified, while the one who has brought a "bonus" is thwarted.[103]

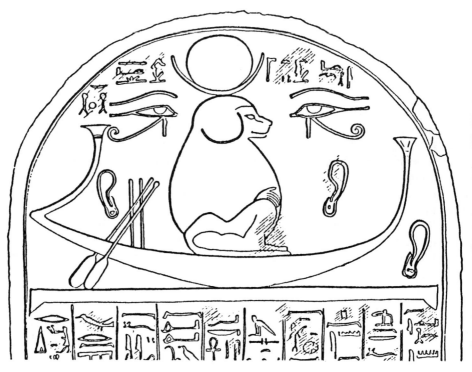

Desirous of encouraging the gods to hear entreaties, worshipers sometimes had ears depicted on the stelae they dedicated to deities. Drawing by B. Bruyère.

Amun-Re, the first to be king, god of the first moment,[104] vizier of the poor man. He does not accept the "bonus" of the guilty one; he does not say, "Bring proof";[105] he pays no heed to pressure.[106] Amun judges the land with his fingers; he speaks according to his heart. He judges the guilty and puts him in hell, and the just one in the West.[107]

You are Amun, the vizier, the vizier who judges every poor man. Amun does not say to the one who has no "bonus," "Leave my tribunal." Amun, turn your face toward the one who pronounces your name, Amun, it is you who make truth emerge.[108]

You are the one who makes truth emerge, who does not accept a "bonus," who sustains the impoverished, who [. . . the po]or man. You would not lend your hand to the powerful one.[109]

The argumentation of these hymns is organized along two contrary lines: criticism of human justice and praise of divine justice. Let us examine this criticism. It is articulated thus:

1. The greed of the judges and all those associated with the judicial system is insatiable.
2. This greed leads to a generalized corruption.
3. When all is said and done, it is the poor man who suffers the consequences of these circumstances. He cannot obtain justice, because he is disadvantaged, if not disqualified, before the tribunals by his very destitution.

We cannot underestimate the critical, even somewhat subversive, import of these texts. If the "poor man" (see pp. 142–43) appeals to the god to grant justice, thus disqualifying the latter's human representatives, it is because he no longer entertains any expectations from a judicial system dedicated to being forever unfavorable to him by virtue of its profound corruption. The praise of the god, which is largely negative, a contrario discredits greedy magistrates, who are as quick as their assistants to demand bribes, susceptible to the pressures of the powerful but inflexible toward those from whom they have nothing to gain, and partial to the point of demanding excessive proof from the innocent or simply dismissing him from the tribunal.

These hymns, which lack the good-natured irony of the older tradition, paint the blackest of pictures of a corrupt judicial system. They condemn it in its entirety, placing no limits on its perversion and crediting it with no capacity for self-correction. In the last analysis, invoking a god as "vizier"[110] entails a very serious implication: it is to proclaim that the terrestrial vizier is performing few, if any, of his duties. The vizier was nothing less than the one who presided over the interlocking complex of administrative offices and institutions by means of which Egypt was administered.[111] Assisted by a veritable army of bureaucrats who were initiated into the arcana of the regulations and who were masters at churning out huge piles of meticulous paperwork, it was he who sat in his office, updating the huge mass of records that kept things going: the records of land holdings that were used to determine taxes, copies of private deeds of transfer of goods and real estate, transcripts of hearings, and so forth. In short, he disposed of the written records of everything that happened in the administration and the judiciary, and he referred to them to resolve disputes between institutions or between institutions and their employees[112] or private individuals, in order to unravel regulatory complications, to decide between plaintiffs, and to exercise jurisdiction over complaints.[113] He also was responsible for making rulings concerning irregularities that had been committed,[114] for getting judicial proceedings under way, and for appointing an interrogatory commission when the gravity of a matter demanded it.[115] In short, he was the chief official responsible for applying the "laws," the complex tapestry of customs justified by their very antiquity and of normative dispositions drawn from royal decrees. By virtue of these activities, the vizier was in a sense the keystone of the arch that assured the smooth functioning of what we today would call, *mutatis mutandis,* the executive and the judiciary.

The office of vizier was thus a hefty responsibility. In fact, in the New Kingdom, it was split between a vizier of the south, whose office was at Thebes and whose authority extended over Upper and Middle Egypt, and a vizier of the north, whose office was in one of the northern capitals (Memphis, Pi-Riamsese) and who had authority over Lower Egypt. In any event, the vizierate was assuredly the supreme authority and the symbol of the judicial system. To speak of a divine vizier was implicitly to besmirch the honor of the human office. It constituted a radical criticism that was potentially capable of leading to a reassessment of the power of Pharaoh himself.[116] As we shall see, this criticism did indeed lead to political change.

Social Basis of the Critique of the Judicial System

It is easy to see that these texts have social connotations;[117] we must determine how wide-reaching they were. The suppliant presents himself using the term *nemeh* (*nmḥ*),[118] the original meaning of which was "orphan"; in judicial terminology, it means "free man," for a *nemeh* was not under the direct control of an institution, just as an orphan is not under the control of parents.[119] But in the terminology of personal piety, the word means "poor man," as opposed to the "rich man" (*wsr*). We must assess the precise implication of this distinction between the rich man and the poor man. These hymns to Amun were included in anthologies that apprentice scribes used to hone their skills. That is to say, the hymns emanated from the ruling class, the men who constituted the hierarchy of the administrative and ideological systems, which were in many ways intertwined. These men were literate, and their position assured them power and affluence. The poverty invoked was thus somewhat theoretical, as it was in other circumstances, as when a courtier wished to glorify the pharaoh who had rewarded him:

> Praises to you, o sovereign who built me, who decreed perfection for me, who formed me, who gave me subsistence, who gave me subsistence through his *ka,* who made me a man . . . who enriched me when I was poor.[120]

O sovereign who made me a man, who formed me with his *ka,* it is a goodly joy for your entourage to hear your instructions. I am a poor man whom you caused to succeed, a dignitary whom you have created.[121]

In the same vein, under Merneptah, Inhermose, first prophet of Onuris of This, a town near Abydos in Upper Egypt, summarized his childhood thus: "I was poor, placed in a school without conducting myself badly."[122] Yet this "poor" person was no less than the son of a "scribe of recruits of the Lord of the Two Lands," a good job that would not have led his son into inevitable poverty. And what are we to say of the aforementioned Simut, surnamed Kyky? Though he was overseer of the cattle count of Amun, possessor of a comfortable patrimony, and someone who had been enriched by many acquisitions, especially servants, when he faced his personal god, he abased his position to the point of declaring himself "a wretch of his town, a poor vagabond of his city."[123]

Declarations of poverty clearly belong to the repertoire of conventions that were employed to emphasize merit, whether one's own or that of one's protector, by stressing the contrast between the supposed modesty of a person's origin and the elevation of the position he attained, or to evoke the beneficence of the human or divine being to whom a request was being directed. Whether someone was requesting a favor from a powerful individual in general or a deity[124] in particular, humility was a requisite. A proclamation of impoverishment, even if fictitious, signified total self-abandonment in the face of omnipotence. In fact, the opposition "poor"/"rich" in these texts is above all rhetorical. Though it reflects a social distinction, it is less a question of the fundamental divide between the masses and the ruling elite than of a secondary distinction within the elite, between the interests of the high officials and those of the middle-level members of the administration, the lower clergy, or even the privileged artisans who worked on the royal tomb.

Advantages of a Personal Relationship with the Divine

In these hymns, we find an opposition between the negative side reflected in their radical criticism of the established order and the positive side constituted by the new ethic that inspired them— that is, the favors bestowed by a personal god. Amun was credited with the behavior of an ideal magistrate, as described in the prescriptions and admonishments that we find in the well-known Instruction of Amenemope, which was undoubtedly written a little later (see the passages translated on p. 135). The help afforded by Amun manifested itself in two ways:

1. Divine justice, free of the defects of human justice, operated in the here-after: "He judges the guilty and puts him in hell, and the righteous man in the West." In this case the divine protection came into play after death and served as the funerary counterpart to intervention by the god in the world of the living. As the ancients conceived it, there was indeed a post-mortem judgment of human action, a "Judgment of the Dead," in the course of which the manner in which the deceased had respected *maat* was evaluated. But the magical techniques by which the scale and the magistrates were ensorceled enabled those who had mastered them to emerge, more or less mechanically, victorious from the test, regardless of what their conduct on earth had been.[125] From then on, just as direct divine intervention in destiny on earth came to replace immanent retribu-tion for human conduct, so belief in the immanent effectiveness of funer-ary mechanisms and magical techniques was replaced by the idea that these mechanisms were intrinsically useless without the protection of a deity, who alone could assure postmortem survival.[126]
2. The deity was transformed into a vizier for the purpose of causing the poor man to triumph:

   May it be found that Amun has transformed himself into a vizier to cause the poor man to overcome! May it be found that the poor man is justified; may the poor man prevail over the rich man.

   He causes the tribunal to be unanimous in order to do justice to the poor. The poor man is justified, while the one who brought a bribe is thwarted.

In this last passage, divine intervention is said to occur in earthly tri-bunals. It is a matter of illustrating, here in the limited and particu-lar case of a tribunal, the belief that the god could, if he wished, act upon the entire existence of someone who chose him as protector and—as an oft-repeated expression put it—placed his destiny en-tirely "in his hands":

Truly, you cannot know the plan of the god; you cannot tell what to-morrow holds. Rest in the hands of the god.[127]

A deity would preserve the faithful from the anguish caused by the uproar and frenzy of a perverted society:

She (i.e., Mut) has suppressed anguish for me, she has protected me in a difficult moment.[128]

Happy is he who relies on her. Misfortune does not descend upon him.[129]

I have abandoned yesterday and today to the hands of Amun; I have found myself well, my condition stable; I have been assured a happy manner of existence until I end my existence, I have given myself entirely to him.[130]

Thus, the new ethic replaced the creator god who had retreated from his creation, which he ruled only through the mediation of *maat* or via sporadic and unpredictable interventions, with a deity of choice with whom an individual could establish a personal relationship and who directly guided his destiny. According to the older concept, love proceeded unilaterally from deities to humans; in the new ethic, it flourished in reciprocity.[131]

The New Ethic and the Reality It Codified

We must take care to distinguish between the historical reality and how it was interpreted by the new ethic. Thus, the cause-and-effect relationship it postulated between the corruption of the established order and personal piety, the former leaving no recourse but the latter, has not been proven,[132] though none would doubt that the two took root in the same soil. Rather, the artifice of doctrinal thinking organized the facts so as to draw an argument from them. After all, these men who denounced their times—these indignant moralists, these deriders of the system who denounced its profound corruption—were at the same time its representatives and the first to draw profit from it. From such people the texts expounding the new ethic in the major mode were derived, and from them alone, for we cannot imagine mastery of the art of writing beyond the ruling class. In other words, the fact that they posed as victims of a corrupt society stemmed as much from rhetorical convention as from the condition of poverty they so complacently declared.

That much said, when it vaunted the advantage of a personal relationship with a deity of choice, the new ethic took into account, if only to lend meaning within a doctrinal argument, of an important phenomenon of the New Kingdom, the growth of personal piety. Previously, such piety had been restricted to certain limited areas,[133] in particular, requests for children made in various ways, votive objects, and personal names, which from the beginning of pharaonic civilization often expressed a relationship between an individual and a deity.[134]

But during the New Kingdom, practices expressing personal piety multiplied and diversified.[135] Chapels appeared in private homes, while in the forecourts of temples, which were open to ordinary individuals, an accumulation of all sorts of votive objects[136] and other private dedications testified to an outpouring of faith. Offerings on the part of the faithful became a regular practice that was even capable of being formally registered,[137] and it was so generalized that the workmen of (the institution of) the Tomb often invoked it to justify their absence from the workplace.[138] But more than these exterior manifestations, it was the enrichment of personal relations between the individual and his god that marked the qualitative leap in personal piety. Witness to this is the interesting dialectic of sin and forgiveness that Egyptology has often invoked under the label—though it is unfortunate in its inaccuracy—of "religion of the poor."[139] This phenomenon is abundantly documented from the Ramesside Period, but it had already appeared at the end of Dynasty 18:[140] the individual interpreted the woes that befell him—such as ill health or blindness—as punishment for sin inflicted by the divine. After this manifestation of the "power of intervention (bau),"[141] the deity showed pity and granted a cure to the repentant sinner:

> Just as the servant is known to be inclined to commit a sin, so the master is known to be inclined to forgiveness.[142]

Confidence in divine omnipotence on earth intensified into a total abandonment that sometimes found concrete expression in legal documents. Thus, in exchange for the protection of Mut, Simut, surnamed Kyky, donated all his goods to her temple and declared that he wished to spend the remainder of his days there; he was thus the precursor of the practice of "self-dedication" that is well attested from a later date.[143]

Characteristic of the flowering of this dialogue between individuals and the divine was the development of channels of communication. Besides inspiration and dreams, which always remained in use, oracles made their appearance.[144] Already in Dynasty 18, unsolicited, exceptional oracles had served to announce important events to Pharaoh. Beginning with the Ramesside Period, there was a multiplicity of oracles, which private people regularly came to consult, following established procedures, on the occasion of festivals, when the divine statue emerged from the sanctuary. The aim of the suppliants was to use these consultations to manage the problems that wracked their lives, not only practical problems of the most prosaic sort, but also quarrels and legal questions.[145] The petitioners even set the oracles in competition with one another by put-

During processions, when he left his temple in a barque, a god—or in this case, Amenophis I, deity and patron of the workmen of the necropolis—was best able to give oracles. Drawing by J.-J. Clère.

ting a question to another oracle when they were dissatisfied with the one they had just consulted. The oracle thus became a decision-making authority that could intervene in matters that otherwise fell within the competence of the tribunals (*qenbet,* see p. 195 nn. 77 and 78). Unfortunately, the relationship between these two authorities is insufficiently clear to us.[146] But it appears that far from being a mere palliative to the corruption of human jurisdictions, as the doctrine of the new ethic would have it, and as proposed by certain Egyptologists writing under its influence,[147] oracles were in particular consulted in matters having to do with real estate.

That much said, regular recourse to oracles in legal matters did not fail to provoke a highly important change in the theory of the established order. In fact, if individuals could have recourse to the direct action of the divine, might not the collective as such also take advantage of this? The way was thus opened to a new concept of political power, "theocracy,"[148] according to which the god ruled the land directly through his terrestrial oracle, with Pharaoh being obliged to submit his decisions for oracular approval.[149] The inauguration of a new era, called Repeating of Births, in year 19 of Ramesses XI,[150] probably masked this change, which we could even call an ideological mutation. The principles of theocracy are concisely manifested in the title "king of the south and the north," which was attributed to Amun, and in a developed form in a hymn that was often reproduced in oracular texts. The hymn exalts both his cosmic lordship over the world he had created and his intervention in the affairs of the human collective, as well as in the destiny of the individuals who composed it.[151]

Thus, the New Kingdom was at one and the same time shaken by serious difficulties that cast doubt on its institutions and rocked by a crisis of values that manifested itself as a conflict within the ideology of the ruling class. The old concept that earthly and postmortem success occurred through adherence to the established order, which the divine had provided with considerable autonomy and with self-regulatory mechanisms, was eroded by a new ethic that recognized individual salvation only in the establishment of deep personal relationships with a deity of choice. The scandals of the period evidently emerged in the context of this crisis of values and generalized corruption of the state; Egyptian ideology interpreted the relationship as one of cause and effect, no doubt somewhat bending reality to serve its argumentation. We should rather think that both of them were more or less direct consequences of Egypt's expansion beyond its natural borders. The opulence that Egypt derived from its empire, together with its inability to make it last, stimulated a propensity that we see firmly rooted in the corruption of moral standards; at the same time, Egypt's contacts with other civilizations—some equally refined—gave rise to a critical reevaluation of a vision of society that was too often contradicted by the facts.

The advent of the theocracy culminated this crisis of values by inviting the god, who was already being asked to guide the destiny of individuals, to take some responsibility for the government. This was indeed a busy creator god, practically overwhelmed by his burden of responsibilities. Not only was he obliged to occupy himself with each person on an individual basis, but also, from this point on, with all of them in the totality of the society they composed. In reality, this submission of the political power to the oracle evidently served the interests of those who were in a position to manipulate it[152]—that is, the high clergy, particularly that of Amun. And everything leads us to think that the denunciation of corruption did not so much provoke this ideological change as serve as a justification for those who imposed it, and that the major crises of the Ramesside Period objectively favored their cause by increasing the discredit of an institution that they intended to reform to their advantage.

Appendix

Terms for Bribe

We have seen how corruption entered into our documentation from the New Kingdom, in both normative or ethical texts and texts reflecting administrative and judicial practices. As we might expect, their vocabulary reflects this preoccupation, for in this period, and in this one only, we find no fewer than five terms designating *bakshish* (the modern Arabic word for bribe) in one way or another.

ḫt

The word *ḫt* is a basic term in the Egyptian language, and its primary sense is "thing." When it is used with the special meaning "bribe," it is followed by a possessive pronoun referring to the person who gives it:

P. Turin 1887, recto 1, 14 (= p. 105): *iw.f (ḥr) dit ḫt.f n p3y ḥm-nṯr r-ḏd imy ʿk.i ḥr p3y nṯr iw p3y ḥm-nṯr sšp ḫt.f*, "He gave his *bakshish* to this prophet, saying, 'Let me approach the god.' This prophet accepted his *bakshish*. He let him approach the god."

P. Turin 1887, verso 1, 3 (= p. 100): *iw p3y h3ty-ʿ sšp n.w ḫt.w*, "This governor received their *bakshish* from them, and he let them go."

P. Turin 1887, verso 2, 16 (= p. 104): *iw.f (ḥr) dit ḫt.f n n3 rwḏw n pr Ḫnmw iw.w (ḥr) tm h3b ḥr.f*, "He gave his *bakshish* to the controllers[1]

151

of the domain of Khnum; they did not make a report on this subject; there has been none to this day."

nkt

The term *nkt* has several connotations. Like *ḫt*, the word means "thing," and as a simple semantic extension of a transitive verb, it serves as the direct object of the verb and has the indefinite meaning "something."[2] From there, by way of a slight twist of meaning, it takes on the sense "a little something," "a nothing," "a trifle,"[3] as in the vizier Ta's speech that was translated on p. 61: "If I have not come to you, was it without a serious reason (lit., "for a trifle")?" Also from there, it means "a little (of)" when it is construed with a possessive.[4] That much said, *nkt* can also have the meaning "advantage, profit."[5] Its use to designate a bribe integrates this polysemy:

> P. Salt 124, recto 1, 17 (= p. 72): [. . .] *P3nb rdit nkt n [sš] Ḳn-ḥr-ḫpš.f mtw.f šd.f*, [Memorandum concerning the fact that . . .] Paneb gave "something" to [the scribe] Qenherkhopshef, and that he (i.e., the scribe) got him (i.e., Paneb) out of trouble."

> Decree of Sethos II (= p. 134): *[wḏ ḥm.f] rdit ḥn.tw t3 f3yt n 'Imn Mw[t Ḥnsw m w3st nfr-ḥtp nṯrw nṯr]yt nbw Šm'w [Mḥw itw-nṯr] w'bw ḥryw-ḥb r tm di wḥ3.tw nkt m-di.sn in ḥm-nṯr nb ḫpr m rk [ḥm.f ir ḥm-nṯr nb nty iw.tw r gmt.f ḥr] wḥ3 nkt m-di.sn iw.tw (r) rwit.f m i3wt.f dd r iḥwty*, "[His majesty commanded] the organization of the corporation of bearers of Amun, Mu[t, and Khons-in-Thebes-Neferhotep, and of all the gods and goddess]es of Upper [and Lower Egypt, the go]d's-[fathers], the pure priests, and the ritualists in order to prevent 'something' from being exacted from them by any prophet who might arise in the time of [his majesty. As for any prophet who might be found] demanding something from them, he will be deprived of his position and be made an agricultural worker."

fk3w

The word *fk3w* is frequently employed in the sense "recompense," "bonus, payment (for work)."[6] Its use to designate a bribe is well established by the following documents; in the translations, the modern term "bonus" hints at the ambiguity of the Egyptian word:

> P. Bologna 1094, 2, 4–2, 7 and P. Anastasi II, 6, 5 (= p. 140): *p3 t3ty n p3 nmḥ bn sw ḥr sšp fk3w n 'd3*, "The vizier of the poor, he does not accept the 'bonus' of the guilty one."

O. IFAO inv. 2181 = O. Wilson (= p. 140): *bw ḏd 'Imn n iwty fḳꜣw pr r-bl m tꜣy.i ḳnbt*, "Amun does not say to the one who has no 'bonus,' 'Leave my tribunal.'"

O. Borchardt (p. 139): *pꜣ nmḥ ḫpr m mꜣꜥ-ḫrw pꜣ fꜣi fḳꜣw snm*, "The poor one is justified, while the one has brought a 'bonus' is thwarted."

O. CGC 25207 (= p. 140): *[ntk] wp mꜣꜥ iwty sšp fḳꜣw*, "[You] are the one who makes truth emerge, who does not accept a 'bonus.'"

Decree of Haremhab, right lateral surface, l. 5 (= p. 137): *m snsn kywy m rmṯ m sšp fḳꜣw n ky*, "Do not associate with those who are answerable (lit., "others among men"); do not accept the 'bonus' of another."

Amenemope 21, 4 (= p. 136): *m-ir šsp fḳꜣw n nḫt mtwk gwꜣ n.f sꜣw*, "Do not accept a 'bonus' from a powerful man in order to reject the case of a weak man in his favor."

ḥsy

This rare word is attested in autobiographies from the beginning of Dynasty 18:

Urk. IV, p. 118, 9–17 (Paheri) (= p. 132): *n sšp.i ḥsy m prw*, "I did not obtain personal benefit from the surpluses."

Urk. IV, 1079, 5–6 (= p. 136): *n sḫ.i ḥr.i r-st r sꜣ-ꜥ ḥr ḥm n sšp.i ḥsy n wꜥ*, "I in no way neglected the weak one, and conversely, I did not accept anyone's bribe."

The writing of *ḥsy*, 𓎛𓐠𓆰, shows that it has to do etymologically with the name of a plant, for which there are several possible identifications. First, it could be connected with *ḥsꜣw/ḥnsꜣy/ḥsy*, which designates a medicinal plant;[7] the fact that it was used for heating could have been the point of departure for its connotation "spices." It could also be connected with 𓃀𓂋𓇌𓈖𓏭𓏥, 𓍿𓇌𓈖𓏥, *Bryonia dioica* (a highly contested identification), a medicinal plant that is often mentioned in medical texts.[8] Another possibility is *ḥsꜣyt, ḥsyt*, if the latter is in fact a separate plant name.[9] In any event, we cannot help but note the analogous use of the word *sm,* "herb," in the sense of "feed, fodder" in the passage from the Tale of the Eloquent Peasant (B 1, 132–4) that was cited on p. 127 in regard to the corruption of judges: "Judges, telling lies is their fodder; they do not weigh on their conscience."

ḏbꜣw

The term *ḏbꜣw*, which means "compensation, remuneration," is derived from the verb *ḏbꜣ*, "to give in exchange," perhaps as a euphemistic designation of a "tip." This meaning is already attested in classical Egyptian, as in the following examples:

autobiography of Mentuweser (New York, Metropolitan Museum of Art)[10] under Senwosret I: *ink . . . tm nmꜥ n nb ḏbꜣw*, "(I was) one who was not partial toward someone who had a remuneration."

Instruction for Merikare P 44:[11] *n ꜥkꜣ.n ḏd hꜣ n.i nmꜥ.f n nb ḏbꜣw[f]*, "The one who says, 'Would that I had!' is unable to be fair, for he is partial toward the one who has a remuneration."

In the New Kingdom, we encounter this meaning in the autobiography of Rekhmire (*Urk.* IV, 1082, 12–14 = p. 136): *iw wp.n.i sprw n rdi.i hr gs n hꜣꜥ.i mꜣꜥwy.i n ḏbꜣw*, "I judged the petitioner, (but) I was not unjust; I was not interested in 'compensation.'"

This use of *ḏbꜣw* is not without analogy to the French word *dédommagement,* which is sometimes used as a discreet term for money paid to someone to arouse his enthusiasm.

Abbreviations

ÄAT	Ägypten und Altes Testament
ADAIK	Abhandlungen des Deutschen Archäologischen Instituts Kairo, Ägyptologische Reihe
AEO	A. H. Gardiner. *Ancient Egyptian Onomastica.* 2 vols. London, 1947.
Äg. Forsch.	Ägyptologische Forschungen
AO	*Archiv Orientální*
AOF	*Archiv für Orientforschung*
ASAE	*Annales du Service des Antiquités de l'Égypte*
BABA	Beiträge zur altägyptische Bauforschung und Altertumskunde
BASOR	*Bulletin of the American Schools of Oriental Research*
BdE	Bibliothèque d'Étude
Bibl. Aeg.	Bibliotheca Aegyptiaca
BIFAO	*Bulletin de l'Institut Français d'Archéologie Orientale au Caire*
BSEG	*Bulletin de la Société d'Égyptologie de Genève*
BSFE	*Bulletin de la Société Française d'Égyptologie*
CAH	*Cambridge Ancient History.* 3d ed., issued in fascicles. Cambridge, 1961–1968.
CASAE	Cahiers des Annales du Service des Antiquités de l'Égypte
CdE	*Chronique d'Égypte*
CLEM	R. A. Caminos, *Late-Egyptian Miscellanies.* Brown Egyptological Studies 1. London, 1954.
CRIPEL	*Cahier de recherches de l'Institut de Papyrologie et d'Égyptologie de Lille*

CT	A. de Buck, *The Ancient Egyptian Coffin Texts,* 7 vols. Chicago, 1935–1961.
DE	*Discussions in Egyptology*
DFIFAO	Documents des Fouilles de l'Institut Français d'Archéologie Orientale au Caire
GM	*Göttinger Miszellen*
GOF	Göttinger Orientforschungen, IV. Reihe: Ägypten
HÄB	Hildesheimer ägyptologische Beiträge
HO	J. Černý and Sir A. Gardiner. *Hieratic Ostraca.* Oxford, 1957.
IEJ	*Israel Exploration Journal*
JARCE	*Journal of the American Research Center in Egypt*
JEA	*Journal of Egyptian Archaeology*
JEOL	*Jaarbericht van het Vooraziatisch Genootschap: "Ex Oriente Lux"*
JESHO	*Journal of the Economic and Social History of the Orient*
JNES	*Journal of Near Eastern Studies*
JSSEA	*Journal of the Society for the Study of Egyptian Antiquities*
KRI	K. A. Kitchen. *Ramesside Inscriptions, Historical and Biographical.* Oxford, 1975–1990.
LAPO	Littératures anciennes du Proche-Orient
LdÄ	W. Helck and E. Otto, eds. *Lexikon der Ägyptologie.* 6 vols. Wiesbaden, 1975–1992.
LES	A. H. Gardiner. *Late-Egyptian Stories.* Bibliotheca Aegyptiaca 1. Brussels, 1932.
LRL	E. F. Wente, *Late Ramesside Letters,* Studies in Ancient Oriental Civilization 33. Chicago, 1967.
MDAIK	*Mitteilungen des Deutschen Archäologischen Instituts, Abteilung Kairo*
MIFAO	Mémoires de l'Institut Français d'Archéologie Orientale au Caire
OA	*Oriens Antiquus*
OBO	Orbis Biblicus and Orientalis
O. DM	Ostracon Deir el-Medina
OIC	Oriental Institute Communications
OLA	Orientalia Lovaniensia Analecta
OLP	*Orientalia Lovaniensia Periodica*
OMRO	Oudheidkundige Mededelingen uit het Rijksmuseum van Oudheden te Leiden
P. BM	Papyrus British Museum
PM	B. Porter and R. L. B. Moss, *Topographical Bibliography of Ancient Egyptian Hieroglyphic Texts, Reliefs, and Paintings.* 7 vols. Oxford,1927–1951. 2d ed. Oxford, 1960–.

Probl. der Äg.	Probleme der Ägyptologie
RAPH	Recherches d'archéologie, de philologie et d'histoire
RdE	Revue d'Égyptologie
RIDA	Revue international des droits de l'antiquité
SAK	Studien zur altägyptischen Kultur
SDAIK	Sonderschrift des Deutschen Archäologischen Instituts, Abteilung Kairo
SHAW	Sitzungsberichte der Heidelberger Akademie der Wissenschaften, philosophisch-historische Klasse
SPAW	Sitzungsberichte der Preussischen Akademie der Wissenschaften, philosophisch-historische Klasse
UGAÄ	Untersuchungen zur Geschichte und Altertumskunde Aegyptens
Urk. IVK.	Sethe, Urkunden der 18. Dynastie. Reprint. Berlin, 1961.
Wb.	A. Erman and H. Grapow, eds. Wörterbuch der ägyptischen Sprache. 5 vols. Reprint. Leipzig, 1972.
YES	Yale Egyptological Studies
ZÄS	Zeitschrift für ägyptische Sprache und Altertumskunde
ZDMG	Zeitschrift der Deutschen Morgenländischen Gesellschaft
ZPV	Zeitschrift des Deutschen Palästina-Vereins
ZRG	Zeitschrift für Religions- und Geistesgeschichte

Notes

Chapter 1. The Plunder of Western Thebes

1. The word "hope" entails a shade of uncertainty, which well suits the situation in pharaonic Egypt, for the exceptional importance of funerary beliefs did not prevent the development of a skeptical attitude toward them. Though this skepticism was overtly expressed by intellectuals, we have every reason to believe that this attitude was not limited to them. Skepticism did not lead to rejection of these beliefs, but rather to a sort of compromise, after the fashion of "Pascal's wager": *postmortem* survival was not assured, of course, but that was all the more reason to increase the odds in its favor by attempting to fulfill all the conditions required by tradition.

2. For an analysis of the grave goods in tombs found intact, see S. T. Smith, *MDAIK* 48 (1992): 193–232.

3. In some instances objects used during the lifetime of the deceased were placed in a tomb.

4. On the hierarchical organization of pharaonic society as evidenced by grave goods, see Smith, *MDAIK* 48.

5. Especially in the Old Kingdom, the tomb furnishings of an official were often at least in part supplied by the workshops of the pharaoh he had faithfully served.

6. Instruction of Hardjedef, II, 2 and 4.

7. This principle is illustrated in a document (P. Turin Strike, verso 7, 6–7, 7) drawn up in connection with the affair of the strikes; see p. 63.

8. See the analyses by A. Gout-Minault, *Le Mastaba d'Ima-pépi* (Cairo, 1992), 201.

9. J. Garstang notes that at Beni Hasan, "[I]n cases where the chambers of adjoining tombs lay alongside, the workmen or others engaged in constructing a new chamber, seem to have consistently plundered that next to it" (*The Burial Customs of Ancient Egypt as Illustrated by Tombs of the Middle Kingdom* [London, 1907], 48).

10. Admonitions, 7, 2; 4, 4; 7; 8.

11. That is, the body itself and the funerary goods buried with it in the heart of the pyramid.

12. Though this is a literary text, the practice it evokes of abandoning plundered mummies on the hillside was quite real, for it is mentioned in almost identical terms in the reports of the proceedings against tomb robbers in the Ramesside Period.

159

13. The expression "white house" designates a treasury; here, it is a room inside the tomb containing the valuable goods buried along with the body.

14. J. Černý, in S. Donadoni, ed., *Le Fonti indirette della storia egiziana,* Studi Semitici 7 (Rome, 1963): 50.

15. We have a great deal of evidence concerning tomb robbery in the Valley of the Kings in Dynasty 19 and the beginning of Dynasty 20; see E. Thomas, *The Theban Necropoleis* (Princeton, 1966), 265–66. Under Ramesses III, in the affair of the strikes (see chapter 2), allusion was made to the plunder of tombs; moreover, one of the workmen vowed to violate a tomb in response to the efforts of the authorities; see p. 60. As for the sinister Paneb, who committed so many misdeeds that we have been obliged to devote chapter 3 of the present work exclusively to him, he did not refrain from violating the tomb of a pharaoh; see p. 83.

16. The documents are published in the fundamental works by T. E. Peet, *The Mayer Papyri A & B: Nos. M.11162 and M.11186 of the Free Public Museum, Liverpool* (London, 1920) and *The Great Tomb-Robberies of the Twentieth Egyptian Dynasty* (Hildesheim, 1977). To these must be added Peet, *JEA* 2 (1915): 173–77 and 204–6; and J. Capart, B. van de Walle, and A. H. Gardiner, *JEA* 22 (1936): 169–93. On details regarding this subject, see E. Thomas, *The Theban Necropoleis,* 265–73; G. A. Wainwright, *JEA* 24 (1938): 59–62; A. H. Gardiner, *Egypt of the Pharaohs* (New York, 1966), 300–2; J. Černý, in S. Donadoni, ed., *Le Fonti indirette della storia egiziana,* 49–52; R. A. Caminos, *LdÄ* II, cols. 862–66, s.v. "Grabräuberprozess"; C. Aldred, "More Light on Ramesside Tomb Robberies," in J. Ruffle, G. A. Gaballa, and K. A. Kitchen, eds., *Glimpses of Ancient Egypt: Studies in Honour of H. W. Fairman* (Warminster, 1979), 92–99; A. G. McDowell, *Jurisdiction in the Workmen's Community of Deir el-Medina,* Egyptologische Uitgaven 5 (Leiden, 1990): 189–200.

17. This expression was intended to designate a new era marked by a new political concept according to which the god Amun would rule directly on earth through the giving of oracles; see pp. 147–48.

18. We have the report of a trial on the verso of P. BM 10053 (K*RI*, vol. 6, 755–63), which is dated to year 9 of a reign or an unidentified era. It is generally attributed to year 9 of the reign of Ramesses XI; see K*RI*, vol. 6, 755–63; A. Niwiński, in I. Gamer-Wallert and W. Helck, eds., *Festschrift für Emma Brunner-Traut* (Tübingen, 1992), 245 n. 2. In any case, we should note that in 4, 11, allusion is made to the *toeyt* of Nefertem, which is to be connected with P. BM 10054, 3, 7, "What do you have to say regarding the gold sheathing of Nefertem of King Usermaatre-setepenre, the great god?", all the more so in that the scribe of the divine book, Sethmose, and the pure priest Pasen appear in both documents. This passage from P. BM 10054 is apparently an intrusion dating to year 18, which could be that of Ramesses IX, since what precedes is dated with certainty to year 16 of that pharaoh; see Peet, *Great Tomb-Robberies,* 58. But, when all is said and done, can it truly be excluded that it is an addition made much later, for example, under Ramesses XI? In any case, the prosopographical data suggest a date in late Dynasty 20; see Peet, *Great Tomb-Robberies,* 112–16. Under these circumstances, is it out of the question that the year 9 of P. BM 10053, verso relates to the era of Repeating of Births?

19. On this problem, see R. Müller-Wollermann, *JESHO* 28 (1985): 121–68; M. Römer, *GM* 108 (1989): 7–20; B. J. Kemp, *Ancient Egypt: Anatomy of a Civilization* (New York, 1989), 249–60.

20. O. DM 556 = J. Černý, *BIFAO* 35 (1935): 52.

21. On this question, the study of which was pioneered by the great Egyptologist J. Černý, see J. J. Janssen, *Commodity Prices from the Ramessid Period: An Economic Study of the Village of Necropolis Workmen at Thebes* (Leiden, 1975), part 3; M. Gutgesell, *Die Datierung der Ostraka und Papyri aus Deir el Medineh und ihre ökonomische Interpretation,* HÄB 18–19 (Hildesheim, 1983), 504–31.

22. On this type of document, see p. 55.

23. Journal of (the institution of) the Tomb, B 1, 6 and 9 = KRI, vol. 6, 571, 2–3 and 7–8. For year 13, see Journal of (the institution of) the Tomb 1, 4 = KRI, vol. 6, 563, 12.

24. Designated as such by the term ḥꜣsty, to be distinguished from the word ꜥꜣw, which is applied to foreigners integrated into Egyptian society; see n. 175.

25. J. Černý, CAH, vol. 2, chap. 35, pp. 14–16 of the fascicle; Haring, VI Congresso Internationale d'Egittologi Atti (Turin, 1993), 202–3, taken up again in R. J. Demarée and A. Egberts, eds., Village Voices (Leiden, 1992), 71–80.

26. The first attestation might date back to year 2 of Ramesses III, according to K. A. Kitchen, RdE 36 (1985): 177–79.

27. See the passage from the deposition of Amenpanefer cited below.

28. The inspection of a ruined tomb and the inventorying of its contents by a commission of officials is attested at the end of the reign of Ramesses III, but this document seems to be an isolated one; see L. M. J. Zonhoven, JEA 65 (1979): 89–98, and D. Valbelle, "Les Ouvriers de la Tombe": Deir el-Médinah à l'Époque Ramesside, BdE 96 (Cairo, 1985), 299.

29. P. Amherst-Leopold II, 2, 12–13, 7.

30. Cf. P. Salt 124, recto 1, 17 (p. 72), in which Paneb is cleared by the scribe Qenherkhopshef, to whom he had given "something (nkt)," and P. Turin 1887, verso 1, 3 (p. 100), in which a governor of Elephantine releases persons he had had arrested after receiving a bribe (ḥt) from them. Conversely, in P. Turin 1887, recto 2, 6–7 (p. 96), a pure priest greases the palm of some followers to get them to arrest a priest whom they had released.

31. The meaning of the expression is not entirely clear; does Amenpanefer mean that all the robbers were recruited from all the groups of society, or that they operated by dividing themselves into gangs? Though the passage contains lacunae, the context in which the same term, wnḏw, occurs in P. BM 10052, recto 1, 21–2 and verso 12, 25 suggests that the second interpretation is the correct one.

32. Anecdote related in P. BM 10054, recto 1, 11 ff.

33. On this individual, see M. L. Bierbrier, JEA 58 (1972): 196, and idem, The Late New Kingdom in Egypt (c. 1300–664 B.C.): A Genealogical and Chronological Investigation (Warminster, 1975), 2.

34. On the organization of the institution of the Tomb, see chapter 2.

35. One papyrus, P. Ambras, contains an inventory of the administrative documents drawn up in the course of the proceedings conducted against the robbers; see KRI, vol. 6, 836–37.

36. On this document, see n. 130.

37. P. Ambras; see Peet, Great Tomb-Robberies, 177–80, and KRI, vol. 6, 836–37.

38. For the problem posed by ḥni and ḥnw in connection with pꜣ ḥr, see E. Thomas, JEA 49 (1963): 57–63, and R. Ventura, Living in a City of the Dead: A Selection of Topographical and Administrative Terms in the Documents of the Theban Necropolis, OBO 69 (Freiburg and Göttingen, 1986), 65–67.

39. Impalement was a punishment employed in cases of serious crimes; see D. Lorton, JESHO 20 (1977): 34–35.

40. P. Abbott, 6, 9–17.

41. On this point, see C. Leblanc, BIFAO 89 (1989): 227, and Ventura, Living in a City of the Dead, 19–21.

42. To indicate a respectful distance, Egyptians did not say "write (or speak) to Pharaoh," but rather "write (or speak) before Pharaoh."

43. Hori and Pabes.

44. On the procedure that was followed, see A. Théodoridès in J. R. Harris, ed., The Legacy of Egypt, 2d ed. (London, 1971), 312.

45. For rwḏw, "controllers" designating the "authorities" of an institution, see J.-M. Kruchten in E. Lipiński, ed., State and Temple Economy in the Ancient Near East: Proceedings of the International Conference Organised by the Katholieke Universiteit

Leuven from the 10th to the 14th April 1978, OLA 6 (Leuven, 1979), 518, and A. Gasse, *Données nouvelles administratives et sacerdotales sur l'organisation du domain d'Amon: XXe–XXIe dynasties,* BdE 104 (Cairo, 1988), 208.

46. P. Abbott, 1, 1–9.

47. The expression *wȝḥ išt* surely refers to the violation of tombs; see J. Capart, A. H. Gardiner, and B. van de Walle, *JEA* 22 (1936): 173, and K. Baer, *Orientalia* 34 (1965): 434–35. Why not attempt to maintain something of its literal meaning, which is "put a cavity (*išt*) in place"?

48. P. Amherst-Leopold II, 1, 3–8.

49. Four officials whose names have been lost.

50. P. Abbott, 1, 9–20.

51. For a comparison of the description from P. Abbott and the archaeological data, the study done long ago by H. E. Winlock, *JEA* 10 (1924): 217–77, remains fundamental.

52. This is Amenophis I (c. 1514–1493 B.C.E.), the second pharaoh of Dynasty 18, whose memory, kept alive by his statue cult, was especially honored in the west of Thebes. His tomb has never been identified with certainty; see PM, vol. 1, 2d ed., 599, and Thomas, *The Theban Necropoleis,* 172–74.

53. This is Inyotef II, Horus name Wah-ankh, of Dynasty 11, who reigned c. 2115–2066 B.C.E.

54. This stela was found by excavators and is now in the Cairo Museum (CGC 20512); see PM, vol. 1, 2d ed., 595. It shows the pharaoh with five dogs at his feet, one of whom is in fact named Bhekai; the author of the report rewrote the name in the syllabic writing system of the New Kingdom.

55. P. Abbott, 2, 1–2, 11.

56. P. Abbott, 3, 15–4, 4.

57. The man in question was in fact named Shury. The scribe of P. Abbott misread the original name; see Winlock, *JEA* 10 (1924): 228.

58. P. Abbott, 2, 12–2, 18.

59. In its list of documents relating to the thefts, P. Ambras 2, 7 (KRI, vol. 6, 837, 8) cites "the inquiry regarding the complex of the pyramid of king Sekhemre-shedtawy," which scholars agree in identifying with P. Amherst-Leopold II.

60. P. Abbott, 4, 5–10.

61. According to K. A. Kitchen, *JEA* 58 (1972): 189 n. 5, she is probably to be identified with Isis, *tȝ-ḥḏrt,* wife of Ramesses III and royal mother, buried in tomb 51 of the Valley of the Queens; see PM, vol. I, 2d ed., 756, and R. Drenkhahn, *LdÄ,* vol. 5, col. 117. According to Kitchen, this queen is probably the royal wife *(tȝ)-ḥbrdt* mentioned in P. BM 10052, 1, 15–16. See also J. Černý, *JEA* 44 (1958): 31; K. C. Seele, *JNES* 29 (1960): 196–97; and Thomas, *The Theban Necropoleis,* 270. On her surname, which is Semitic in origin, see T. Schneider, *Asiatische Personennamen in ägyptischen Quellen des Neuen Reiches,* OBO 114 (Freiburg and Göttingen, 1992), 165.

62. In the official terminology, *nȝ swt,* "the places," designated a sector of tombs.

63. Černý, *A Community of Workmen at Thebes* (Cairo, 1973), 11, proposes "a common *ḥr* of the king's children."

64. Probably Ramesses III.

65. P. Abbott, 4, 17–5, 10.

66. The block that obstructed the entrance.

67. The eight thieves are known from P. BM 10068 and P. BM 10053; see Černý, *Community of Workmen,* 19.

68. On this word, see Thomas, *The Theban Necropoleis,* 268–69. The word, which is otherwise unknown, is perhaps to be connected with *mnyty,* "porter"; see Peet, *Great Tomb-Robberies,* 173, and J. Černý, *Coptic Etymological Dictionary* (Cambridge, 1976), 86.

69. Journal of (the institution of) the Tomb, B 8, 4–11 = KRI, vol. 6, 579, 5–11.

70. The reading follows that of Kitchen, *JEA* 58 (1972), who plausibly suggested that this is the wife of Ramesses III and not his mother, *ḫbrḏt*.

71. P. BM 10052, recto 1, 14–17.

72. P. BM 10053, recto 1, 1–1 6 = K*RI*, vol. 6, 506.

73. The restoration suggested by Kitchen is assured, because the expression is used several times in the same document, e.g., 4, 1.

74. What remains shows that a queen or a noble lady was named here.

75. P. BM 10068, 1, 3–1, 5 = K*RI*, vol. 6, 497.

76. Yet, the punishment inflicted on other robbers implicated in the scandal was so severe that it still weighed on the collective memory thirty years later. Thus, one suspect attempted to establish his innocence with the following argument: "I have seen the punishment that was inflicted on the robbers in the time of the vizier Khaemwese. What, then, would it mean that I went out in search of death, since I know it?" (P. BM 10052, verso 8, 19 = K*RI*, vol. 6, 787, 6–8); see Aldred, in Ruffle, Gaballa, and Kitchen, eds., *Glimpses of Ancient Egypt*, 92; E. D. Bedell, "Criminal Law in the Egyptian Ramesside Period" (Ph.D. diss., Brandeis University, 1973), 146; Lorton, *JESHO* 20 (1977): 31. For a reduced sentence as a reward for informing on others, see the case of Hori, pp. 119–20.

77. P. Abbott, 5, 10–11.

78. For the word *ḥr* in this passage, see Černý, *Community of Workmen*, 20.

79. Lit., "in a place far removed," if we follow the interpretation suggested by A. Alcock and S. M. Petty, *JEA* 56 (1970): 193, for the expression *m bw wꜣ*.

80. P. Abbott, 5, 14–15 and 6, 1–9.

81. The objectivity of administrative and judicial documents is of course illusory, as we shall see again in the case of the papyrus recounting the strikes in year 29 of Ramesses III (chapter 2). On this point, see P. J. Frandsen, in S. I Groll, ed., *Studies in Egyptology Presented to Miriam Lichtheim* (Jerusalem, 1990), 166–99, esp. p. 172.

82. See p. 33 for the cases of Pawerkhetef and Panefer, who suggested heists to the gangs to which they belonged during the reign of Ramesses XI. One of their targets was the tomb of Queen (Ta-)Heberdjet.

83. The violations of private tombs by the same gang that robbed the tomb of King Sebekemzaf were, however, the subject of administrative documents. Thus, P. BM 10054 contains notes on depositions taken on this subject; one deposition recounts the robbery of the tomb of the third prophet of Amun, Tjanefer, which is well-known to archaeologists (PM, vol. 1, 2d ed., 268–71, no. 158). But it is not a properly drawn up document.

84. So far as we can tell, the historical role of this pharaoh was quite limited; see J. von Beckerath, *Untersuchungen zur politischen Geschichte der zweiten Zwischenzeit in Ägypten,* Äg. Forsch. 23 (Glückstadt, 1964), 290–92, and A. Dodson, *GM* 120 (1991): 35. He lived during the darkest moments of the Second Intermediate Period, when much of Egypt, including Memphis, the ancient, prestigious capital, was under the thumb of the Hyksos kings. In retrospect, however, he had the merit of belonging to the line of nationalist pharaohs of Dynasty 17, whose last member, Kamose, would win the first significant victories in the war of liberation; see P. Vernus and J. Yoyotte, *Les Pharaons: Les Noms, les thèmes, les lieux* (Paris, 1988), 50. Not only his prestige at Thebes but also the limits of his power are indicated by his epithet *šd wꜣst*, "who saved Thebes," in the Royal Canon of Turin, instead of *šd tꜣwy*, "who saved the Two Lands."

85. P. Abbott, 2, 1–2, 7, regarding the tomb of Amenophis I.

86. P. Abbott, 7, 8–7, 16.

87. P. Amherst-Leopold II, 4, 10–11.

88. A. Théodorides, in J. R. Harris, ed., *The Legacy of Egypt*, 312.

89. Bedell, "Criminal Law," 24–26; Lorton, *JESHO* 20 (1977): 31–32; W. Boochs, *GM* 109 (1989): 24.

90. This episode in Egyptian history has been the subject of a number of studies and reconstructions that often differ considerably from one another. Without following them slavishly, we have relied on the recent advances made by Niwiński, in Gamer-Wallert and Helck, eds., *Festschrift für Emma Brunner Traut,* 235–62, and especially by K. Jansen-Winkeln, *ZÄS* 118 (1992): 22–37. For an excellent summary with bibliography, but which appeared before the two studies just cited, see K. A. Kitchen, *The Third Intermediate Period in Egypt* (Warminster, 1973), 248.

91. On this point, see D. O'Connor, in B. G. Trigger, B. J. Kemp, D. O'Connor, and A. B. Lloyd, *Ancient Egypt: A Social History* (Cambridge, 1983), 229–32.

92. Černý, *CAH,* vol. 2, chap. 25, p. 30 of the fascicle; Valbelle, *"Les Ouvriers de la Tombe,"* 220.

93. P. M. Chevereau, *Prosopographie des cadres militaires égyptiens de la Basse Époque: Carrières militaires et carrières sacerdotales en Égypte du XIe au IIe siècle avant J.-C.* (Antony, 1985), 5, 7; M. C. Perez-Die and P. Vernus, *Excavationes en Ehnasya el Medina (Heracleopolis Magna): Introduccion general, inscripciones (informes arqueologicos)* (Madrid, 1992), 40.

94. P. Mayer A, 6, 5–8. This well-known passage has often been commented on and glossed; see the works cited in n. 16.

95. K*RI,* vol. 6, 537, 16.

96. In his account, Amenhotpe first calls on Amun for help with a supplication that falls into the category of personal piety. Pharaoh's intervention is only the instrument of divine mercy, which is the ultimate cause of every event. See my study on *L'Idéologie égyptienne face à l'individualité historique* (forthcoming).

97. From P. Mayer A, 13 B1–B4, it seems that before he took control of Thebes, seven tomb robbers had already been impaled. Otherwise, we have a document dated to year 9, which could be that of Ramesses XI, if it is not from the era of the Repeating of Births, and another one dated to a year 18, which could be that of Ramesses XI; see n. 18. As for Panehsy, he executed three robbers. It is possible that on this occasion he got hold of the archives of the trials from the reign of Ramesses IX, which were apparently carried off by his partisans after his defeat, only to be recovered later; see p. 7.

98. For an analogous use of this graphic indication of infamy in the case of Mesy, who was undoubtedly a usurper, see p. 74.

99. K*RI,* vol. 6, 538, 5, *th3.f pw th3 wi.* The expression illustrates the oft-expressed theme that a misdeed returns to haunt the one who performed it, thus: *iw.i r dit phr w3w3 r ir s(w) sdb r š3 s(w),* "I shall cause the plot to turn back on the one who made it, the evil on the one who originated it" (*Urk.,* vol. 6, 57, 20–21); or *iw.w (hr) dit mt n3 di mt.w,* "They put to death the ones who had put to death," P. Jur. Turin, 216 n. 7.

100. H. Kees, *Die Hohenpriester des Amun von Karnak von Herihor bis zum Ende der Äthiopenzeit,* Probl. der Äg. 4 (Leiden, 1964), 6–18; Černý, *CAH,* vol. 2, chap. 35, 35–38; *Tanis: L'Or des pharaons* (Paris, 1987), 55. On the origin of this name, see Černý, *JEA* 15 (1929): 198.

101. See p. 194.

102. This Qashuty, who plays a good role here, was otherwise implicated in the thefts from the Ramesseum and the temple of Ramesses III; see P. BM 10053, 4, 10, and P. BM 10383, 1, 4.

103. P. Mayer A 6, 8–12.

104. P. BM 10052 and P. Mayer A.

105. For the intermingling of the two investigations in P. Mayer A, see C. Cannuyer, in Groll, ed., *Studies in Egyptology,* 103. We must also reckon with enigmatic passages that seem to contain extracts from trials from the reign of Ramesses IX; for P. BM 10052, verso 14, 11–16, see the remark by J. Capart, B. van de Walle, and A. H. Gardiner, *JEA* 22 (1936): 187 n. 7, to which we can add that this passage has an echo in P. Mayer A 5, 9.

106. P. Mayer A 2, 10–12.

107. P. Mayer A 2, 18–21; see also 10, 21.

108. For the problem posed by these indications given by the witnesses regarding their ages at the time of these thefts, see C. Aldred, in Ruffle, Gaballa, and Kitchen, eds., *Glimpses of Ancient Egypt,* p. 95; A. Niwiński, in *Festschrift,* 246–47; and K. Jansen-Winkeln, *ZÄS* 119 (1982): 28.

109. To exculpate himself, one accused man went so far as to claim that the terror this precedent inspired in him would have dissuaded him from engaging in theft; see n. 76.

110. For indications suggesting that certain robbers had already been brought to trial before the Repeating of Births, see n. 97.

111. Town south of Thebes, not far from Gebelein, at the site of modern El Mahamid. Magnificent monuments from this town are on display in the Luxor Museum.

112. Town south of Thebes, not far from present-day Moalla.

113. P. BM 10052, verso 8, 14–16.

114. This is the conventional translation of *miḥt,* which often designated an Abydene "cenotaph" in the Middle Kingdom; see W. K. Simpson, *The Terrace of the Great God at Abydos: The Offering Chapels of Dynasties 12 and 13,* Publications of the Pennsylvania-Yale Expedition to Egypt 5 (New Haven, 1974), 10–13. In the documents from Dynasty 20, however, it is clearly applied to the tombs of private persons; see Černý, *Community of Workmen,* 14.

115. Thus, in P. BM 10053, 3, 27, "the scribe *Pn*[. . .]." In P. Ambras, 2, 8, the tomb of the general whose name is not cited is called a *ḥr.*

116. Bukhaaf admitted to violating three tombs, "three in all," counting that of Nesimut and Bake(t)werel (P. Mayer 4, 4). The third tomb seems to have been that of Isis (Ta-)Heberdjet. Černý, however, wonders whether it was not that of the reigning pharaoh, Ramesses XI; see n. 124.

117. P. Mayer A, 4, 2–4.

118. Sethos I scarcely seems to have had a wife with this name. Moreover, at this time, he was called "King Menmaatre Sethos" and not simply Menmaatre, probably to distinguish him from Ramesses XI, as cleverly suggested by Černý, *JEA* 15 (1929): 195.

119. A usurper who contested the rule of Sethos II; see chap. 3, n. 36.

120. PM, vol. 1, p. 518 (no. 10); A. Dodson, *DE* 2 (1985): 7–11; N. Reeves, *Valley of the Kings: The Decline of a Royal Necropolis* (London, 1991), 104.

121. Thus *LdÄ,* vol. I, col. 201; R. Krauss, *SAK* 5 (1977): 168–69.

122. See A. Dodson, *JEA* 73 (1987): 225; Dodson makes her the wife of Ramesses IX and maintains that the queen in our text is another Baketwerel, wife of Ramesses XI.

123. Černý, *Community of Workmen,* 19; Valbelle, *"Les Ouvriers de la Tombe,"* 220; Krauss, *SAK 5* (1977); Dodson, *JEA* 73 (1987).

124. P. Mayer B 6–15 (without date). The date proposed by Aldred, in Ruffle, Gaballa, and Kitchen, eds., *Glimpses of Ancient Egypt,* 92, is based on a conjecture. Černý, *Community of Workmen,* 19, maintains that P. Mayer A alludes to theft from the tomb of the reigning pharaoh, Ramesses XI; see n. 97. In another passage, Ahautynefer is accused of having plundered in "the tombs of Pharaoh, life, prosperity, health" (*n3 ḥr n pr-ꜥ3 ꜥnḥ wd3 snb,* P. Mayer A, 4, 16–17); the plural poses a problem to which Černý (*Community of Workmen,* 15) has turned, hypothesizing that two tombs were prepared during the reign of Ramesses XI.

125. See the preceding note.

126. Not to mention houses. We have a list of the inhabitants of this sector of Thebes on a papyrus that also contains a document relating to the thefts, P. BM 10068, verso 2, 1–8, 8 = KRI, vol. 6, 749–55.

127. On this important feature of religious architecture, see P. Lacau, *ASAE* 53 (1955): 221–50.

128. The reference is to the funerary temple of Ramesses III at Medinet Habu.

129. The term *ḥtri* undoubtedly designates the jambs and lintel that frame a doorway; see Christophe, *Mélanges Maspero*, vol. 1, MIFAO 66 (Cairo, 1961), 23; P. Spencer, *The Egyptian Temple: A Lexicographical Study* (London, 1984), 203–5; and especially S. Sauneron, *BIFAO* 64 (1964): 16 (o) = *KRI*, vol. 6, 532, 7, regarding the restoration of a portico at Karnak by the high priest Amenhotpe, and thus a document contemporary with our papyrus. On the etymology of the word, see J.-M. Kruchten, *Annuaire IPHOS* 24 (1980): 40.

130. P. BM 10053, verso 3, 1–30. For the problem posed by the date (year 9) of this document, see n. 18.

131. P. BM 10383 1, 8–12.

132. For the ratios of gold/silver/copper/barley, see Černý, *Cahiers d'histoire mondiale* 1 (1954): 905–6.

133. P. BM 10053, verso 3, 1–30.

134. The term *kꜣwty*, originally "laborer, carrier," tends to designate a temple servant who not only performed the duties of a porter but also those of a factotum, like the *bawab* of modern Egypt. The translation "sacristan" has been proposed by J. Leclant, *Enquêtes sur les sacerdoces et les sanctuaires égyptiens à l'époque dite "éthiopienne,"* BdE 17 (Cairo, 1954), 68; see also P. Vernus, *RdE* 37 (1986): 146 n. 41.

135. P. BM 10403, recto 1, 3–20.

136. *škw*; see Janssen, *Commodity Prices,* 308–9.

137. The reference is to Ramessesnakht, first prophet of Amun, who dedicated a portable *naos* that was placed in the funerary temple of Ramesses III.

138. P. BM 10403, recto 1, 19–23. In P. Mayer A, 2, 7, the surprised thieves also give rings to those who caught them to buy their silence.

139. See the suggestion of C. Cannuyer, in Groll, ed., *Studies in Egyptology,* 102 n. 6, regarding *miw* in P. Mayer A 1, 24.

140. P. BM 10053, verso 4, 18.

141. P. BM 10053, verso 4, 21–2.

142. For the "silver floor," which was intended to render a place propitious for oracular rituals, see J.-M. Kruchten, *BSFE* 103 (1985): 14–18, and especially idem, *Le Grand texte oraculaire de Djéhoutymose intendant du domaine d'Amon de Pinedjem II,* Monographies Reine Élisabeth 5 (Brussels, 1986), 325–36.

143. Ramesses II.

144. P. BM 10053, verso 4, 15–16.

145. Lit., "one gave value back to the unguent vase"; that is to say, the material that had been taken from it (more than 58 percent of its mass!) was replaced so as to give it a presentable appearance.

146. P. BM 10383, 1, 4–10.

147. The expression *gs-pr* originally meant "workshop," a meaning that does not suit here. The context leads us to think that this is a cult object analogous to a portable naos, all the more so in that it is probably the same object that is called "naos (*kꜣr*) of King Menmaatre Sethos, l.p.h." in another document, P. Turin Cat. 1903, verso 2, 12; see Černý, *JEA* 15 (1929): 195. This meaning would be a stage along the route that led *gs-pr* toward the sense "temple," for which see F. Daumas, *Les Moyens d'expression du grec et de l'égyptien comparés dans les décret de Canope et de Memphis,* CASAE 16 (Cairo, 1952), 228.

148. That is, the treasury.

149. P. Mayer A 1, 1–4 and 1, 4–15.

150. Another deposition could allow some doubt to persist: "My mother said to me, 'The chief of the Medjay Nesamun gave some *mꜣ*-objects of copper (or, "some *mꜣn*-objects") to your father. And when the chiefs of the troops of foreign auxiliaries killed your father, they seized me to interrogate me, and that was when Nesamun seized the pieces of copper that he (= your father) had given to me'" (P. Mayer A, 2,

19–20). Unfortunately, the passage is highly unclear; apparently, Nesamun first gave some objects to a robber, and then after the latter's death, he took them back from his wife. We should note that in the list of accomplices designated as such by the thieves of the portable naos, P. Mayer A, 13 A, mentions "the two chiefs of the Medjay of the House, and that a chief of the Medjay, Nesamun, participated in the pillage of the west of Iuemiteru"; P. BM 10052, 8, 14.

151. A first list was presented to the king in year 1 of the Repeating of Births (Abbott Docket = KRI, vol. 6, 764–67). A detailed summary follows the reports on the interrogations conducted in years 1 and 2 preserved in P. Mayer A, 11–13 (KRI, vol. 6, 824–28).

152. Vernus and Yoyotte, Les Pharaons, 34–35; Reeves, Valley of the Kings, 183–92.

153. This person's son, Pakhar, would in his turn be implicated in the second scandal entailing theft; see P. BM 10052, verso 10, 4–10, 9, and J. Capart, A. H. Gardiner, and B. van de Walle, JEA 22 (1936): 183.

154. Tuthmosis IV, a king of Dynasty 18.

155. In pharaonic Egypt, the term ḥm, which is conventionally translated "slave," did not indicate the same status as an ancient Roman servus; see the treatment by C. Eyre in M. A. Powell, ed., Labor in the Ancient Near East, American Oriental Series 68 (New Haven, 1987), 208–11.

156. P. Amherst-Leopold II, 3, 7–16.

157. W. Helck, Materialien zur Wirtschaftsgeschichte des Neuen Reiches (Mainz, 1961), 120; for what remains of this temple, see B. M. Bryan, A Study of the Reign of Thutmose IV (Baltimore, 1991), 188.

158. See van Heel, in R. J. Demarée and A. Egberts, eds., Village Voices: Proceedings of the Symposium "Texts from Deir el-Medîna and Their Interpretation," Leiden, May 31–June 1, 1991 (Leiden, 1992), 24–26.

159. This is the conventional, but not necessarily entirely gratuitous, translation of the term ḥrty, which means, etymologically, "one belonging to the necropolis," and which is often used to designate those who worked in the tombs, often including the workers of (the institution of) the Tomb; see Černý, Community of Workmen, 251; Valbelle, "Les Ouvriers de la Tombe," 100–1 and 212 n. 9. See also P. Salt 124, recto 2, 7–10 (= p. 80), which tells of quarriers taking stones from Pharaoh's tomb and reusing them to construct the tomb of Paneb.

160. The paraphrase is inelegant, but it gives the sense of the Egyptian term nšdw/nšdty, Gardiner, AEO, vol. 1, *67–*68.

161. On the sense of p3 ḥr in this expression, see Černý, Community of Workmen, 19, where the arguments presented are not always convincing. It is genuinely difficult to deny that the term can mean "(royal) necropolis" in the larger sense, including both the Valley of the Kings and the Valley of the Queens; a detailed discussion with abundant documentation is made by Ventura, Living in a City of the Dead, 1–37; see esp. p. 34 for the expression it3w n p3 ḥr. Note also the expression p3 ḥr n n3 ḥmwt-nsw, P. Turin Strike, recto 3, 19, Ventura, Living in a City of the Dead, 218 n. 112.

162. As a matter of interest, we can note that the Egyptian employs the word basically meaning "give" in the sense "denounce," just as in French argot.

163. This detail is furnished by P. BM 10052, recto 7, 2.

164. P. BM 10052, recto 2, 1; the titles and names have been completed as necessary on the basis of other passages in the document.

165. P. BM 10052, recto 1, 15.

166. Proper names are sometimes abbreviated in this type of document. For example, Perpatjauemope (Prp3t3wmipt, Abbott Docket A 4) is usually designated by the shorter form Perpatjau; Userhetnakht (wsrḥ3tnḫt, P. BM 10052, 6, 1) is usually called by the short form Userhat; and Panekhyenope (P. Mayer A 5, 1) is called Panekhy in P. BM 10052, 10, 16. Peet, Great Tomb-Robberies, 74, notes a different kind of abbreviation: "[W]e find a deputy whose name is written indifferently Paken or Paanken."

167. The text definitely reads *p₃ šr n p₃ nfr*; he could thus be the son of Panefer. But given that Panefer himself is mentioned in this deposition (see also P. Mayer A 9, 16–19, which mentions the same incident), I wonder whether *p₃ šr* should be taken literally here, or whether it is a familiar designation of the sort "young Panefer."

168. P. BM 10052, verso 8, 10–11.

169. For the term *gs-pr*, see n. 147.

170. A locale in Upper Egypt, for which see Gardiner, *AEO*, vol. II, p. *48.

171. P. Mayer A.

172. That the foreigner Pakamen resided at Hermonthis is indicated in another document, Abbott Dockets, verso A 17.

173. P. BM 10383, 1, 6.

174. P. BM 10052, recto 7, 10.

175. The term used is *ꜣ῾w*, which originally designated foreign auxiliaries; see L. Bell, "Interpreters and Egyptianized Nubians in Ancient Egyptian Foreign Policy: Aspects of the History of Egypt and Nubia" (Ph.D. diss., University of Pennsylvania, 1976). On the presence of a number of them in legal and administrative documents of the Ramesside Period, see Gardiner, *JEA* 27 (1941): 25 n. 4. At this time, the term could be applied to Nubian troops; see O'Connor, in Trigger, Kemp, O'Connor, and Lloyd, *Ancient Egypt: A Social History*, 231. *ꜣ῾w*, which could almost be translated "immigrant," must be distinguished from *ḫꜣsty*, which, in the same documents, is applied to unintegrated foreigners—for example, the Libyans, whose incursions became numerous during Dynasty 20; see n. 24. For the integration of foreigners into Egyptian society, see D. Valbelle, *Les neuf arcs: L'Égyptien et les étrangers de la préhistoire à la conquête d'Alexandre* (Paris, 1990), 189–99.

176. Aldred, in Ruffle, Gaballa, and Kitchen, eds., *Glimpses of Ancient Egypt*, 96–99, attributes the pillage of the tomb of Ramesses VI to bands of soldiers: "[T]he tomb was plundered not by the usual furtive fraternity of Thebes with their contacts among the workmen of the royal tombs, but by a large and powerful force of men who were ignorant of the exact arrangements of a royal burial." This thesis, which is in itself not improbable, does not impose itself ineluctably.

177. There was definitely a sense of the risks incurred; one accused man defended himself by pointing out that he well knew the punishments inflicted on thieves; see n. 76.

178. P. BM 10052, recto 2, 17–24.

179. Nespare sold Iufenamun some beer that he had most likely diverted from its intended destination, the cult of Re; see P. Mayer A 8, 21–22, cited in note 184.

180. P. Mayer A 8, 11–13.

181. P. BM 10052, verso 11, 4–6.

182. See n. 126.

183. P. BM 10052, verso 10, 14–16.

184. P. Mayer A 8, 21–2.

185. For a comparison with other evidence concerning the price of honey, see Janssen, *Commodity Prices*, 352–53. See also ibid., 131–32 and 227 n. 53, regarding the theft of honey intended for the divine offering.

186. P. BM 10052, recto 2a, 9–13.

187. P. BM 10052, recto 2a, 4–6.

188. Including temples, for in pharaonic Egypt, there was no separation of church and state.

189. P. BM 10052, verso 11, 8. This well-known passage is often cited in Egyptological literature. Černý, *AO* 6 (1934): 177, was the first to explain it by analyzing the economic situation in this period. For a more recent discussion, see Niwiński, in *Festschrift*, 244.

190. P. BM 10403, recto 3, 5–6.

191. P. BM 10052, verso 10, 7–8.

192. P. BM 10052, recto 1, 8–10.
193. It seems that the expression used is colloquial, if not slang.
194. P. BM 10052, recto 3, 3, 2–5.
195. P. Mayer A 6, 23–5; cf. 2, 7–8.
196. P. Mayer A 9, 16–17.
197. Respectively, P. BM 10052, verso 8, 6, and recto 6, 7.
198. Thus, a workman could threaten to rob a tomb if he was forcibly prevented from manifesting his discontent; P. Turin Strike, recto 2, 8; see p. 60.
199. Thus, Iufenamun, who, along with his brother Ihymeh, was a troop chief; P. BM 10052, 7, 11.
200. For the archaeological problem posed by the reuse and plunder of tombs, see D. Polz, in J. Assmann, G. Burkard, and V. Davies, *Problems and Priorities in Egyptian Archaeology* (London, 1987), 119–40.
201. For the meaning of ḥmꜥ, see P. Posener-Kriéger, *RdE* 33 (1981): 56 aah.
202. P. Mayer B, 9.
203. The existence of fortified posts is assured by the texts and by some archaeological traces; see, for example, Thomas, *The Theban Necropoleis,* 51, and *JEA* 49 (1963): 61–62. On the problem of the five "redoubts," see chapter 2.
204. *Theban Ostraca* A 11, 21–2.
205. Cf. the scandal of Paneb, in which workers attempting to remove stone for the benefit of that scoundrel were seen by passersby; P. Salt 124, recto 2, 7–8: "[I]t was while they were at the construction site of Pharaoh, l.p.h., that those who passed by on the hillside saw the quarrymen" (see p. 81).
206. On absenteeism at Deir el-Medina, see J. J. Janssen, *SAK* 8 (1980): 127–50; Valbelle, "Les Ouvriers de la Tombe," 95–96; and Eyre, in Powell, ed., *Labor in the Ancient East,* 177–78.
207. On this title, *ms-ḥr*, see Černý, *Community of Workmen,* 28; Ventura, *Living in a City of the Dead,* 35–37.
208. The use of the conjunctive is all the more notable in that the sentence seems to begin with a passive or perfective *sḏm.f*. It would be more common if it were in fact a matter of a prospective ("(I) shall kill"), but the context scarcely favors this interpretation.
209. P. Mayer B, 8.
210. Tuthmosis III.
211. P. Abbott, 3, 1–9.
212. The funerary temple of Ramesses III, which is still standing at Medinet Habu.
213. P. Amherst-Leopold II, 1, 16–3, 2.
214. Bibliography in PM, vol. 1, 2d ed., 603–4; the fundamental study is that by H. E. Winlock, *JEA* 10 (1924): 237–43.
215. The necropolis is located on a hillside.
216. P. BM 10052, recto 3, 5–13.
217. Lit., "I heard among them"; the unusual construction of *sḏm* plus *m-di.w* surely has a special meaning; undoubtedly, it indicates that the narrator heard statements that were not intended for him.
218. Aside from its literal meaning, "silver," the word *ḥḏ* in these texts clearly also indicates an ensemble of objects and valuable materials representing a certain value; see Janssen, *Commodity Prices,* 499–500. The translation "sum of money" is proposed here *faute de mieux,* for this expression unfortunately suggests the existence of coinage, which was not the case.
219. P. Mayer A, 9, 18–19.
220. P. BM 10052, verso 8, 9–10; see n. 168.
221. On the conjunctive in this passage, see J. F. Borghouts, *ZÄS* 106 (1979): 21 (16).
222. P. Mayer B 1–2.
223. P. BM 10053, verso 3, 11.

224. See n. 218.

225. P. BM 10052, recto 6, 5–7. In what precedes, allusion is made to the use of "five sticks" to divide the shares, indicating a procedure that is not clear.

226. For example, P. BM 10052, verso 14, 7: "The basket was put into a branch of water, with objects in it."

227. This use of a stone weight was not peculiar to thieves; rather, it was a basic practice in Egyptian society. A goodly number of the weights have survived to us, each bearing a brief inscription recalling the transaction, the beneficiary, or even tools that were temporarily entrusted, the sum of which was represented by the stone. See D. Valbelle, *Catalogue des poids à inscriptions hiératiques de Deir el-Médineh n° 5001–423*, DFIFAO 16 (Cairo, 1977). For a translation of one of the preserved inscriptions, which is especially important for understanding the role of these weights, see A. Lemaire and P. Vernus, *Semitica* 28 (1978): 58.

228. P. BM 10052, recto 3, 7–13.

229. P. BM 10052, recto 5, 18–21.

230. In the thesis "Les Poids dans l'Égypte ancienne" (Paris IV, 1989), 212, A. Cour-Marty points out that in the land of Akan, the interest on a debt is represented by the difference between the masses of two weights having the same nominal value.

231. P. BM 10052, recto 6, 18–19.

232. P. BM 10052, verso 10, 4–8.

233. Or, "for the foreigner Pais was living with me." The suggestion of confusion of pronouns is entirely plausible in the context of an embedded quotation.

234. P. Mayer B 3–6.

235. P. BM 10053, verso 2, 15–18.

236. See p. 25 regarding the sheathing of architectural elements with precious metals.

237. For data regarding the price of an ox, see Janssen, *Commodity Prices,* 73 (table) and 174–75, and B. Vachala, *ZÄS* 114 (1987): 91. Regarding the passage here, Janssen makes the following excellent comment: "Now it is possible that the man who sold the ox knew that the gold was stolen, and as a 'receiver' he would not of course pay the real value for it—in which case 5 kite of gold, i.e. 60 deben of copper, would not be a genuine price. There is, however, no hint in the text that the theft was known to the seller of the ox."

238. P. BM 10053, verso 3, 12–3, 15.

239. P. BM 10053, verso 3, 17: "[T]hey took a (bit) of gold from the frames; we took it and we gave it to the scribe Sedy; he took it, he had it melted down, and he gave it to Pameniu."

240. The choice that the thieves made among what was available to them was often guided, at least in part, by their desire to avoid what was too easily recognizable; see Reeves, *Valley of the Kings,* 275.

241. Lit., "that one speak against me." The speaker, a woman, points out that giving her husband's share would earn her criticism.

242. P. BM 10052, recto 6, 7–13.

243. See, for example, "And when the chiefs of the troops of foreigners killed your father" (P. Mayer A 2, 20–1), and more generally, Valbelle, *"Les Ouvriers de la Tombe,"* 305–6.

244. P. BM 10052, verso 8, 6–7.

245. Here, the verb *gmi* seems to have a sense of this sort, rather than its literal meaning "to find."

246. P. Mayer A, 9, 16–18.

247. See Janssen's comment on the price of an ox in n. 237.

248. The accounts of the investigations employ technical terms whose precise meanings are unknown to us: *bdn, mnini, dnn, iq, ir m ni*. The translations here are,

of course, conventional. For the references, see L. Lesko, *A Dictionary of Late Egyptian* (Berkeley, 1982), s.v., and W. Boochs, *GM* 109 (1989): 23.

249. P. BM 10053 and 10068, see p. 28.

250. Lit., "the neighborhood of the share of valuable items." The use of *p3 h3w* to indicate the extent of the booty's dispersion is interesting. Cf. P. Turin 1887, verso 2, 11: *iw.w (ḥr) ir(t) h3w m n3yw h3w n ḥʿww*(?) (p. 103, with n. 65).

251. Lit., "silver"; see n. 218.

252. P. BM 10052, recto 2, 17–19.

253. P. BM 10068, verso 4, 12.

254. P. BM 10068, 4, 14; this is unlikely to be Ptah of Thebes.

255. P. BM 10068, verso 4, 16; see D. Kessler, *SAK* 2 (1975): 128.

256. P. BM 10053, 2, 12.

257. P. BM 10053, 4, 4.

258. P. BM 10068, 4, 18.

259. In Egyptian, *šwty*: see M. Megally, *Recherches sur l'économie, l'administration et la comptabilité égyptiennes à la XVIIIᵉ dynastie d'après le papyrus E. 3226 du Louvre*, BdE 71 (Cairo, 1977), 255, and W. F. Reineke, *AOF* 6 (1979): 5–14. In the Elephantine affair, some pure priests reproach a newly appointed prophet for being the son of a broker; see P. Turin 1887, recto 1, 13, p. 137. During the same affair, a broker seems to have been appointed captain of a barge by the prophet; see P. Turin 1887, verso 1, 9, p. 104 below.

260. See p. 133.

261. P. Mayer A, 10, 2–8.

262. P. Mayer A, 12, 9 (list B 3).

263. P. BM 10053; there is also an exceptional mention of gold, silver, and bronze.

264. Stolen items had been used to make funerary objects; thus, P. BM 10053, verso 4, 15–16, cited above, p. 28 with n. 144.

Chapter 2. The Strikes

1. With the exception of the pharaohs of Dynasty 18 who preceded Tuthmosis I, and with the exception of Akhenaten.

2. For a table giving the dimensions of the Ramesside royal tombs, see J. Černý, *The Valley of the Kings: Fragments d'un manuscrit inachevé*, BdE 61 (Cairo, 1973), 8.

3. See E. Hornung, *The Tomb of Pharaoh Seti I / Das Grab Sethos' I.* (Zurich, 1991). In fact, the undertaking was so huge that it could not be entirely completed, and certain parts received only preliminary sketches.

4. The facts are brought together in J. Černý, *A Community of Workmen at Thebes in the Ramesside Period*, BdE 50 (Cairo, 1973), and D. Valbelle, *"Les Ouvriers de la Tombe": Deir el-Médineh à l'époque ramesside*, BdE 96 (Cairo, 1985); see also the excellent contributions and systematic bibliography in R. J. Demarée and J. J. Janssen, eds., *Gleanings from Deir el Medîna* (Leiden, 1982), and R. J. Demarée and A. Egberts, eds., *Village Voices* (Leiden, 1992).

5. See chap. 1 n. 159, and chap. 2 n. 9.

6. For the respective roles of these two specializations in the preparation of inscriptions, see P. Vernus, *BSFE* 119 (1990): 49 n. 12.

7. See A. G. McDowell, *Jurisdiction in the Workmen's Community of Deir el-Medîna*, Egyptologische Uitgaven 5 (Leiden, 1990), 215.

8. For an overall study of the social status of persons engaged in artisans' work, see F. Steinmann, *ZÄS* 107 (1980): 137 ff.; idem, *ZÄS* 109 (1982), 66 ff. and 149 ff.; idem, *ZÄS* 111 (1984): 30 ff.; and idem, *ZÄS* 118 (1991): 149–61.

9. Note that in the wording of oaths, being made a "quarryman" occurs as a punishment in cases of perjury; see P. Salt 124, verso 1, 6–7 = p. 84.

10. See the bibliography given in chap. 1, n. 206.

11. On the wages of the workmen, see J. J. Janssen, *Commodity Prices from the Ramessid Period: An Economic Study of the Village of Necropolis Workmen at Thebes* (Leiden, 1975), 455–93; idem, *SAK* 3 (1975): 166–70; and D. Valbelle, *"Les Ouvriers de la nécropole,"* 148–57.

12. R. Miller, *GM* 115 (1990): 63–74. See p. 63 for the mention of loaves of bread that were given to the workers after having been consecrated to the funerary cult of Ramesses II.

13. See M. Malaise, *Anthropologica: Second numéro spécial 1988*, 68.

14. R. O. Faulkner, *CAH*, vol. 2, chap. 23, p. 32 of the fascicle attributes the difficulties in the provisioning to "probably less positive misconduct than inefficiency or neglect of duty on the part of those whose business it was to keep the supplies in the storehouses up to date and to issue them to the workmen." This explanation is partially acceptable, but shortsighted, for it underestimates the general bad state of the economy in this period.

15. M. Gutgesell, *LdÄ*, vol. 6, col. 82.

16. For the vizier To, see *KRI*, vol. 5, 369, along with K. A. Kitchen and B. Ockinga, *MDAIK* 48 (1992): 99–105. On pp. 61–64, we see how this vizier met his responsibilities.

17. On this personage, see J. Černý, *A Community of Workmen at Thebes*, 212.

18. A measure representing one-fourth of a "sack"; that is, about seventeen and a half dry quarts.

19. O. Chicago 16991; see E. F. Wente, *JNES* 20 (1961): 252; idem, *Letters from Ancient Egypt* (Atlanta, 1990), 50–51; and S. Allam, *Hieratische Ostraka und Papyri aus der Ramessidenzeit* (Tübingen, 1973), 76.

20. The hyperbolic use of *mwt*, "to die," is well attested in the classical tradition: thus, Maxims of Ptahhotep, P 585, "dying while alive every day"; P. Lansing 10, 8, "he is dead while alive"; and in an administrative report, Semna Dispatch 4, 10, "the desert is dying of hunger."

21. On this scribe, see Černý, *A Community of Workmen at Thebes*, 339–50; A. Roccati, in *Hommages à Serge Sauneron*, vol. 1, BdE 81 (Cairo, 1979), 282; C. J. Eyre, in J. Ruffle, G. A. Gaballa, and K. A. Kitchen, eds., *Glimpses of Ancient Egypt: Studies in Honour of H. W. Fairman* (Warminster, 1979), 84; M. L. Bierbrier, *The Late New Kingdom in Egypt (c. 1300–664 B.C.): A Genealogical and Chronological Investigation* (Warminster, 1975), 39–42; J. J. Janssen, in R. J. Demarée and J. J. Janssen, eds., *Gleanings from Deir el-Medîna*, 149–53; P. W. Pestman, in *Gleanings from Deir el-Medîna*, 174.

22. P. Turin "Strike"; hieroglyphic transcription in A. H. Gardiner, *Ramesside Administrative Documents* (Oxford, 1948), 45–58. For translations of the papyrus, see W. Spiegelberg, *Arbeiter und Arbeitbewegung im Pharaonenreich unter den Ramessiden (ca. 1400–1100 v. Chr.): Eine kulturgeschichtliche Skizze* (Strasbourg, 1895), 18; B. Lourie, *Vestnik* 34/4 (1950): 81–88; Z. Žába, *Prao du vijstavou Deir el Medinai*, 4; W. F. Edgerton, *JNES* 10 (1951): 137–45; S. Allam, *Hieratische Ostraka und Papyri*, 310, no. 276 (recto 3, 6–13 and verso 5, 2–6, 5); A. K. Graysen and D. B. Redford, eds., *Papyrus and Tablet* (Englewood Cliffs, N.J., 1973), 37–40; P. J. Frandsen, in S. I. Groll, ed., *Studies in Egyptology Presented to Miriam Lichtheim* (Jerusalem, 1990), vol. I, 166–99.

23. O. Berlin P. 10633; O. CGC 25530; O. IFAO 1255 + O. Varille 39; P. Turin Cat 2006 + 1961. For other allusions to strikes, see C. J. Eyre, in J. Ruffle, G. A. Gaballa, and K. A. Kitchen, eds., *Glimpses of Ancient Egypt*, 80–91 (O. Sydney Nicholson Museum); O. CGC 25533; O. DM 36; O. DM 38; O. DM 571; *Giornale della Necropoli*, pl. 14, recto 1, p. 53, recto 2, 16 (Ramesses XI); J. J. Janssen, *OA* 18 (1979): 301–8 (O. Turin 57072, shortages in the deliveries of food rations). See also C. J. Eyre, *GM* 98 (1987): 11–18 (P. DM XXIV: under Ramesses I, Ramesses V, or Ramesses VI, the gang made a report about the delivery of its clothing, its unguents, its wood, its fish, its salt,

and its lamp oil). On the strikes in general, see M. Gutgesell, *LdÄ*, vol. 6, cols. 82–84, s.v. "Streik"; J. Černý, in S. Donadoni, ed., *Le Fonti indirette della storia egiziana*, Studi Semitici 7 (Rome, 1963), 48; R. O. Faulkner, in *CAH*, vol. 2, chap. 23, p. 32 of the fascicle; C. J. Eyre, in M. A. Powell, ed., *Labor in the Ancient Near East* (New Haven, 1987), 178; D. Valbelle, *"Les Ouvriers de la Tombe,"* 190–93; and P. Vernus and J. Yoyotte, *Les Pharaons: Les noms, les thèmes, les lieux* (Paris, 1988), 58.

24. On this sentence, see J. J. Janssen, *OA* 18 (1979): 306–7.

25. O. Berlin P. 10633; S. Allam, *Hieratische Ostraka und Papyri*, 29, no. 8.

26. For the remains of this temple, see PM, vol. 2, 2d ed., 426–29. For information regarding its administration, see W. Helck, *Materialien zur Wirtschaftsgeschichte des Neuen Reiches* (Mainz, 1961), 95–97. For the remains of this temple, see PM, vol. 2, 2d ed., 457–60; for information regarding its administration, see W. Helck, *Materialien,* 102.

27. P. J. Frandsen, *JEA* 75 (1989): 117–21, proposes to restore a mention of the causeway of Mentuhotpe Sankhkare in the lacuna.

28. O. Varille + O. IFAO 1255 = K*RI*, vol. 7, 301.

29. O. CGC 25530.

30. The expression used, *p3 nfrw*, could be understood as "the heart of," by analogy with the sense of *nfrw* in *nfrw grh*, "the dead of night," for which see D. Meeks, *Année lexicographique 1978*, vol. 2 (Paris, 1981), 195. But I am hesitant to select this interpretation here, for it would imply that the workmen penetrated into the heart of the funerary temple of Ramesses III. Such a possibility cannot be excluded, but we may think that the mention of such an incident would have been more detailed, for it would have been no small matter for them to have penetrated into the funerary temple of the reigning pharaoh. Two days later, were not the workers obliged to wait in front of the gate before entering the Ramesseum? When all is said and done, it is preferable to give *nfrw* the meaning "rear, extremity," for which see A. H. Gardiner, *JEA* 22 (1936): 178 (with regard to a nearly contemporaneous document), and E. Hornung, *Eranos* 49 (1980): 413.

31. P. Turin "Strike," verso 3, 1.

32. Since the writing is ambiguous, several interpretations are possible. J. J. Janssen, *OA* 18 (1979): 306–8, and P. J. Frandsen, in S. I. Groll, ed., *Studies in Egyptology*, 168–69, after detailed discussions using all existing bibliography, prefer to understand *ʿk* as a pseudoparticiple, given that the Future III is not very probable; yet the sense obtained is not very satisfying in the context. There are, however, two other possibilities that have not been envisaged. The first is to read *iw 18 n hrw (hr) ʿk*, that is, a present circumstantial with *hr* + infinitive, "eighteen days entering in the month." The second is to read *iw 18 n hrw (m) ʿk*, the construction *m* + infinitive expressing, with a verb of motion, unaccomplished action, "eighteen days being in the process of entering in the month," that is, eighteen days remained before the twenty-eighth, the possible date of payment of the rations, the tenth day being considered as having already "entered," since it had begun. For the variation between subject + pseudoparticiple and subject + *m* + infinitive in an analogous expression, see P. Vernus, *Future at Issue, Tense, Mood and Aspect in Middle Egyptian: Studies in Syntax and Semantics*, YES 4 (New Haven, 1990), 156–57, (311) and (312). For a related use of *ʿk*, see *iw m-dy ʿk hrw wʿw wʿw m p3y.sn diw m p3y.sn sgnn*, "do not allow to pass even a single day of their rations and of their unguent," P. Turin PuR 4, 9.

33. That is, inside the territory of the Tomb; here, the workmen are being bidden to return to their village.

34. P. Turin "Strike," recto 1, 1.

35. For other possibilities, see R. Ventura, *Living in a City of the Dead: A Selection of Topographical and Administrative Terms in the Documents of the Theban Necropolis*, OBO 69 (Freiburg and Göttingen, 1986), 132 n. 76. For the remains of this temple, see PM, vol. 2, 2d ed., 426–29, and for information regarding its administration, see W. Helck, *Materialien,* 95–97.

36. In addition to its basic sense "tomb of the king," *p3 ḥr* came to designate the apparatus that was set in place to administer it, and the territory that belonged to it; see K. Baer, *Orientalia* 34 (1965): 431 n. 4, and R. Ventura, *Living in a City of the Dead,* 14–15.

37. W. Helck, *JESHO* 7 (1964): 136 ff.

38. W. F. Edgerton, *JNES* 10 (1951): 133 n. 10; E. Thomas, *The Royal Necropoleis of Thebes* (Princeton, 1966), p. 51, and eadem, *JEA* 49 (1963): 61.

39. P. J. Frandsen, *JEA* 75 (1989): 113–23.

40. R. Ventura, *Living in a City of the Dead,* 120–44.

41. P. Turin "Strike," recto 1, 6 = A. H. Gardiner, *Ramesside Administrative Documents* (Oxford, 1948), 53.

42. P. Turin "Strike," verso 1, a–b = A. H. Gardiner, *Ramesside Administrative Documents,* 48–49.

43. Unfortunately, we do not know exactly how many workmen composed the gang; for this problem, see P. J. Frandsen, in S. I. Groll, ed., *Studies in Egyptology,* 184 n. 46.

44. O. Varille + O. IFAO 1255 = *KRI,* vol. 7, 301.

45. P. Turin "Strike," recto 1, 7–2, 5.

46. The "Enclosure of (the institution of) the Tomb" was the administrative center of the institution of the Tomb, where the captains stayed and the foodstuffs to be distributed were stored; see R. Ventura, *Living in a City of the Dead,* 83–106, and idem, *JEA* 73 (1987): 149–60, where it is situated "on the slope leading from the Ramesseum to Deir el-Medina, within 300m of the south-western corner of the temenos of the Ramesseum." See also C. Sturtewagen, in S. I. Groll, ed., *Studies in Egyptology,* 938.

47. On this meaning of *wšbt,* see J. F. Borghouts, in R. J. Demarée and J. J. Janssen, eds., *Gleanings from Deir el-Medîna,* 77.

48. Confirmed by another account, that of O. Varille + O. IFAO 1255 = *KRI,* vol. 7, p. 301, 8–10: "(Year 29), [month 2 of winter, day 30]; same thing, (but) they had brought their wives. . . . List of what was payable to them." What follows is ridden with lacunae; for an attempted interpretation, see P. J. Frandsen, in S. I. Groll, ed., *Studies in Egyptology,* 179–81.

49. P. Turin "Strike," recto 4, 23–4, 16 (text written in reverse direction).

50. O. Varille + O. IFAO 1255, 7 = *KRI,* vol. 7, p. 300, 11–12.

51. O. Varille + O. IFAO 1255, 11–13 = *KRI,* vol. 7, pp. 300, 15–301, 1.

52. P. Turin "Strike," verso 3, 24.

53. The simple insertion of *p3 ḥtm n* before *p3 ḥr* resolves the topographical difficulties in the interpretation of this passage, for it is difficult to imagine that *p3 ḥr* in this passage could designate the village of Deir el-Medina, as suggested by P. J. Frandsen, *JEA* 75 (1989): 115. If the latter were the case, it would be difficult to imagine how Mose could have said, "if I am taken from here to up there," given that in these texts, "up there" (*r-ḥr*) usually refers to the village, as opposed to the plain (see A. H. Gardiner, *Ramesside Administrative Documents,* 56, 16). It cannot be excluded, of course, that "up there" refers to the construction site as opposed to the village, but such an identification would ill accord with the other information we have regarding the strikes; for instance, we would not understand why the captains would have set out to look for them in their own village. Note that O. DM 571 mentions a protest movement that is analogously marked by the fact that the workmen passed by "four (!) redoubts" and spent the day in the Enclosure of the Tomb; the date of this ostracon is uncertain (see P. J. Frandsen, *JEA* 75 [1989]: 122 n. 51).

54. For the expression *w3 is,* see K. Baer, *Orientalia* 34 (1965): 425–31, and C. Sturtewagen, in S. I. Groll, ed., *Studies in Egyptology,* 940. See also P. Salt 124, verso 1, 1, cited on p. 83 of the present volume.

55. P. Turin "Strike," recto 2, 6–2, 10.

56. D. Valbelle, *"Les Ouvriers de la Tombe,"* 191, citing P. Turin Cat 2006 + 1961.

57. For the "Enclosure of the Tomb," see n. 46.

58. Following Z. Žába, *Ar. Or.* 20 (1952): 642–45; but this thesis has been contested by J. J. Janssen, *OA* 18 (1979): 307, who notes that of the twenty-two known dates for the payment of rations, the twenty-eighth day is attested only once. The argument, however, is perhaps not cogent; see the following note.

59. It is clear that for technical reasons, the payment of rations could be made on various days; see p. 60 of the present volume, and F. Neveu, *RdE* 41 (1990): 144, § 4, regarding the spreading out of payments to the workers in P. DM 28.

60. That is, he took the statues of the gods.

61. This jubilee was the *sed*-festival, celebrated by the pharaoh after thirty years (in principle) of rule; see, in general, E. Hornung and E. Staehelin, *Studien zum Sedfest,* Aegyptiaca Helvetica 1 (Geneva, 1974). In the present instance, the vizier went to el-Kab for divine statues that he took to Pi-Riamsese in the delta, where Ramesses III was going to celebrate his first jubilee.

62. Or, "who was promoted (recently) for the purpose of taking away," according to the interpretation of P. J. Frandsen, in S. I. Groll, ed., *Studies in Egyptology,* 188.

63. P. Turin "Strike," recto 2, 18–3, 4, studied in detail by P. Vernus, *RdE* 32 (1980): 121–24.

64. For a logical analysis of one of these sentences, see A. Loprieno, in D. Mendel and U. Claudi, eds., *Ägypten im Afro-orientalischen Kontext: Aufsätze zur Archäologie, Geschichte und Sprache eines unbegrenzten Raumes, Gedenkschrift Peter Behrens* (Cologne, 1991), 231–32.

65. We have seen that a workman's ration of emmer wheat consisted of four "sacks."

66. The word *mryt* has been studied in detail by R. Ventura, *Living in a City of the Dead,* 79–82, 90, etc. (see the index to the book); see also A. Théodoridès, *RIDA* 28 (1981): 14 n. 8, and A. G. Macdowell, *Jurisdiction in the Workmen's Community,* 221.

67. The text employs the word *nꜣ ḥrdw,* literally, "the children"; this is evidently a colloquial and deprecatory designation of the informers who reported the actions of the workmen to the vizier.

68. Note the use of the first person; see the comments in the next paragraph.

69. P. Turin "Strike," recto, 3, 6–13.

70. J. J. Janssen, *OA* 18 (1979): 305.

71. There is a similar change in P. Turin 1887, recto 2, 4–5; cf. p. 183 n. 4.

72. P. Turin "Strike," recto 3, 14–18.

73. Restore *šm.*

74. Once again, there is a shift to the first person.

75. This was added at a later date, after the preceding statement was written down (A. H. Gardiner, *Ramesside Administrative Documents,* 51 a, 16 c), hence the shift back to the third person.

76. P. Turin "Strike," verso 7, 1–7, 7. There is a partial translation in W. Helck, *Materialien,* 463–64.

77. See p. 3.

78. Compare P. Turin Giornale 52, recto 2, 8 = *KRI,* vol. 6, 690, where offering loaves from the funerary temple of Ramesses III are divided among the workers. On the use and consumption of offerings, see in general J. J. Janssen, in E. Lipinski, ed., *State and Temple Economy in the Ancient Near East: Proceedings of the International Conference Organised by the Katholieke Universiteit Leuven from the 10th to the 14th April 1978,* OLA 6 (Louvain, 1979), 512–15, citing documents in which it appears that the workmen of (the institution of) the Tomb received meat that came from offerings consecrated on the occasion of the Opet festival.

79. Thus, at the end of Dynasty 20, the scribe Djehutimose was caught stealing

grain owed to the workmen of (the institution of) the Tomb by falsifying accounts; see p. 133.

80. O. DM 36, 9; O. DM 38, 21; O. CGC 2553, verso 9–10.

81. See the next text cited.

82. Restored after the passage from the journal of the necropolis cited on p. 65.

83. O. Sydney = C. Eyre, in M. A. Powell, ed., *Labor in the Ancient Near East,* 89. The date is uncertain, but the attribution to the reign of Ramesses IV is not impossible; still, M. Gutgesell, *LdÄ,* vol. 6, col. 84, inclines toward a later date.

84. See A. G. McDowell, *Jurisdiction in the Workmen's Community,* 234. We saw earlier that the scribe Amennakht threatened the gang in these terms: "If you leave, I shall have you found in the wrong in any tribunal before which you go" (p. 62).

85. P. Mallett II, 5–6 = KRI, vol. 6, 69. For this passage, see W. Helck, *Materialien,* 616, and S. I. Groll, in S. I. Groll, ed., *Studies in Egyptology,* 387. The syntax of the passage is worth attention: the second tense *i.ri.tw-ḏd,* itself converted into a circumstantial, lays the focus on the circumstantial *iw bn twtw ḥr dit,* while *ḥr* introduces two clauses that prolong this circumstantial.

86. Texts relating to the nonpayment of rations in year 17 of Ramesses IX are translated on p. 6.

87. The royal necropolis.

88. For the tomb of Ramesses IX, see F. Abitz, in N. Reeves, ed., *After Tutankhamun: Research and Excavations in the Royal Necropolis at Thebes* (London, 1992), 165–85.

89. Journal of (the institution of) the Tomb B 9, 6–11 = KRI, vol. 6, 580.

90. Read *r-ḥȝt,* rather than *di.*

91. O. DM 571; see n. 53.

92. Shift from the impersonal style to a more engaged notation; the writer betrays his membership in the institution of the Tomb.

93. That of the first prophet of Amun?

94. Each Egyptian month consisted of thirty days.

95. For this individual, see A. G. McDowell, *Jurisdiction in the Workmen's Community,* 77.

96. For the word *rȝ-ꜥ,* see F. Neveu, *RdE* 41 (1990): 150.

97. Journal of (the institution of) the Tomb, P. Turin 1898, recto 3, 23–4, 4 = KRI, vol. 6, 694.

98. It took no fewer than six woodworkers to fashion the two coffers and the box for papyri, according to P. Turin 1898, recto 5, 6, as judiciously noted by Neveu, *RdE* 41 (1990): 150.

99. See, in general, I. Pomorskai, *Les Flabellifères à la droite du roi en Égypte ancienne* (Warsaw, 1987). That a fan bearer could be charged with a mission of a judicial nature is proved by the Judicial Papyrus of Turin, 6, 7, where the fan bearer *Kr* belongs to the commission constituted by Ramesses III to inquire into a plot (see pp. 110 and 188 n. 5). Elsewhere, it is also a fan bearer whom Pharaoh sends to force the governor of Thebes to return a wooden mast in P. BM 10383, 3, 5–6 (see McDowell, *Jurisdiction in the Workmen's Community,* 238), a document concerning the sack of western Thebes.

100. On the topographical problems posed by the passage, see R. Ventura, *Living in a City of the Dead,* 122 n. 17, and P. J. Frandsen, *JEA* 75 (1989): 114.

101. Once again, the author of the document allows himself to forget to employ the required impersonality of the administrative style.

102. For the grammatical form, see J. F. Borghouts, in R. J. Demarée and J. J. Janssen, eds., *Gleanings from Deir el-Medîna,* 76 n. 10.

103. In front of their superiors, the two workmen confirm the statement they had made to their messengers. For the formulation *ḏd . . . mȝꜥt,* see P. Turin 1887, recto 1,

13, "[I]t was found that he had said it truly" (p. 105), and O. IFAO 502 = J. Černý, *BIFAO* 35 (1935): 52, *ḏḏ.f t3y mdt m mȝʿt*, "[D]id he really say this thing?" P. J. Frandsen, in S. I. Groll, ed. *Studies in Egyptology*, 187, proposes another interpretation, "Tell it as it is."

The text is P. Turin "Strike," recto 2, 11–2, 17.

104. For the procedure to be followed by workmen reporting accusations, see A. G. McDowell, *Jurisdiction in the Workmen's Community*, 211.

105. For the passage, see K. Baer, *JEA* 50 (1964): 180. The problematic of the expression *sdf3-tryt*, long considered as the designation of a form of oath, has been entirely renewed in an article by S. N. Morschauser, *JARCE* 25 (1988): 93–103, where the bibliography is to be found (add A. G. McDowell, *Jurisdiction in the Workmen's Community*, 202–8, and B. Menu, *Le Serment*, vol. 1: *Signes et fonctions*, Paris, 1991, 331). Morschauser holds that "*sdf3-tryt* is a technical expression referring to the issue of a legal pardon for a crime."

106. The expression designates the royal tombs, according to Černý, *BIFAO* 35 (1935): 69, while according to K. Baer, *JEA* 50 (1965): 180, it designates the Valley of the Kings, the Ramesseum, and Deir el-Medina. Note also the same expression, but in the singular, in P. Lee 1, 4 (see p. 190 n. 44).

107. For the obligation to denounce, see P. Abbot 6, 16–17: "For it would be a fault for someone in my position, that I learn of an affair and that I conceal it" (see p. 8); and the judicial papyrus of Turin 4, 8: "[H]e was arrested because of plans that he had knowledge of and concealed" (see p. 111); and ostracon CGC 25556, 7–8: "[T]here was no accusation against [him] regarding Pharaoh, l.p.h., and if we conceal it today to report it later, may our (lit., "his") nose and our (lit., "his") ears be cut off." For reporting crimes as obligatory, see S. N. Morschauser, *JARCE* 25 (1988): 100 n. 70.

108. For the term utilized, see p. 76.

109. For references to judicial precedents in the texts, see A. G. McDowell, *Jurisdiction in the Workmen's Community*, 217, and chap. 1 n. 76. For the precedent noted here, see J. Černý, *A Community of Workmen*, 304, and M. L. Bierbrier, *The Late New Kingdom in Egypt (c. 1300–664 B.C.): A Genealogical and Chronological Investigation* (Warminster, 1975), 23.

110. P. Turin "Strike," recto 4, 1–4, 16a.

111. Another example of the ambiguity of *p3 ḥr*; here, the term could designate either a collective tomb for the wives of the reigning king, or, more likely, the necropolis of the queens in general. See chap. 1 n. 161.

112. P. Turin "Strike," recto 3, 18; for the position of this addition, see P. J. Frandsen, in S. I. Groll, ed., *Studies in Egyptology*, 197.

113. This is the interpretation of D. Valbelle, *"Les Ouvriers de la Tombe,"* 192.

114. See K. Baer, *Orientalia* 34 (1965): 435–37, where the passage is studied.

115. It had already been Penanukis who, by his statements, had been at the origin of a scandal that obliged the vizier to make an on-the-spot inquiry in the third month of the inundation season of a year that is thought to be year 26 of Ramesses III; see O. DM 148 and D. Valbelle, *"Les Ouvriers de la Tombe,"* 192. We know nothing about this scandal except that it was considered to be quite important, given the high rank of the commission brought together to look into it; see A. G. McDowell, *Jurisdiction in the Workmen's Community*, 217–19. But it is not out of the question to think that it had some connection with tomb violations.

116. The most natural interpretation is to think that "my father" in "the foreman of the gang Paneb, my father" refers to Penanukis, as most commentators have done; see P. J. Frandsen, in S. I. Groll, ed., *Studies in Egyptology*, 193 n. 74.

117. C. J. Eyre, *JEA* 70 (1984): 94.

118. See chapter 5.

Chapter 3. Paneb

1. The chronology of Paneb's career has not been clearly established. For a document (O. DM 594) that undoubtedly portrays him running wild as early as the reign of Merneptah, see n. 64.

2. The basic edition is that by J. Černý, *JEA* 15 (1929): 243–58. The text is transcribed into hieroglyphs in K*RI*, vol. 4, 408–14. For translations and commentaries, see S. Allam, *Hieratische Ostraka und Papyrus aus der Ramessidenzeit* (Tübingen, 1973), 281–87, no. 266, with photographs on pls. 84–85, and A. Théodoridès, *RIDA* 28 (1981): 11–79.

3. On this problem, see Théodoridès, *RIDA* 28 (1981): 73–77.

4. On this vizier, see W. Helck, *Zur Verwaltung des Mittleren und Neuen Reiches* (Leiden, 1958), 327 and 460, and R. Krauss, *SAK* 4 (1976): 197. For the relevant hieroglyphic texts, see K*RI*, vol. 5, 279–81.

5. P. Salt 124, recto 1, 1–4.

6. On the organization of (the institution of) the Tomb, see chapter 2.

7. Another highly fragmentary source seems to confirm this information. On O. DM 697, recto 4, we can make out: ". . . killed the foreman [of the gang] . . ."; on the date of the ostracon, see M. L. Bierbrier, *JSSEA* 8 (1978): 138–39.

8. W. Helck, *ZDMG* 105 (1955): 43 (= bedouin or Libyan). For *ḥrw* as a designation of foreigners who made incursions at Thebes, see B. J. J. Haring, *Sesto congresso internationale di egittologia* (Turin, 1993), 203, who points out that K. A. Kitchen, *RdE* 36 (1985): 177–79, noted a document attesting this usage as early as the reign of Ramesses III. But in an expanded version of this communication, which appeared in R. J. Demarée and A. Egberts, eds., *Village Voices* (Leiden, 1992), 71–80, Haring attempted to return to the interpretation of "civil strife."

9. J. Černý, *A Community of Workmen at Thebes in the Ramesside Period,* BdE 50 (Cairo, 1973), 289, and S. Donadoni, ed., *Le Fonti indirette della storia egiziana,* Studi Semitici 7 (Rome, 1963), 39. In favor of the identification with Amenmesse, see R. Krauss, *SAK* 4 (1976): 184–87; against the identification, see J. Osing, *SAK* 7 (1979): 270–71.

10. An example is the office of governor of el-Kab, which fell to Iymeru "as property of his mother's brother, the governor of el-Kab Ay the Younger, who died childless." See P. Lacau, *Une stèle juridique de Karnak,* CASAE 13 (Cairo, 1949), p. 8, l. 5.

11. Bribery as a means of obtaining a promotion or causing a promotion to be made seems to have been a frequent practice. Thus, O. CGC 25800 cynically inventories the goods given to the "agents" in order, it seems, to speed the promotion of a young man; see J. Černý, *A Community of Workmen at Thebes,* 255.

12. For the formulation with *sḫ³*, "memorandum," see 225 n. 6.

13. On this meaning of ʿ*rk*, see A. G. McDowell, *Jurisdiction in the Workmen's Community of Deir el-Medîna,* Egyptologische Uitgaven 5 (Leiden, 1990), 33.

14. A number of texts allude to these chapels (*ḥnw*) in which the workmen celebrated the festivals of their deity of choice: "As for me, I was in my chapel (on the festival) of the birth of Taweret," O. Gardiner 166, recto; "On the (festival) of *Mḥt*, he went to stay in his chapel," O. P. Berlin 10637. See also J. J. Janssen and C. Pestman, *JESHO* 11 (1968): 123, and A. G. McDowell, *Jurisdiction in the Workmen's Community,* 123.

15. P. Salt 124, verso 1, 13–16.

16. J. Černý, *A Community of Workmen at Thebes,* 301, citing O. CGC 25237, verso = K*RI,* vol. 4, p. 530, 5–10.

17. This is the equivalent, in the formal language, of the title "man of the gang." The "Place of Truth" designates the Theban necropolis; see R. Ventura, *Living in a City of the Dead: A Selection of Topographical and Administrative Terms in the Documents of the Theban Necropolis,* OBO 69 (Freiburg and Göttingen, 1986), 38–63.

18. On this point, see J. J. Janssen, in R. J. Demarée and J. J. Janssen, eds., *Gleanings from Deir el-Medîna* (Leiden, 1982), 110.

19. P. Salt 124, recto 1, 18.

20. Thus, the decree of Sethos II forbids the prophets from exacting "something" (*nkt*) from the pure priests or the ritualist priests; see KRI, vol. 4, p. 266, 3.

21. O. Gardiner 197, verso 3–6, according to J. Černý, *A Community of Workmen at Thebes,* 332. Analogously, the agents of the domain of Khnum did not report on the fact that a captain burned his barge because "he gave his *bakshish* (*iw.f (ḥr) dit ḫt.f*)," P. Turin 1887, verso 2, 16; see p. 104.

22. P. Amherst-Leopold II, 3, 3–4, and P. BM 10054, recto 1, 11; see p. 7.

23. P. Salt 124, recto 14.

24. Probably the temple of Hathor at Deir el-Medina; see PM, vol. 2, 2d ed., 695, and D. Valbelle, *"Les Ouvriers de la Tombe": Deir el-Médineh à l'Époque ramesside,* BdE 96 (Cairo, 1985), 168–70.

25. *Smn* is probably used here in its well-known sense of "to fix in writing." That much said, there are two possible interpretations. One is that Qenherkhopshef wrote down a misdeed of Paneb. The other is that the scribe registered a pious act, probably an offering made by Paneb using fraudulently acquired foodstuffs. The practice of registering offerings is in fact clearly attested, for example, in the Instruction of Any on P. Boulaq III, 3, 5 = A. H. Gardiner, *JEA* 45 (1959): 12; *sᶜḥᶜ mtrw m-ḫt wdn.k sp tpy n p3 ir(t).f twtw iw r wḥ3 šnw.k imy sw dit h3.k ḥr ᶜrt,* "produce witnesses when you have offered, the first time you do it; one will come to examine your inventory; accept that he sets you down on a papyrus." Given that Qenherkhopshef seems afterward to have been an accomplice of Paneb, the second interpretation seems preferable.

26. Undoubtedly the temple of Ptah in the Valley of the Queens, though the god had a large number of cult monuments in the region; see D. Valbelle, *"Les Ouvriers de la Tombe,"* 315.

27. For this scribe, see J. Černý, *A Community of Workmen at Thebes,* 329–37; M. L. Bierbrier, *The Late New Kingdom in Egypt (c. 1300–664 B.C.): A Genealogical and Chronological Investigation* (Warminster, 1975), 26–29; and C. Pestman, in R. J. Demarée and J. J. Janssen, eds., *Gleanings from Deir el-Medîna,* 160.

28. According to the best authorities in the matter; see J. Černý, *A Community of Workmen,* 332, "at times unreadable or almost so," and A. H. Gardiner, *Ramesside Administrative Documents* (Oxford, 1948), xxiv n. 1.

29. P. Vernus, *BSFE* 119 (1990): 36.

30. I. E. S. Edwards, *JEA* 54 (1968): 155–60; see also Y. Koenig, *RdE* 33 (1981): 29.

31. P. Salt 124, verso 1, 4–5.

32. For this vizier, see W. Helck, *Zur Verwaltung,* 326–27; G. A. Gaballa, in J. Ruffle, G. A. Gaballa, and K. A. Kitchen, eds., *Glimpses from Ancient Egypt: Studies in Honour of H. W. Fairman* (Warminster, 1979), 49; R. Krauss, *SAK* 5 (1977): 154–56; KRI, vol. 4, 204–6.

33. E. D. Bedell, "Criminal Law in the Egyptian Ramesside Period" (Ph.D. diss., Brandeis University, 1973), 29–30 and 36; A. G. McDowell, *Jurisdiction in the Workmen's Community,* 226–27 and 238. The text is P. Salt 124, recto 2, 16–18.

34. See pp. 141–142.

35. This name is written with the determinative that indicates an enemy, as noted by R. Krauss, *SAK* 4 (1976): 186; see the additional remarks by A. Théodoridès, *RIDA* 28 (1981): 23–24. This orthographic indication of infamy was also used against Panehsy after he deposed Amenhotpe, the first prophet of Amun; see p. 20.

36. J. Černý, *JEA* 15 (1929): 255–56, first suggested this identification. The thesis has been developed at length by R. Krauss, *SAK* 5 (1977): 161–99 and *SAK* 6 (1978): 131–74; also see the reservations of R. O. Faulkner, *CAH,* vol. 2, chap. 23, p. 22 of the

fascicle, and of J. Osing, *SAK* 7 (1979): 253–71. On Amenmesse, see also K. A. Kitchen, *GM* 97 (1987): 23, and A. Dodson, *GM* 117/118 (1990): 151.

37. On this point, see J. J. Janssen, in R. J. Demarée and J. J. Janssen, eds., *Gleanings from Deir el-Medîna,* 125.

38. For analogous acts in the same period, see D. Valbelle, *"Les Ouvriers de la Tombe,"* 308, and A. G. McDowell, *Jurisdiction in the Workmen's Community,* 187. Note that Paneb's own son, Aapehty, was also the victim of this sort of treatment: "Year 1, month 2 of inundation season, day 15 . . . Aapehty was attacked"; O. CGC 25517, recto 3–6. In fact, his father could have been the one who beat him; on the complex relations between the two, see pp. 76–77.

39. P. Salt 124, recto 2, 21.

40. Here, Paneb, who directed the proceeding, is explicitly named, though most often, he is not named (see, "the tribunal said to them," at the beginning of the passage). On this interesting detail, see A. G. McDowell, *Jurisdiction in the Workmen's Community,* 168.

41. O. CGC 2556. According to J. J. Janssen, *Commodity Prices from the Ramessid Period: An Economic Study of the Village of Necropolis Workmen at Thebes* (Leiden, 1975), 18 n. 11, the ostracon "dates from a year 5, clearly of Sethos II." For translations, see S. Allam, *Hieratische Ostraka und Papyri aus der Ramessidenzeit* (Tübingen, 1973), 61–63, and A. G. McDowell, *Jurisdiction in the Community of Workmen,* 251–53.

42. P. Salt 124, recto 2, 14–16.

43. One of the many causes of the conflict could have been the fact that Paneb made use, for his own benefit, of the workmen belonging to the half of the gang supervised by Hay, as cleverly suggested by J. Černý, *A Community of Workmen,* 304.

44. For the use of the conjunctive in past narrative, here and elsewhere in P. Salt 124, see J. F. Borghouts, *ZÄS* 106 (1976): 22–23 (20); see also P. Rollin, 2–3, on which see 190 n. 36.

45. J. J. Janssen, in R. J. Demarée and J. J. Janssen, eds., *Gleanings from Deir el-Medîna,* 109–15, has studied the life of this workman, showing that he had been brought up by the foreman Neferhotep, just like Paneb himself; the latter thus added to the pleasure of adultery the spice of flaunting his revenge on his rival in front of their father, even if only an adoptive one. Note that Hel divorced Hessunebef in year 2 of Sethnakhte; see Janssen, *Gleanings from Deir el-Medîna,* 115. This divorce could have been related to the adultery.

46. Hel and Ubekhet are in fact well attested as the wife and daughter on the stela Manchester 4588 and on a cloth in the Meters collection in Washington; see J. J. Janssen, ibid., 111.

47. P. Salt 124, recto 2, 1–4.

48. On this point, see A. G. McDowell, *Jurisdiction in the Workmen's Community,* 46.

49. P. Turin "Strike," recto 4 (A. H. Gardiner, *Ramesside Administrative Documents,* 57); see also pp. 67–68.

50. P. Turin 1887, recto 1, 5 (A. H. Gardiner, *Ramesside Administrative Documents,* 74); see also p. 97.

51. On this problem, see C. J. Eyre, *JEA* 70 (1984): 93, and C. Desroches Noblecourt, *La Femme au temps des pharaons* (Paris, 1986), 210 and 215–18.

52. Afroasiatic is a group of related languages divided into five branches: Egyptian, Semitic (including, inter alia, Hebrew and Arabic), Libyco-Berber, the Kushitic languages, and Chadic. Egyptian is thus somewhat distantly related to Arabic.

53. Other examples are *bled, chouia,* and *flous.*

54. See S. Morschauser, *Threat-Formulae in Ancient Egypt: A Study of the History, Structure and Use of Threats and Curses in Ancient Egypt* (Baltimore, 1991), 229.

55. Adulterous affair from P. Deir el-Medina 27, recto 11; for a translation, see P.

Vernus, *Chants d'amour de l'Égypte antique* (Paris, 1992), 165. For the grammatical interpretation of this passage, which is characteristic for the meaning of *n(i)k*, see P. Vernus, *RdE* 41 (1990): 179 n. 97; it should be added that taking *f*ɜ*y(.i)* as a perfective *sḏm.f* cannot be excluded.

56. P. Salt 124, recto 1, 19.

57. On the expression, see P. Vernus, *RdE* 36 (1985): 159 (22).

58. The syntax of the whole poses two alternatives: should we understand the conjunctive as the apodosis of a protasis constituted by *wnn iw.tw (ḥr) ḏd*, or should it be attached to *sḥr r p*ɜ . . . ? The translation differs according to the preferred solution; here, we have chosen the second alternative. For detailed discussions, see K. Baer, *JEA* 51 (1965): 138; P. J. Frandsen, *An Outline of the Late Egyptian Verbal System* (Copenhagen, 1974), 184–92; J. F. Borghouts, *ZÄS* 106 (1979): 23 n. 49; H. Satzinger, *Neuägyptische Studien: Die partikel ir, das Tempussystem* (Vienna, 1976), 91; F. Neveu, "La Particule *ḥr* en néo-égyptien: Étude synchronique" (Ph.D. diss., École Pratique des Hautes Études, 1985), 59.

59. P. Salt 124, recto 2, 13.

60. A proceeding concerning the theft of "three chisels of Pharaoh, l.p.h." is known from O. Nash 2 = J. Černý and A. H. Gardiner, *Hieratic Ostraca*, pl. 47, L.

61. D. Valbelle, *Catalogue des poids à inscriptions hiératique de Deir el-Médineh n. 5001–5423*, DFIFAO 16 (Cairo, 1977), 5.

62. For *ḥʿty*, see J. J. Janssen, *Commodity Prices*, 180–84. The fact is confirmed by O. CGC 25516, verso 8.

63. P. Salt 124, recto 2, 19–20.

64. We have an analogous reference on O. DM 594: "Year 8, month 3 of winter, day 5, day when the designer Neferhotep was there to decorate the funerary equipment of Paneb." To the reign of which pharaoh is this date to be attributed? S. Sauneron, *Catalogue des ostraca hiératiques non littéraires de Deir el-Médineh (n° 550–623)*, DFIFAO 13 (Cairo, 1959), xi, suggested Sethos II, which is impossible, for he reigned no longer than six years, as noted by M. L. Bierbrier, *The Late New Kingdom in Egypt*, 123 n. 31, who thought (p. 23) that "this date may be tentatively assigned to Tewosret who probably counted her years from the accession of Siptah." Bierbrier later returned to the question in *JSSEA* 8 (1978): 138, where he was inclined to attribute this year 8 to the reign of Merneptah, following a suggestion made independently by R. Krauss and J. J. Janssen.

65. O. CGC 25516, verso 3–8.

66. O. CGC 25517, recto 9–10.

67. O. CGC 25519, verso 21.

68. The words *ḥr sš t*ɜ *ḏb*ɜ*t n P*ɜ*nb* are inserted interlinearly.

69. J. Černý, *ASAE* 27 (1927): 192 did not translate *r-ʿ-pd*. The word is surely formed with the prefix *r-ʿ*, for which see L. Pantalacci, *OLP* 16 (1985): 5–20, and F. Neveu, *RdE* 41 (1990): 149, § 5.2.1.12.

70. O. CGC 25521, recto 3–verso 20.

71. On Paneb's use of the workmen for his own profit, see J. Černý, *ASAE* 27 (1927): 198–99, and S. Sauneron, *Catalogue des ostraca hiératiques non littéraires*, xi–xii.

72. The personnel of (the institution of) the Tomb often used their skills, as well as Pharaoh's equipment and materials, to create funerary objects for their own benefit or that of a third party; see A. P. Kozloff and B. M. Bryan, *Egypt's Dazzling Sun: Amenhotep III and His World* (Cleveland, 1992), 329–30, no. 71.

73. J. Černý, *A Community of Workmen at Thebes*, 322. P. Harris I, 59, 8–60, also seems to allude to the fact that a vizier supposedly misappropriated, for his own benefit, personnel of the temple of Athribis, aside from the usual encroachments of other institutions; see P. Vernus, *Athribis: Textes et documents relatifs à la géographie, aux cultes et à l'histoire d'une ville du delta égyptien à l'époque pharaonique*, BdE 78 (Cairo, 1978), 50–52, and J.-M. Kruchten, *Annuaire IPHOS* 23 (1979): 39–51.

74. For *krḏn*, see J. J. Janssen, *Commodity Prices,* 318–21.

75. P. Salt 124, recto 1, 5–2, 12.

76. For the tomb of this pharaoh, which is in the Valley of the Kings, see PM, vol. 1, 2d ed., pp. 532–33, no. 15; H. Altenmüller, *SAK* 10 (1983): 52–61; N. Reeves, *Valley of the Kings: The Decline of a Royal Necropolis* (London, 1991), 103–4.

77. The judicial action conducted by the vizier after this exaction by Paneb is mentioned in the examination of the strikes under Ramesses III; see p. 68.

78. PM, vol. 1, 2d ed., 307–9, no. 211; the hieroglyphic texts are in K*RI,* vol. 4, 189–93.

79. See J. Černý, *A Community of Workmen at Thebes,* 305, and M. L. Bierbrier, *JSSEA* 8 (1978): 4. In K*RI,* vol. 4, 189–93, it is dated to the reign of Merneptah.

80. For this title, see n. 17.

81. A daughter of Ramesses II, according to H. Sourouzian, *ASAE* 69 (1989): 365–71; for her tomb, no. 75 in the Valley of the Queens, see C. Leblanc, *BIFAO* 88 (1988): 131–33.

82. Surely a goose intended for a rite carried out in the course of the ceremony. On the use of geese in religious practices, see P. Vernus, *RdE* 42 (1991): 246–49.

83. P. Salt 124, verso 1, 10–11.

84. This passage has attracted various comments. C. Aldred, *JEA* 49 (1963): 47, thinks that the burial of Sethos II was the occasion of a renewal of the burial of Amenmesse and his family: "Could the expression *nswtyw ḏrw* have been used here to refer to 'majesties' or 'royalties', i.e. a king, his queens, and children removed to more honoured burial in the royal cemeteries at the same time as Sethos II was interred?" A. Théodoridès, *RIDA* 28 (1981): 24–28, attempts to escape the difficulty by suggesting a generic meaning: "the funerals which are those of all the kings." See also N. Reeves, *Valley of the Kings,* 112 n. 16.

85. Or "that were found in his possession"; *i.ir.tw-gmt.w* could be either a second tense or a relative form.

86. Allam and Théodoridès have followed the second of the interpretations proposed by J. Černý, *A Community of Workmen,* 247, that is, to attribute a literal meaning to *šꜥ ḏrt.* But the first interpretation, "part with," has the advantage of being based on a text of the same genre from a point close in time, P. Turin 1887, recto 1, 2 = A. H. Gardiner, *Ramesside Administrative Documents,* p. 74, 3; the text is cited on p. 184 n. 29.

87. P. Salt 124, recto 1, 4–8.

88. Cf. P. Turin B, verso 1, 19, and R. A. Caminos, *Late Egyptian Miscellanies* (Oxford, 1954), 468. For Pharaoh's funerary chariot, see *Ramsès le grand* (Paris, 1976), 243–62.

89. P. Salt 124, recto 1, 17.

90. O. CGC 25518, recto 5–8.

91. See p. 174, n. 54.

92. The expression *r-iwd* here can have a sense derived from its meaning "as an obligation upon," for which see J. Černý and S. I. Groll, *A Late Egyptian Grammar,* Studia Pohl Series Maior 4 (Rome, 1978), 123, § 7.3.26. If we wish at all costs to give it a locative meaning, we can arrive at something like "hiding it," for which see K. Baer, *Orientalia* 34 (1965): 428 n. 3, or, more simply, "in its vicinity."

93. P. Salt 124, verso 1, 1–3.

94. PM, vol. 1, 2d ed., p. 291 and map VII (d 6).

95. The speculations of A. Théodoridès, *RIDA* 28 (1981): 52 n. 197, according to whom Paneb stole this stela, rest on a grammatical confusion: in the formulation *iw wn, wn* is not the past converter, but rather the predicate of existence. Even if we wished to read *i.wn,* with the relative form of the past converter, that would simply imply that the presence of the stela was anterior to the action, but not necessarily that it was no longer there when the action occurred. See P. Vernus, *RdE* 41 (1990): 3.2.5.

96. See W. A. Ward, *The Four Homographic Roots b-ꜣ: Etymological and Egypto-Semitic Studies,* Studia Pohl, Series Maior 6 (Rome, 1978), 40.

97. Designation of the royal necropolis, according to E. Thomas, *The Royal Necropoleis of Thebes* (Princeton, 1966), 266.

98. For the expression *sdfꜣ-tryt,* see 177 n. 105. For the passage, see K. Baer, *JEA* 50 (1965): 180, and S. N. Morschauser, *JARCE* 25 (1988): 100 n. 1.

99. P. Salt 124, recto 1, 16.

100. G. Charpentier, *Lexique bibliographique,* vol. 1 (Paris, 1981), 90–91 n. 35.

101. P. Salt 124, recto 1, 11–12.

102. Since the Egyptians were great lovers of wine and skilled cultivators of it, we should not be surprised that the pharaoh's tomb furnishings included amphorae of wine. Such amphorae were found in the tomb of Tutankhamun; see C. Desroches Noblecourt, *Toutankhamon: Vie et mort d'un pharaon* (Paris, 1965), p. 206, no. 127.

103. See H. Altenmüller, *SAK* 10 (1983): 57.

104. PM, vol. 1, 2d ed., 555. Precious objects bearing the names of Sethos II and his wife Twosre were found in a cachette in the Valley of the Kings; see PM, vol. 1, 2d ed., p. 567, no. 56, and H. Altenmüller, *SAK* 10 (1983): 58–61.

105. See p. 29.

106. For the sake of conciseness, the scribe did not write the first, stereotyped part of the protosis of the oath: "As Amun endures, and as the sovereign, l.p.h., endures."

107. On this passage, see J. Winand, *BSEG* 15 (1991): 107–13. The text is P. Salt 124, verso 1, 6–8.

108. For this difficult passage, I have benefited from the suggestions of F. Neveu. The interpretation of *irt wḏꜣt* is uncertain. I view *sw ḥr irt wḏꜣt* and *sw mi-ḳd wšš* as two clauses in asyndetic relationship.

109. P. Salt 124, verso 2, 1–7.

110. P. Turin "Strike," recto 4, 11; see p. 68.

111. For the chronological uncertainties regarding the end of Paneb's career, see M. L. Bierbrier, *JSSEA* 8 (1978): 138.

112. A. G. McDowell, *Jurisdiction in the Workmen's Community,* 211.

113. D. Valbelle, *"Les Ouvriers de la Tombe,"* 184.

Chapter 4. A Provincial Scandal

1. See in general H. Kees, *Ancient Egypt: A Cultural Topography* (London, 1961), 308–13; J. Baines and J. Málek, *Atlas of Ancient Egypt* (New York, 1980), 72–73.

2. It is perhaps not a coincidence that two tusks figure in the inventory of a bribe paid by the pure priest Penanukis: P. Turin 1887 recto 2, 6; see p. 96.

3. On these goddesses, see D. Valbelle, *Satis et Anoukis,* SDAIK 8 (Mainz, 1981).

4. P. Turin 1887. For the hieroglyphic text, see A. H. Gardiner, *Ramesside Administrative Documents* (Oxford, 1948), 73–82. For translations, see W. Spiegelberg, *ZÄS* 29 (1891): 73–75; T. E. Peet, *JEA* 10 (1924): 120–27. See also S. Sauneron, *The Priests of Ancient Egypt* (Ithaca, 2000), 14–17; idem, *RdE* 7 (1950): 19–50 and 53–62; A. H. Gardiner, *JEA* 27 (1941): 60–62; idem, *Egypt of the Pharaohs: An Introduction* (Oxford, 1961), 295–96; J. Černý, in S. Donadoni, ed., *Les Fonti indirette de la storia egiziana,* Studi Semitici 7 (Rome, 1963), 48–49; and P. Vernus, *Annuaire EPHE IVᵉ* section (1978–79): 67–69.

5. A. H. Gardiner, *Ramesside Administrative Documents,* xxiii.

6. The word *sḫꜣ* is the usual term for designating a fact mentioned as an element of a complaint. See the examples given by J. Černý, in *Studies Presented to F. Ll. Griffith* (London, 1932), 49–50 n. 1; S. Allam, *Hieratische Ostraka und Papyri aus der Ramessidenzeit* (Tübingen, 1973), 35 n. 1, 93 n. 6, 96 n. 2, 285 n. 34; A. Théodoridès, *RIDA* 28 (1981): 35–37; and M. Green, *Orientalia* 49 (1980): 24. For further examples, see D.

Valbelle, *Poids à inscriptions hiératiques de Deir el-Médineh,* DFIFAO 16 (Cairo, 1977), pl. 26, no. 5196.

7. There is a similar change in the Turin Strike Papyrus; see 175 n. 71.

8. For this vizier, see *LdÄ,* vol. 4, col. 378; K*RI,* vol. 6, 78–79, 348.

9. The phyles were groups into which the priests were divided to carry out their service on a monthly basis. For the meaning of *ꜥḥ,* "to be in service," see U. Kaplony-Heckel, *Ägyptische Handschriften,* vol. 10, Verzeichnis der orientalischen Handschriften in Deutschland 19 (Wiesbaden, 1986), 244; P. Vernus, *Future at Issue: Tense, Mood, and Aspect in Middle Egyptian, Studies in Syntax and Semantics,* YES 4 (New Haven, 1990), 149.

10. J. J. Janssen, *Commodity Prices from the Ramessid Period: An Economic Study of the Village of Necropolis Workmen at Thebes* (Leiden, 1975), 191–94 and 292.

11. W. Helck, *JARCE* 6 (1967): 136.

12. P. Turin 1887, recto 2, 4–7. Here, the palms of hired hands are greased so as not to release an accused person. Usually the opposite occurs: officials are bribed to release persons who have been arrested; see pp. 7 and 72, p. 161 n. 30, and p. 185 n. 45.

13. See pp. 67–68 and 76.

14. P. Turin 1887, recto 1, 5–6.

15. For *ḥꜣi pꜣ iwr,* see *Wb.,* vol. 2, p. 473, 15.

16. P. Turin 1887, verso 3, 1.

17. In regard to magic, see *LdÄ,* vol. 3, col. 204; for medicine, see *LdÄ,* vol. 3, col. 1158, and C. Desroches Noblecourt, *La Femme au temps des pharaons* (Paris, 1986), 246.

18. G. Charpentier, *Receuil de matériaux épigraphiques relatifs à la botanique de l'Égypte antique* (Paris, 1986), 570.

19. P. Ebers 94, 14–15; there are analogous texts in H. von Deines, H. Grapow, and W. Westendorf, *Grundriss der Medizin der alten Ägypter,* vol. 4/1 (Berlin, 1958), 278–79, and hieroglyphic texts in ibid., vol. 5 (Berlin, 1958), 478–81.

20. In P. Ebers 94, 10–11, however, the text has to do "möglicherweise um Abort," according to H. von Deines, H. Grapow, and W. Westendorf, *Grundriss der Medizin der alten Ägypter* vol. 4/2, 212, relying on the expression *dit r tꜣ,* while recognizing that in later texts, this expression is used for "der normalen Niederkunft." See also H. Grapow, *Grundriss der Medizin der alten Ägypter,* vol. 3 (Berlin, 1956), 16.

21. See *LdÄ,* vol. 2, col. 296 (without reference).

22. For contraception, see the article "Empfängnisverhütung" in *LdÄ,* vol. 1, cols. 1227–28.

23. P. Turin 1887, recto 2, 10–11.

24. Paneb also knew how to share the mother's fate with the daughter, but in his case, the fate was less cruel; see P. Salt 124 recto 2, 1–4, and p. 77.

25. P. Turin 1887, recto 2, 3.

26. On mutilation as punishment, see D. Lorton, *JESHO* 20 (1977): 40; E. D. Bedell, "Criminal Law in the Egyptian Ramesside Period" (Ph.D. diss., Brandeis University, 1973), 173–76; W. Boochs, *GM* 109 (1989): 23. It was inflicted on certain of those charged in the affair of the harem conspiracy against Ramesses III; see p. 119.

27. J.-M. Kruchten, *Le Décret d'Horemheb: Traduction, commentaire épigraphique, philologique et institutionnel,* Université Libre de Bruxelles, Faculté de Philosophie et Lettres 82 (Brussels, 1981), 160 n. 544: "toute peine entraînant au minimum une mutilation était de la compétence du souverain."

28. See in general J. J. Janssen, in E. Lipinski, ed., *State and Temple Economy in the Ancient Near East: Proceedings of the International Conference Organised by the Katholieke Universiteit Leuven from the 10th to the 14th April 1978,* OLA 6 (Louvain, 1979), 505–15.

29. P. Turin 1887, recto 1, 7.

30. P. Turin 1887, verso 1, 1.

31. P. Turin 1887, verso 1, 7.

32. Ramesses IV.

33. P. Turin 1887, recto 2, 14–15.

34. The meaning of *ir hꜣw* + suffix (or indirect genitive) is well illustrated by P. BM 10052, 5, 6–7: "You, you took money outside, and you disposed of it (*iw.tn ḥr*) *irt hꜣw.f*)."

35. For *šꜥ ḏrt*, see 182 n. 86.

36. For *di m šbw*, see H.-W. Fischer-Elfert, in H. Altenmüller and R. Germer, eds., *Miscellanea Aegyptologica: Wolfgang Helck zum 75. Geburtstag* (Hamburg, 1989), 47–48.

37. For the use of the sequential in this and analogous passages, see J. F. Borghouts, *ZÄS* 106 (1979): 24.

38. P. Turin 1887, recto 1, 2–3.

39. G. Daressy, *ASAE* 18 (1918): 196–210 and 211–17; see also L. Kákosy, *LdÄ*, vol. 4, col. 166.

40. "Prophet," the conventional translation of the Egyptian expression "servant of the god," designates the highest rank of clergy, that which carried out the liturgies and manipulated the oracles (see pp. 105–6), thus the Greek designation "prophet = he who speaks in the name (of the god)," which has nothing to do with the prophecy of the Hebrew Bible. The prophet also administered the goods of the temple and thus possessed important administrative and even judicial powers (see 196 n. 88).

41. P. Turin 1887, verso 1, 5.

42. J. J. Janssen, *Commodity Prices*, 284–86.

43. Lit., "He found them in their possession when they had given them. . . ."

44. For the Place of Truth, see 178 n. 17. This carpenter is in fact mentioned in P. BM 10053, recto 7, 8, as husband of one of the many persons found to be in possession, in year 17 of Ramesses IX, of copper stolen from the Valley of the Queens; see J. Černý, *A Community of Workmen at Thebes in the Ramesside Period*, BdE 50 (Cairo, 1973), 62–63.

45. P. Turin 1887, verso 1, 2–3. For analogous instances, see 161 n. 30.

46. The restoration is practically certain because of the address: "to the governor Montuher[khopshef]."

47. As often, the Egyptian here employs direct address, but with a second-person pronoun by attraction: "cause that you (= he) be well."

48. Measure of capacity, about half a quart.

49. The translation of P. Posener-Kriéger, "And look, if you find a good one (honey), let it be brought to me," implies that she considers *ptr* to be a particle and the conjunctive *mtw.k-dit* to be the apodosis of a conditional sentence whose protasis would be *inn iw.k (r) gm*. We observe, on the one hand, that *ptr* is surely the full verb, here an auxiliary infinitive as part of the conjunctive, as shown by the preceding *mtw.k,* and on the other hand, that the use of the conjunctive as the apodosis of a conditional sentence with a protasis introduced by *inn* is highly doubtful. See P. J. Frandsen, *An Outline of the Late Egyptian Verbal System* (Copenhagen, 1974), 148–52. The text is P. Louvre E 27151; see P. Posener-Kriéger, *JEA* 64 (1978): 84–87 and pl. 14, and S. Allam, *ZÄS* 114 (1987): 101.

50. Honey was a highly appreciated foodstuff; see P. BM 10052, 2a, 9–13 (168 n. 185), which relates how robbers hastened to exchange their loot for honey.

51. There were periodic inventories of the furniture and goods stored in the temples. Thus, in year 15 of Ramesses III, Paenpata, overseer of caretakers and scribe of the white house of Pharaoh, l.p.h., "made the inventory of the domains of the temples from Memphis to Elephantine"; see KRI, vol. 5, p. 232, 1–14, and P. Grandet, *RdE* 41 (1990): 95–99.

52. On this person, see W. Helck, *Zur Verwaltung des Mittleren und Neuen Reiches*, Probl. der Ägypt. 3 (Leiden, 1958), 519, and S. Sauneron, *RdE* 7 (1950): 53–57;

on the meaning of his name, see P. Vernus, *Annuaire EPHE IVᵉ* section 1978 (1979): 68.

53. P. Turin 1887, recto 2, 1–2.

54. Rough translation of the term *d₃iw*; we do not know exactly what garment it designated. See J. J. Janssen, *Commodity Prices*, 265–71, who suggests that rather than a loincloth, it could be a sort of skirt worn by both men and women.

55. For the term, see P. Vernus, *BIFAO* 75 (1975): 50 (a); see also F. de Cénival, *Papyrus démotiques de Lille III*, MIFAO 90 (Cairo, 1984), 58, whose discussion is unfortunately burdened by confusion due to use of P. Berlin 10096, and all the more unfortunate in that it is based solely on the translation by A. Scharff and not on the Egyptian text.

56. See R. A. Caminos, *Late-Egyptian Miscellanies*, Brown Egyptological Studies 1 (London, 1954), 403.

57. On this passage, see A. H. Gardiner, *JEA* 27 (1941): 62; the text is P. Turin 1887, verso 1, 4.

58. P. Vernus, *RdE* 37 (1986): 146.

59. For this title, see p. 48. It seems that Khnumnakht had another title, which is difficult to identify; J. Černý suggested *f₃i nwb*, "transporter of gold"; see A. H. Gardiner, *Ramesside Administrative Documents*, p. 79 a, 6a–b.

60. Ramesses IV.

61. M. Mégally, *Notions de comptabilité à propos du papyrus E 3226 du Louvre*, BdE 72 (Cairo, 1977), 69–78.

62. The reference is to the sacred staff of the god Khnum; see S. Sauneron, *BIFAO* 58 (1958): 37. This god, like many others, had a sacred staff in which he was supposed to be able to hypostatize himself. Not only did this staff receive a cult; it also disposed of an institution that included personnel and equipment.

63. In the Ramesside Period, the designation "Pharaoh, l.p.h.," unaccompanied by a personal name, applied to the reigning pharaoh, in this case Ramesses V.

64. For the use of *rwḏw* in connection with the administration of temple domains, see J.-M. Kruchten, in E. Lipinski, ed., *State and Temple Economy*, 519–20.

65. The expression *iw.w (ḥr) ir(t) h₃w m n₃y.w h₃w n ḥʿw.w* deserves to be noted. A. H. Gardiner translated "for their own purposes"; see the commentary by M. Römer, *GM* 108 (1989): 11, who does not propose a translation. In P. BM 10052, recto 2, 17, *p₃ h₃w p₃ ḥḏ* in some way designates the area of diffusion of the booty (see p. 171 n. 250); hence the translation "circles of acquaintances" proposed here.

66. P. Turin 1887, verso 1, 13–2, 11. On this passage, see A. H. Gardiner, *JEA* 27 (1941): 60–61.

67. For *šd b₃kwt*, see J. J. Janssen, *SAK* 3 (1974): 174. According to E. Bleiberg, *JARCE* 25 (1988): 168, "*b₃kw(t)* is an economic transaction between foreign lands or groups of foreigners or Egyptians and the temple."

68. P. Turin 1887, verso 2, 12. On the passage, see A. H. Gardiner, *JEA* 27 (1941): 62.

69. According to J.-M. Kruchten, in E. Lipinski, *State and Temple Economy*, 519–20, *rwḏw* here would designate the "autorités mêmes du temple à Éléphantine."

70. P. Turin 1887, verso 2, 15–16. On *bn sw* in this passage, see P. Vernus, *RdE* 36 (1985): 158 (18).

71. The expression is *ʿk ḥr*, and not the extremely frequent *ʿk ḥr*. The use of the preposition *ḥr*, lit. "under," is no doubt due to the fact that inside temples, the priests found themselves at the foot of effigies or emblems of the god, which rested on a pedestal or a base. Cf. *Urk.*, vol. 3, p. 112, 9: "to cause that all the prophets and all the pure priests who approach the god be struck with respect because of the greatness of his power."

72. P. Turin 1887, recto 1, 9–11.

73. See D. Meeks, *Dictionnaire de la Bible, Supplément IX* (Paris, 1979), cols.

440–41, where our document should be added because of its especially explicit character.

74. The principal contributions to the study of oracles in pharaonic Egypt are: J. Černý, in R. A. Parker, *A Saite Oracle Papyrus from Thebes in the Brooklyn Museum: Papyrus Brooklyn 47.218.3* (Providence, 1962), 35–39; J. Leclant, in A. Caquot and M. Leibovici, eds., *La Divination*, Rites et pratiques religiouses, vol. 1 (Paris, 1968), 1–31; L. Kákosy, *LdÄ*, vol. 6, cols. 600–6; J.-M. Kruchten, *Le grand texte oraculaire de Djéhutymose intendant du domaine d'Amon de Pinedjem II*, Monographies Reine Élisabeth 5 (Brussels, 1986), 337–54; and A. G. McDowell, *Jurisdiction in the Workmen's Community of Deir el-Medîna*, Egyptologische Uitgaven 5 (Leiden, 1990), 107–47.

75. O. IFAO 562 = J. Černý, *BIFAO* 35 (1935): 47.

76. O. IFAO 854 = J. Černý, *BIFAO* 72 (1972): 52.

77. The most recent discussion focusing on this problem is that of A. G. McDowell, *Jurisdiction in the Workmen's Community*, 114–32.

78. A private person could exercise, temporarily, a duty that would qualify as clerical, if only bearing the barque of a deity during a festival procession. In such cases, the only requirement was a state of ritual purity, and the person thus invested with this honor received the designation w^cb, "pure priest."

79. For the guild organization of these bearers, see p. 195 n. 66.

80. The evidence relating to Bekenkhons and Nebwenenef has been drawn together by S. Sauneron, *RdE* 7 (1950): 57–62. For Nebwenenef, see also L. Habachi, *JEA* 51 (1965): 135.

81. For *bsy*, see J. Černý and S. I. Groll, *A Late Egyptian Grammar*, Studia Pohl, Series Maior 4 (Rome, 1978), 556, and H. Satzinger, *Neuägyptischen Studien: Die Partikel ir, das Tempussystem* (Vienna, 1976), 115. T. E. Peet, *JEA* 10 (1924): 121 n. 6, S. Sauneron, *RdE* 7 (1950): 57, and L. Habachi, *JEA* 51 (1965): 135, have interpreted *bsy* as a form of the verb *bsi*, "to introduce," wrongly in my opinion, for no satisfying interpretation results.

82. For this term, see p. 171 n. 259.

83. P. Turin 1887, recto 1, 12–14. For this passage, see S. Donadoni, *La Religione dell'antico Egitto* (Bari, 1959), 466–67.

84. An analogous situation explains the complaint against Paneb written by Amennakht; see p. 71.

85. In this hypothesis, $h^{3c}\ r$-bl would be the colloquial equivalent of *rwi*. The relationships between administrative power and oracular jurisdiction in nomination to office need to be clarified for the New Kingdom, when the ideological base was not yet that of the Third Intermediate Period. Let us recall that the first prophet of Amun Nebwenenef was chosen by oracle from a list of names enumerated by the pharaoh; see K*RI*, vol. 3, 282–85.

86. This passage does not seem to me to have been well understood by its translators. For the error regarding *bsy*, see n. 81. Otherwise, *p³y w^cb in p³y w^cb (ḥr) ḍd n w^cb nbwnnf* probably refers to Penanukis, as elsewhere in the document, and not to Bekenkhons, who, we just learned, had been promoted to prophet.

87. For the manipulation of oracles, see W. Kaiser, *ZRG* 10 (1958): 204, and A. G. McDowell, *Jurisdiction in the Workmen's Community*, 111.

88. In the preceding memoranda, Penanukis is simply designated by the anaphoric third-person pronoun, so that in this passage, the pronoun has a good chance of referring to him rather than to Bekenkhons.

89. Despite A. H. Gardiner's note in *Ramesside Administrative Documents*, p. 75 a, 3 a–b, it is quite likely that we are dealing with a writing of *hnn*.

90. P. Turin 1887, recto 1, 8.

91. On this theme, see P. Vernus, *Hathor* 1 (1989): 38.

92. Formula used to deny retrospectively that an individual had occupied an of-

fice of which he had proved to be unworthy by committing a serious wrong; see P. Vernus, *RdE* 26 (1974): 121–23. It is frequently used in reference to persons who participated in the plot against Ramesses III; see p. 117.

93. For *wȝḥ* in oracular procedure, see Bedell, "Criminal Law in the Egyptian Ramesside Period," 322 n. 3. See, for example, P. Turin 1975, 3 = *LRL*, p. 52, where it is specifically a question of the oracle of Khnum.

94. P. Turin 1887, recto 1, 4.

95. For *irw nfr*, see E. F. Wente, *LRL*, 19–20.

96. An interlocutor whose identity is no longer accessible.

97. P. Turin 1887, recto 2, 17.

98. L. Habachi, *JEA* 51 (1965): 136, pertinently observes: "A man with relations of this order could hardly fail to prove himself innocent, even if he was actually guilty."

Chapter 5. The Harem Conspiracy under Ramesses III

1. P. Vernus and J. Yoyotte, *Les Pharaons: Les Noms, les thèmes, les lieux* (Paris, 1988), 44–46, s.v. "conspiration"; M. Weber, *LdÄ*, vol. 2, cols. 987–91, s.v. "Harimver-schwörung."

2. Certain documents are accessible to us only in mediocre copies made by an adventurer named J.-J. Rifaud. For Rifaud texts A–C, see S. Sauneron and J. Yoyotte, *BIFAO* 50 (1952): 107–17, and Y. König, *CRIPEL* 12 (1990): 67–69 (Rifaud text A). For Rifaud text E, see Y. König, *CRIPEL* 11 (1989): 55–58; see p. 118.

3. T. Devéria, *Le Papyrus judiciare de Turin et les papyrus Lee et Rollin*, B. E. 5 (Paris, 1868), 97–99. There is a hieroglyphic transcription in *KRI*, vol. 5, pp. 350–60. For translations, see A. de Buck, *JEA* 23 (1937): 156, and J. A. Wilson, in J. B. Pritchard, ed., *Ancient Near Eastern Texts Relating to the Old Testament* (Princeton, 1955), 214–16. I see no solid reasons for including Papyrus Varzy in this dossier, *pace* Weber, *LdÄ*, vol. 2, col. 990, n. 24.

4. According to whether we read *iw.i (ḥr) dit m-ḥr* or *iw.i (r) dit m-ḥr . . .*, the interpretation of the document changes. In the second case, it would be a Future III, "it will be necessary for me to entrust . . . ," and Ramesses III would be getting the judicial process going; while this interpretation can be envisaged if we limit ourselves to this single statement, it is difficult to maintain it the further we advance into the passage. In the first case, that which we have chosen, the verb is a sequential form, and the text is an account, placed in the mouth of Ramesses III, of his conduct in reaction to the conspiracy.

5. This document is not listed by I. Pomorska, *Les Flabellifères à la droite du roi en Égypte ancienne* (Warsaw, 1987); nevertheless, it seems that in this passage, it is necessary to read *ṭȝy ḥw*, and not the *ṭȝy sryt* written differently a little later in the same passage (2, 4). For the judicial role of the fan bearers, see p. 176 n. 99.

6. A Semitic name meaning "Baal is a warrior"; see T. Schneider, *Asiatische Personennamen in ägyptischen Quellen des Neuen Reiches,* OBO 114 (Freiburg and Göttingen, 1992), 86.

7. For the idea that a misdeed returns against its doer, see p. 164 n. 99. This is a fossil of an old concept of the immanent punishment of wrongdoing, for which see p. 126 and p. 193 n. 20.

8. For the meaning of *ḥr iw* in this passage, see F. Neveu, *La Particule ḥr en néo-égyptien: Étude synchronique,* Diplôme de l'EPHE, IVᵉ sec. (Paris, 1985), 12.

9. To be compared with the instructions given by Haremhab to his judges in his decree, pp. 136–37; see also, further in the document, the indication that judges forgetful of their duties were punished "because of the fact that they had neglected the goodly instructions that I had formulated for them" (6, 1).

10. Judicial Papyrus of Turin, 2, 2–3, 5.

11. As noted by D. Lorton, *JESHO* 20 (1977): 28–30.

12. That is, humanity, whose "herdsman" is the creator god. The text is P. Westcar 8, 15–8, 17.

13. For the grammatical structure of this passage, see S. I. Groll, in G. Rendsburg et al., eds., *The Bible World: Essays Dedicated to Cyrus Gordon* (New York, 1980), 69–70.

14. In context, a manifestly pejorative connotation of one meaning of *ḥwi sw*, for which see E. Otto, *Das Verhältnis von Rite und Mythus im Ägyptischen*, SHAW 1958/1 (Heidelberg, 1958), 19 n. 38.

15. The fault was thus not having exposed the criminal intentions; see p. 177 nn. 104 and 107. For the interesting negative form *iw.f (ḥr) tm pr ḥr.w*, see S. I. Groll, in G. Rendsburg et al., eds., *The Bible World*, 69–70.

16. On this foreign name, the meaning of which remains uncertain, see T. Schneider, *Asiatische Personennamen*, 212–13.

17. Literally, "he hid them." The sequential *iw.f (ḥr) ḥꜣp.w* continues a sequence implicitly opened by the relative form *i.sḏm.f*. That it is indeed a sequential form, and not the present circumstantial, is proved by the parallel form *iw.f (ḥr) tm pr ḥr.w* in 4, 6 and by *iw.f (ḥr) tm ḏd sm i.w* in 4, 12. See S. I. Groll, in G. Rendsburg et al., eds., *The Bible World*, 73–75.

18. For this name, see T. Schneider, *Asiatische Personennamen*, 80–81.

19. That is, Pabekkamen.

20. This name means "the Lycian."

21. Libu designates one of the Libyan ethnic groups with which the Egyptians had dealings beginning with the New Kingdom.

22. A Semitic name; see T. Schneider, *Asiatische Personennamen*, 152–53.

23. Also called "overseer of cattle" in the papyrus.

24. For the title, see J. Quaegebeur, in S. I. Groll, ed., *Pharaonic Egypt, the Bible, and Christianity* (Jerusalem, 1985), 162–72.

25. On this person, see L. Habachi and P. Ghalioungui, *CdE* 46 (1971): 59–71, and F. von Kaenel, *Les Prêtres-ouab de Sekhmet et les conjurateurs de Serket*, Bibliothèque de l'EPHE 87 (Paris, 1984), 60–66.

26. Probably the name under which he would rule; see A. de Buck, *JEA* 23 (1937): 156 n. 1: "It is, however, more probable that Pentawere was his real name and that 'that other name' refers to the royal titulary which was given him by the conspirators when they proclaimed him king." See also G. Posener, *RdE* 4 (1946): 52.

27. Grammatically, this is a sequential continuing a relative form; see n. 15.

28. Judicial Papyrus of Turin, 4, 1–5, 10.

29. See D. Lorton, *JESHO* 20 (1977): 28.

30. For this queen, see R. Drenkhahn, *LdÄ* 5, col. 118, n. 25.

31. See n. 26.

32. For the harem in pharaonic Egypt, see E. Reiser, *Die königliche Harim im alten Ägypten* (Vienna, 1972). For the harem at Medinet Habu, see U. Hölscher, *Medinet Habu Studies*, OIC 7 (Chicago, 1930), 26–28; cf. B. J. Kemp, *ZÄS* 105 (1978): 122–33.

33. It is well established that pure priests of Sakhmet were capable of practicing black magic; see P. Vernus, *RdE* 33 (1981): 97 (y).

34. On the "House of Life," see the excellent summary, with bibliography, by M. Weber, *LdÄ*, vol. 3, cols. 954–57, s.v. "Lebenshaus"; see also, inter alios, G. Burkard, *Bibliothek* 4 (1980): 90.

35. For hieroglyphic transcriptions, see K*RI*, vol. 5, 360–63. There is a highly questionable translation by H. Goedicke, *JEA* 49 (1963): 71–92; Goedicke must have had a great love of paradox and a taste for doomed causes to strive as he did to deny that these documents allude to the use of magic. See G. Posener, *Annuaire du Collège de France* 76 (1976): 435–37.

36. An artifice of translation intended to mark the use of the conjunctive *mtw.w-dit* in a narrative sequence; see p. 180 n. 44.

37. Restoring *ḥr sw (ḥr) dit ꜥk.w*, rather than what I proposed in *RdE* 26 (1974): 121. The apodosis corresponding to this protasis is *ir n³ bin.w*, and not *iw.tw (ḥr) smtr.f*.

38. P. Rollin.

39. On this passage, see K. Baer, *JEA* 50 (1964): 179–80, and S. N. Morschauser, *JARCE* 25 (1988): 101–2. The interpretation is not assured, but it seems that it is a direct quotation of the commitment by which one of the accused bound himself and then violated.

40. See F. Neveu, *RdE* 41 (1990): 150.

41. For *iw.f ḥr ḫpr*, see S. I. Groll, in G. Rendsburg et al., eds., *The Bible World*, 75–76.

42. For *pḥ nṯr*, see J.-M. Kruchten, *BSFE* 103 (1985): 12, and idem, *Le grand texte oraculaire de Djéhoutymose intendant du domaine d'Amon de Pinedjem II,* Monographies Reine Élisabeth 5 (Brussels, 1986), 329–30. According to him, the guilty party would have revealed "l'avenir à des 'gens' malintentionnés."

43. The term is unclear; see G. Fecht, *Orientalia* 24 (1955): 292 n. 2; J.-M. Kruchten, *Le grand texte oraculaire,* 330 n. 2, translates "follement." It is perhaps to be compared with *srḥ*, *Urk.* VI, p. 133, 5, but the reading is uncertain; see P. Vernus, *Athribis: Textes et documents relatifs à la géographie, aux cultes et à l'histoire d'une ville du delta égyptien à l'époque pharaonique,* BdE 78 (Cairo, 1978), 306, and J. F. Borghouts, *The Magical Texts of Papyrus Leiden I 348,* OMRO 51 (1971), 47 (29). The least implausible interpretation is perhaps to take it as derived from the causative of the verb *iḥ*, "to be plunged into darkness, to drowse," for which see P. Vernus, *RdE* 32 (1980): 131–32; we would understand something like *(ḥr)* (or *m) siḥ n n³ rmṯ* "making darkness for people," or "during a sleeping of people," or "by putting people to sleep," that is, "without people knowing."

44. In *t³ kt st*, *kt* is probably to be given the idiomatic meaning "and also," for which see P. Venus, *Cahiers de Karnak* 6 (1980): 228 (an). The "deep great place" is to be compared with "the deep great places" probably designating the royal tombs; see p. 177 n. 106. The hypothesis of H. Goedicke, *JEA* 49 (1963): 85, according to which the expression refers to the "High-Gate" of Medinet Habu, has been subjected to doubt by K. Baer, *JEA* 50 (1964): 180.

45. The reading and thus the etymology of this foreign name remain uncertain; see T. Schneider, *Asiatische Personennamen,* 51–52.

46. For the opposition *int/iṯ³* with regard to communications, see P. CGC 58059.

47. The restoration suggested in KRI, vol. 5, p. 363, 7–8, is not entirely satisfying. What I propose is scarcely more so, for although we can easily postulate the omission of a preposition such as *m,* we would expect *p³ nty*, not *nty*.

48. See E. D. Bedell, "Criminal Law in the Egyptian Ramesside Period," 152. The text is P. Lee.

49. E. Chassinat, *Le Temple d'Edfou,* vol. 6 (Cairo, 1931), 131–33; E. Drioton, *ASAE* 39 (1939): 35; S. Quirke, *The Administration of Egypt in the Late Middle Kingdom: The Hieratic Documents* (New Malden, 1990), 31; G. Posener, *Annuaire du Collège de France* 76 (1976): 436. See also n. 58.

50. J. E. Harris and K. R. Weeks, *X-Raying the Pharaohs* (London, 1973), 163–65.

51. G. Posener, *RdE* 5 (1946): 51–56.

52. On the relationship between the creator god and his creation, see pp. 123–25.

53. On this formula, see P. Vernus, *RdE* 26 (1974): 119–21; and p. 187 n. 92. For a new example, see P. Rifaud E, published by Y. Koenig, *CRIPEL* 11 (1989): 55.

54. P. Rollin 3.

55. P. Rifaud E; see Y. Koenig, *CRIPEL* 11 (1989): 55–58.

56. The reading of the name is uncertain, perhaps *Idy*, "the deaf one," a pejorative name attributed as a punishment.

57. For the formula denying a troublesome reality, see p. 117.

58. It seems probable to me that Rifaud omitted *pnꜥ* here, taking into account P. Ri-

faud A 5, *iw.f (ḥr) ḫpr ḥr pn⁽ n³ mkw*, as judiciously noted by Y. Koenig, *CRIPEL* 11 (1989): 56. The expression can be interpreted in two ways: (1) as an allusion to a precise fact, for example, the erection of the magical apparatus protecting the pharaoh, in which case *mkw.f* means "the protection from which he (i.e., Pharaoh) benefits"; or (2) as a euphemism designating the pharaoh's betrayal by his protégé, in which case the verb *pn⁽*, literally "to overturn," would mean "to return a good deed with a bad one," with *mkw.f* meaning "the protection that he (i.e., Pharaoh) accords." It seems to me that the context favors the second possibility.

59. For the theme of the pharaoh who "builds" his protégé by lifting him from his original poverty and promoting him, see p. 142.

60. For the verb *b⁽*, "to neglect, disregard," see p. 195 n. 78.

61. For this punishment, see, p. 184 n. 26.

62. I am not convinced by the argument presented by S. I. Groll, in G. Rendsburg et al., eds., *The Bible World*: "Classifying *iw n³ ḥmw.t šm* as a circumstantial first present (i.e., *šm* is the stative form) and not as an *iw n³-ḥmw.t (ḥr) šm* of the past is due to the fact that *iw n³-ḥmw.t* . . . lacks a resumptive element referring back to the antecedent, *rmṯ*."

63. For this foreign name, see T. Schneider, *Asiatische Personennamen,* 141.

64. Judicial Papyrus of Turin 6, 1–5.

65. See p. 184 n. 26.

66. They are mentioned in the Judicial Papyrus of Turin 2, 2 and 2, 3.

67. R. O. Faulkner, *CAH*, vol. 2, chap. 23, p. 33 of the fascicle: "It is an eloquent commentary on the standards of conduct then current that five of the bench of twelve judges were arrested for carousing with the accused women and one of the male offenders." J. A. Wilson, in J. B. Pritchard, ed., *Ancient Near Eastern Texts,* 215 n. 20: "Two of the following four had been judges in the court of examination, two were of the military or police, perhaps attached to that court. The instructions which they had 'abandoned' were those of the pharaoh in constituting the court."

68. Judicial Papyrus of Turin, 6, 6–7.

Chapter 6. The Crisis of Values in the New Kingdom

1. We have described five particularly spectacular scandals that are well documented. But we know of a number of analogous scandals from the same period, though the texts are more allusive, more obscure, or less well-preserved than those studied here. Still others are related in documents that have yet to be published, such as P. Turin 1966 (D. Valbelle, *"Les Ouvriers de la Tombe": Deir el-Médineh à l'Époque ramesside,* BdE 96 [Cairo, 1985], p. 198) or a papyrus in Milan (kindly pointed out to me by F. Tiradritti). Moreover, similar scandals occurred in other periods. Thus, for the Old Kingdom, we have a letter denouncing the exactions of a governor of Elephantine during the reign of Pepy II; see P. Smither, *JEA* 28 (1942): 16–19, and A. Roccati, *La Littérature historique sous l'Ancien Empire égyptien,* LAPO 12 (Paris, 1982), 288–89.

2. J. Leclant, in M. Duverger, ed., *Le Concept d'empire* (Paris, 1980), 57–61; B. Kemp, in P. D. A. Garnsey and C. R. Wittaker, eds., *Imperialism in the Ancient World: The Cambridge University Research Seminar in Ancient History* (Cambridge, 1978), 7–57 and 84–297. A theoretical essay on Egyptian imperialism in Nubia has been attempted by S. T. Smith, *GM* 122 (1991): 77 ff.

3. A. Q. Mohammad, *ASAE* 56 (1959): 105–37; W. Helck, *Die Beziehungen Ägyptens zu Vorderasien im 3. und 2. Jahrtausend v. Chr.,* Äg. Abh. 3 (Wiesbaden, 1971), 107–494; J. Weinstein, *BASOR* 241 (1981): 1–28; N. Na'aman, *IEJ* 31 (1981): 172–85.

4. E. Bleiberg, *JARCE* 21 (1984): 155–64, and *JARCE* 25 (1988): 157–214.

5. J. Černý, *Cahiers d'Histoire mondiale* 1 (1954): 920–21, ascribes the growing

shortage of silver during the reign of Ramesses III to the incursion of the Sea Peoples into the Near East.

6. On the temple of Amun of Ramesses III in Canaan and its domains, see C. Uehlinger, *ZPV* 104 (1988): 6–25. Egypt's prosperity during the reign of Ramesses III can be measured above all by the enormous donations inventoried in Papyrus Harris; see R. O. Faulkner, *CAH,* vol 2, chap. 23, p. 30 of the fascicle.

7. This concept can of course be applied only *mutatis mutandis* to pharaonic Egypt. It is nevertheless pertinent, if we evaluate it in terms of funerary equipment in the case of individuals and monumental constructions (temples, royal tombs) in the case of the state.

8. No one has ever dreamed of underestimating the Asiatic, and more specifically, Semitic, influence on Egyptian culture in the New Kingdom; see, inter alios, W. Helck, *Beziehungen.*

9. Fundamental works are J. Assmann, *Maât: L'Égypte pharaonique et l'idée de justice sociale* (Paris, 1989); idem, *Ma'at: Gerechtigkeit und Unsterblichkeit im alten Ägypten* (Munich, 1990); and the excellent essay by E. Hornung, "Maat Gerechtigkeit für Alle? Zur altägyptische Ethik," *Eranos* 56 (1987): 385–427.

10. Myth of the Heavenly Cow; see E. Hornung, *Die ägyptische Mythos von der Himmelskuh: Eine Ätiologie des Unvollkommenen,* OBO 46 (Freiburg and Göttingen, 1982).

11. These lineages of demigods and the lengths of their reigns are inserted between the era of the gods and that of the pharaohs in the Royal Canon of Turin, a chronological summary of their history as the Egyptians conceived it. See U. Luft, *Beiträge zur Historisierung der Götterwelt und der Mythenschreibung,* Studia Aegyptiaca 4 (Budapest, 1978), 215–18; D. B. Redford, *Pharaonic King-lists, Annals and Daybooks: A Contribution to the Study of the Egyptian Sense of History,* SSEA Publications 4 (Mississauga, 1986), 1–18.

12. Egyptian thought on this point is particularly subtle: being is characterized by order, but also by a correlative principle of disorder represented by the god Seth, who is "die Kehrseite der Notwendigen, positiven Auseinander-Setzung, durch die Schöpfung . . . erst möglich wird"; see E. Hornung, *Symbolon* n.F. 2 (1974): 54.

13. Differentiation was in fact the original principle of creation; see P. Derchain, *LdÄ,* vol. 2, col. 753.

14. $wd^c.i$ m^3r m-^{c} wsr, "I separated the weak from the strong," *CT,* vol. 7, 466e (monologue of the creator god). In chapter 126 of the Book of the Dead, the same role is assigned to the baboons in the sun barque in similar terms: wp m^3r hn^c wsr, "who separate the weak and the strong"; see J. Assmann, *Maât,* 119; idem, in W. K. Simpson, ed., *Religion and Philosophy in Ancient Egypt,* YES 3 (New Haven, 1989), 61.

15. J. Assmann, *Der König als Sonnenpriester: Ein kosmographischer Begleittext zur kultischen Sonnenhymnik in thebanischen Tempeln und Gräber,* ADAIK 7 (Glückstadt, 1970), 35; idem, in W. K. Simpson, ed., *Religion and Philosophy,* 59–66. A new version of the text has been published by C. Betro, *I Testi solari del portale di Pascerientaisu (BN 2),* Saqqara 3 (Pisa, 1990).

16. The god engenders the one who will become pharaoh by uniting with a woman whom he has chosen to be the mother. In other words, the pharaoh is predestined to his office by the very manner in which he was conceived.

17. Instruction for Merikare, P 135–6.

18. iw $nhm.n.i$ m^3r m-^{c} wsr, "I rescued the weak from the strong"; J. Janssen, *De traditioneele egyptische autobiografie vóór het Nieuwe Rijk,* vol. 2 (Leiden, 1946), 72–73, Bh; A. Roccati, *OA* 12 (1973): 32; K. Jansen-Winkeln, *Ägyptische Biographien der 22. und 23. Dynastie,* ÄAT 8 (Wiesbaden, 1985), 373 (3.9.17); E. Otto, *Die biographischen Inschriften der ägyptischen Spätzeit* (Probleme der Ägyptologie 2), 95. There is a good example in the autobiography of Aba.

19. See the admirable analyses of H. Brunner, in *Les Sagesses du Proche-Orient*

ancien: *Colloque de Strasbourg, 17–19 mai 1962* (Paris, 1963), 103–20, and E. Otto, *Wesen und Wandel der ägyptischen Kultur* (Berlin, 1969), 60–62.

20. For similar formulations, fossils of the older concept in periods when it no longer prevailed, see p. 164 n. 99, p. 188 n. 7, and this chapter, nn. 25 and 54.

21. Book of the Dead, chapter 17, version from the sarcophagus of Queen Mentuhotpe. It is typical that the versions of the New Kingdom replace the reading "(evil or *maat*) is attributed" with the reading "he (i.e., the god) attributes (evil or *maat*)," illustrating the transition from the older to the later concept. For the variation, see K. Sethe, *Dramatische Texte zu altägyptische Mysterienspielen,* UGAÄ 10 (Leipzig, 1928), 65 n. 1. A similar variation has been judiciously noted by E. Otto, *Wesen und Wandel,* 62, involving an "appeal to the living" from the First Intermediate Period and its reinterpretation under Dynasty 26.

22. Ptahhotep, P 88–93; this passage has often been commented on; for a detailed study, see the following note.

23. G. Fecht, *Der Habgierige und die Maat in der Lehre des Ptahhotep (5. und 19. Maxime),* ADAIK 1 (Glückstadt, 1958), 11–25.

24. It is symptomatic that a religious spirit such as S. Morenz felt that "their pragmatic character . . . sometimes embarrasses modern readers"; *Egyptian Religion* (Ithaca, 1973), 123.

25. Stela of Baki, Turin 156, ll. 3 and 14, attributable to the reign of Amenophis III (the older concept, of course, still inspired many texts in Dynasty 18). That the person who had this stela erected could be presented as a mystic is one of the curiosities of Egyptology; see the translation proposed by A. Varille, *BIFAO* 54 (1954): 129–35.

26. See P. Vernus, *RdE* 39 (1988): 147–54.

27. Memphite Theology, l. 57; see H. Beinlich, *GM* 122 (1991): 18–20, for an attempt to elucidate this passage. In fact, the passage can be understood only if we take *ir mrrt r msd(dt)* as entailing the expression *ir . . . r,* "to distinguish something from." Cf. J. F. Borghouts, *The Magical Texts of Papyrus Leiden I 348,* OMRO 51 (Leiden, 1971), plate section, recto 8, 1 and pp. 103–4; and *iw grt n.tn ir ꜥd r mꜣꜥty,* "it is (up) to you to distinguish the guilty from the just," Decree of Haremhab, lateral surface, l. 7.

28. Lit., "he who is with peace."

29. Lit., "he who is with crime."

30. Theodicy, in the form of a monologue, of the All-Lord, that is, the creator god, *CT,* vol. 7, p. 464a–b. For the problem of evil, see S. Morenz, *Egyptian Religion,* 57–60; E. Hornung, *Les Études philosophiques* 2–3 (1987): 125; J. Assmann, *The Search for God in Ancient Egypt* (Ithaca, 2001), 175–76; J. Baines, in B. E. Shafer, ed., *Religion in Ancient Egypt: Gods, Myths, and Personal Practice* (Ithaca, 1991), 163–64.

31. Nevertheless, the rich man is no longer easygoing when he is seized by a desire for power, as we learn from a passage in the Instruction of Ptahhotep.

32. Tale of the Eloquent Peasant, B 1, 122–6. The text dates to Dynasty 12, but there is an allusion to it in a literary composition copied in Dynasty 20; see R. B. Parkinson, *The Tale of the Eloquent Peasant* (Oxford, 1991), xxix–xxx. A similar theme, according to which it is need that explains the transgression of justice, is developed in the Instruction for Merikare, P 43–44: "The rich man cannot be partial in his house; (for) he is a possessor of goods who has no need. (But) the poor man cannot speak according to a justice that is his."

33. That is to say, there was never an end to greasing their palms, just as a leaky bucket is never filled.

34. Lit., "so that they find themselves light in their spirits"; Tale of the Eloquent Peasant, B 1, 132–4.

35. In the Egyptian, "the possessor of character."

36. Ptahhotpe, P 167–8.

37. On the juridical background of the Tale of the Eloquent Peasant, see N. Shupak, *JNES* 51 (1992): 1–18.

38. Eloquent Peasant, B 1, 105–6, 113–14, 221–3.

39. Thoth, who could be represented as either an ibis or a baboon, was god of all that is ruled by norms, regularity, and equilibrium: moon, calendar, writing system. For an Egyptian, laxity would contradict Thoth's very essence and function.

40. Eloquent Peasant, B 1, 179–81. In the same work, there is already skepticism with regard not to high officials, but to judges at a lower level; see p. 128.

41. Instruction of Ptahhotpe, P 116.

42. Ptahhotpe, P 545–6; see S. Morenz, *Egyptian Religion,* 66; W. Barta, *SAK* 1 (1974): 24–25; H. Brunner, *Saeculum* 12 (1961): 196–97.

43. See, in general, J. Assmann, in W. K. Simpson, ed., *Religion and Philosophy,* 69–71.

44. Sinuhe, B 37–43 and 261–62; on this mention of divine intervention, see J. Baines, *JEA* 68 (1982): 39–42.

45. J. Vandier, *Mo'alla: La Tombe d'Ankhtifi et la tombe de Sébekhotep,* BdE 18 (Cairo, 1950), 163; G. Fecht, in *Festschrift für Siegfried Schott zu seinem 70. Geburtstag am 20. August 1967* (Wiesbaden, 1968), 50–56. This could be an allusion to an oracle, as suggested by J. Baines, *JEA* 73 (1987): 91, who otherwise studies similar indications from before the New Kingdom. But it could also have to do with some manifestation of the god with respect to the individual. In any case, if it was an oracle, it was certainly spontaneous; the deity took the initiative to make his will known, without solicitation, as would be the case with oracles later, in the New Kingdom. For the notion of "going in search of" and "bringing" (*in*) with regard to the promotion of a king by the god or the promotion of a private individual by the king, see P. Vernus, *RdE* 40 (1989): 159 n. 26, and Y. Koenig, *CRIPEL* 11 (1989): 56.

46. Lit., "an excellent man."

47. Lit., "his original smallness."

48. Lit., "according to what has happened to him."

49. Ptahhotpe, P 176–81 (and cf. the L 2 version).

50. P. Vernus and J. Yoyotte, *Les Pharaons: Les Noms, les thèmes, les lieux* (Paris, 1988), 77, s.v. "loyalisme."

51. P. Chester Beatty IV, recto 4, 2–3.

52. P. Lansing, 8, 1–2.

53. See P. Vernus, *BSFE* 59 (1970): 31–47.

54. Of course, vestiges of the older concept crop up here and there, not only in the New Kingdom, as in the Judicial Papyrus of Turin, p. 118, but also later; see p. 164 n. 99 and also nn. 20 and 25.

55. A designation for large expanses of water; here, the term is probably applied to the Mediterranean Sea, into which the Nile inundation flows.

56. *Urk.* IV 118, 9–17 (Pahery).

57. See M. Megally, *Notions de comptabilité à propos du papyrus E.3226 du Musée du Louvre,* BdE 72 (Cairo, 1977).

58. *prw;* cf. T. G. H. James, *The Hekanakhte Papers and Other Early Middle Kingdom Documents,* The Metropolitan Museum Egyptian Expedition Publications 19 (New York, 1962), pp. 24 (39) and 29 (74).

59. This was precisely the role of the "brokers" mentioned on p. 48.

60. A. H. Gardiner, *JEA* 27 (1941): 49, 54, 58.

61. We would love to know what is hidden behind an apparent anomaly noted by Gardiner, ibid., p. 34, in which the same quantity of grain is registered in two granaries at the same time; "strange are the ways of Egyptian book-keeping," he notes.

62. On this personage, see J. Černý, *A Community of Workmen at Thebes in the Ramesside Period,* BdE 50 (Cairo, 1973), 357–83.

63. See chapter 2.

64. The *s* is enigmatic, but a restoration *[i]s[t]* is not out of the question. In fact, the particle often introduces a description supplying the background or the context in

which a deed of Pharaoh is accomplished, which well suits the context here. According to a literary tradition known as the "Königsnovelle," Pharaoh is busy with his pious duties when an event occurs, in this case a divine inspiration that leads to the deed commemorated in the document.

65. Kitchen's restoration [*hrw pn iw wd.n ḥm*] is scarcely plausible, for the expression *hrw pn* does not occur before *wd.n ḥm*.

66. For *f3yt*, see Gardiner, *JEA* 34 (1947): 22 n. 19; idem, *JEA* 38 (1952): 19 n. 5; H. Kees, *ZÄS* 85 (1960): 53; *KRI*, vol. 6, p. 735, 1 (P. Turin 1896).

67. Kitchen's restoration [*iw.tw r sdm r-dd*] is grammatically untenable and incompatible with the *wḫ3 nkt* that follows. We would prefer something like [*ir ḥm-nṯr nb nty iw.tw r gmt.f ḥr*], relying on the Nauri Decree = *KRI*, vol. 1, p. 55, 11.

68. PM, vol. 2, p. 136; *KRI*, vol. 4, pp. 263–66; W. Helck, *ZÄS* 81 (1956): 82–86; idem, *ZÄS* 83 (1958): 145–46.

69. For placement as a "cultivator" (*iḥwty*), see D. Lorton, *JESHO* 20 (1977): 25, with n. 117. A similar punishment was to place the guilty party as a "quarryman"; see p. 84.

70. J.-M. Kruchten, *Le Décret d'Horemheb: Traduction, commentaire épigraphique, philologique et institutionnel,* Université Libre de Bruxelles, Faculté de Philosophie et Lettres 82 (Brussels, 1981), 159, suggests "que le *nkt* en question était versé entre les mains du haut clergé pour obtenir la nomination en tant que prêtre ordinaire (*w'b*) ou ritualiste (*ḥry-ḥb*)."

71. Instruction of Amenemope, 1, 14–2, 3.

72. This interpretation, which accords with the uses of the Conjunctive, was suggested to me by F. Neveu. A similar idea occurs again in prescriptions addressed to officiants in the Ptolemaic Period: "Do not collect taxes by discriminating against the humble in favor of the powerful"; *Edfou*, vol. 3, p. 361, 1 = M. Alliot, *Le Culte d'Horus à Edfou,* BdE 20, vol. 1 (Cairo, 1949), 184–85. The text is the Instruction of Amenemope, 15, 20.

73. It has been estimated that 1 percent of the population was literate; see J. Baines and C. Eyre, *GM* 61 (1983): 65–74; J. Baines, *Man,* n.s., 18 (1983): 584–86. Since it rests on extrapolations, this figure is clearly approximate.

74. Inscription of Mes, N 7 ff.

75. A. Théodoridès, in J. Harris, ed., *The Legacy of Egypt,* 2d ed. (London, 1971), 310; D. O'Connor, in B. G. Trigger, B. J. Kemp, D. O'Connor, and A. B. Lloyd, *Ancient Egypt: A Social History* (Cambridge, 1983), 218. S. Allam, *JEA* 75 (1989): 103–12, denies that Khay's documents were falsified.

76. P. Berlin 9010; K. Sethe, *ZÄS* 61 (1926): 67–79; H. Goedicke, *ZÄS* 101 (1974): 90–95; M. Green, *GM* 39 (1980): 33–39; A. Théodoridès, *RIDA* 24 (1977): 44–64.

77. For instance, it has been noted that the term *qenbet* (*qnbt*), which we translate here as "tribunal" according to Egyptological usage, designated an assembly that was also supposed to be familiar with administrative problems, such as irrigation; see S. Allam, *JEA* 72 (1986): 194–95. This is undoubtedly so, but it remains no less true that the Egyptians themselves considered the *qenbet* to be the appropriate authority over matters at law.

78. There are at least two terms written *b'*. One has a meaning along the lines of "to be attentive to" (P. Harris 79, 10; the meaning "to neglect" is excluded) and might be related to the particle *b'*; see A. Erman, *ZÄS* 42 (1905); *CLEM,* p. 9; *Wb.* I, 446, 1–2; P. Berlin 10463, recto 5 and verso 2 = R. A. Caminos, *JEA* 49 (1963), p. VI. Another of these terms quite likely has the meaning "to neglect" in three other passages from the Instruction of Amenemope; see M. Lichtheim, *Ancient Egyptian Literature: A Book of Readings,* vol. 2: *The New Kingdom* (Berkeley, 1976), 163 n. 14. It also occurs in P. BM 10375, 27 = *LRL* 46, 14, notwithstanding the suggestion of E. Wente, ibid., p. 63; see also the proposal by Y. Koenig, *CRIPEL* 11 (1989): 57 and 12 (1990): 67. In our passage here, since the Conjunctive might or might not continue the preceding negation, both meanings are more or less suitable, but the second seems to be the pertinent one.

79. Instruction of Amenemope, 20, 21–22, 6.

80. *Urk.* IV, 1082, 14; see N. Shupak, *JNES* 51 (1992): 16.

81. For the use of *ḥr*, cf. *LES* 7, 6 (Tale of the Two Brothers), cited by F. Neveu, *La Particule ḥr en néo-égyptien: Étude synchronique* (Paris, 1985), 15–16, and see also p. 126 on coordination of grammatical structures of the same nature.

82. *Urk.* IV, 1079, 5–6.

83. On the range of Haremhab's "reforms," see A. M. Gnirs, *SAK* 16 (1989): 95–96.

84. There is a distinct analogy with the instructions given by Ramesses III to the judges he charged with inquiring into the plot that had been hatched against him; see the Judicial Papyrus of Turin, 2, 8–9 (p. 108) and 6, 9, where the alleged reason for the punishment of the judges who had shown themselves unworthy of their responsibility is that they had neglected the king's instructions.

85. *ḥrwwyt*, etymologically "journal."

86. *kywy*, "others," hence "those who are not part of a group," as opposed to a delimited group. Thus, *k3wy* designates an ordinary person, as opposed to those initiated into the secrets of the House of Life, as in Magical Papyrus Harris, VI, 10: *m wb3 ib im.f n k3wy sšt3 m3ꜥ n pr-ꜥnḥ*, "do not divulge any of it to an ordinary (i.e., profane) person; it is a true secret of the House of Life."

87. Decree of Haremhab, right side surface, l. 5; see Kruchten, *Le Décret d'Horemheb,* 148–61. On this passage, see also N. Shupak, *JNES* 51 (1992): 9 n. 33, and G. Husson and D. Valbelle, *L'état et les institutions en égypte des premiers pharaons aux empereurs romains* (Paris, 1992), 127.

88. It is not surprising that prophets, who had important administrative responsibilities, including the administration of the temple domains (see p. 185 n. 40), were members of tribunals (*qenbet*); see A. Théodoridès, *RIDA* 27 (1980): 17–19.

89. See n. 68.

90. Decree of Haremhab, right lateral surface, ll. 6–7.

91. The death penalty was a frequent punishment for serious crimes, such as tomb robbery (see p. 19). That much said, in this passage, certain scholars have felt that this allusion should not be taken literally; see D. Lorton, *JESHO* 20 (1977): 62.

92. For instance, in the autobiography on the stela University College 14440, col. x + 10–11, we read, "I did not receive fraudulent goods." This is possibly an allusion to corruption, but the matter is uncertain.

The allusion seems clearer in the autobiography of Montuweser in the Metropolitan Museum of Art; K. Sethe, *Lesestücke,* p. 79, 19: "(I am) one who was not partial in favor of the one who possessed something to pay (lit., 'possessor of compensation,' *nb ḏb3w*)."

A passage from the Instruction for Merikare denounces, in similar terms, a propensity to be partial toward someone who can satisfy a need: "The one who says, 'I want!' cannot be equitable, for he is partial to his partisan and he inclines toward the one who has something to pay"; p. 44; see J. F. Quack, *Studien zur Lehre für Merikare,* GOF, IV. Reihe (Göttingen, 1992), 30. Context, however, shows that this passage has especially to do with avoiding intrigues on the part of the dignitaries constituting the king's entourage. Otherwise, upon examination of the texts, it seems to me that many of the allusions to corruption that W. Barta, *JEOL* 24 (1975–1976): 57 n. 50, believes he has noted in the pessimistic literature are not actually such.

93. J. Yoyotte, in *Le Jugement des morts: Égypte ancienne, Assour, Babylone, Israel, Iran, Islam, Inde, Chine, Japon,* Sources Orientales 4 (Paris, 1961). For the text, see the in part obsolete edition by C. Maystre, *Les Déclarations d'innocence,* RAPH 8 (Cairo, 1937).

94. G. Posener, *RdE* 27 (1975): 195–210; J. Assmann, *The Search for God in Ancient Egypt* (Ithaca, 2001), 221–22.

95. Inscription of Simut, surnamed Kyky, Theban Tomb 409. For the hieroglyphic text, see *KRI,* vol. 3, pp. 331–45; for a translation and commentary, see P. Vernus, *RdE* 30 (1978): 115–46.

96. Here the lion goddess Sakhmet represents the redoubtable form assumed by Mut to punish the magistrate who has misused his power in a legal matter to harm the interests of one who has placed himself under divine protection.

97. Inscription of Simut, A, ll. 12–15 = Vernus, *RdE* 30 (1978): 123–28, with reference to a parallel in a graffito expressing personal piety.

98. Inscription of Simut, A, ll. 17–19 = Vernus, *RdE* 30 (1978): 130–32.

99. The fundamental study on this topic is that of G. Posener, *BABA* 12 (1971): 59–63.

100. Lit., "your ear."

101. The title probably designates a sort of clerk of the court.

102. P. Anastasi II, 8, 5–9, 1.

103. Ostracon Borchardt.

104. These epithets evoke Amun as god of the "first occasion," that is, as creator god, for as the Egyptians conceived it, the creator always remained master of his creation; see E. Otto, *Forschungen und Fortschritt* 35 (1961): 279.

105. This is an allusion *a contrario* to the fact that human judges are both so partial and so accusatory toward the poor man that they demand superfluous evidence that they well know he cannot produce. Other scholars have understood the passage to mean "it does not speak to the one who has brought evidence," but the sense seems less suitable.

106. The term used, *šʿr*, of Semitic origin, means both "promise" and "threat." In either case, allusion is being made to pressures put on judges.

107. P. Bologna 1094, 2, 3–2, 7, and P. Anastasi II, 6, 5.

108. O. IFAO inv. 2181.

109. O. CGC 25207.

110. Amun is quite often called "vizier"; one example, which is highly significant because it occurs in a scene depicting an oracle, has been studied by J. J. Clère, *Festschrift für Siegfried Schott*, 45–49. Elsewhere in expressions of personal piety, Amun is also called the "shepherd of every unfortunate man" and "the shepherd who saves the unfortunate one"; see G. Posener, *RdE* 27 (1975): 205 n. 24.

111. See P. Vernus and J. Yoyotte, *Les Pharaons*, 174–75; T. G. H. James, *Pharaoh's People: Scenes from Imperial Egypt*, chap. 2; G. P. F. van den Boorn, *The Duties of the Vizier: Civil Administration in the Early New Kingdom* (London, 1988).

112. We have seen that the vizier was constrained to respond to the demands of the workmen of (the institution of) the Tomb; see p. 61.

113. The following question, addressed to an oracle, is symptomatic: "Should I set the affair down in writing to address it to the vizier?" O. Gardiner = J. Černý, *BIFAO* 72 (1972): 51.

114. For example, A. G. McDowell, *Jurisdiction in the Workmen's Community of Deir el-Medîna*, Egyptologische Uitgaven 5 (Leiden, 1990), 131.

115. See the role of the vizier in the tomb robbery scandal, chap. 1.

116. In fact, from this same period, we have evidence of the questioning of Pharaoh. Aside from a case of blasphemy against Sethos II, which is known from an ostracon (O. CGC 25556; see A. G. McDowell, *Jurisdiction in the Workmen's Community*, 251–53), there are texts that treat kings inconsiderately; for example, *LRL* 36, 11–12. See also E. F. Wente, *JNES* 25 (1966): 261, and idem, in W. K. Simpson, ed., *The Literature of Ancient Egypt: An Anthology of Stories, Instructions, and Poetry* (New Haven, 1972), 152 n. 28. See also, in general, D. O'Connor, in B. G. Trigger, B. J. Kemp, D. O'Connor, and A. B. Lloyd, *Ancient Egypt: A Social History*, 229–32; A. Niwiński, in I. Gamer-Wallert and W. Helck, eds., *Festschrift für Emma Brunner-Traut* (Tübingen, 1992), 261; K. Jansen-Winkeln, *ZÄS* 119 (1992): 31 n. 79.

117. For the imperative in appeals for help for the poor, see E. Brunner-Traut, in G. K. Schafer and T. Strohm, eds., *Diakonie, Biblische Grundlagen und Orientierungen:*

Ein Arbeitsbuch zur theologischen Verständigung über den diakonischen Auftrag (Heidelberg, 1990), 23–43.

118. An excellent study of this term has been made by A. M. Gnirs, *SAK* 16 (1989): 104–10.

119. J.-M. Kruchten, in E. Lipinski, ed., *State and Temple Economy in the Ancient Near East: Proceedings of the International Conference Organised by the Katholieke Universiteit Leuven from the 10th to the 14th April 1978*, OLA 6 (Louvain, 1979), 523, even proposes the meaning "private person" in the expression *ꜣht nmḥ*.

120. Tomb of Panehesy at Tell el-Amarna; M. Sandman, *Texts from the Time of Akhenaten*, Bibl. Aeg. 8, p. 24. King Akhenaten's adherents were fond of posing as people who had been elevated from poverty; see J. Assmann, *SAK* 8 (1980): 9–19. While this pharaoh certainly favored the rise of "new men," where we are able to tell, the lowliness of the origin of certain of his officials turns out to be quite relative. Thus, Ay might have been a member of the family of Queen Tiye; see D. B. Redford, *Akhenaten, the Heretic King* (Princeton, 1984), 151. At a later date, this theme of the king whose good will has "built" someone who had been nothing was used in stigmatizing the ingratitude of a conspirator; see p. 118 on P. Rifaud and E. Koenig, *CRIPEL* 11 (1989): 55–58.

121. Inscription of Hormin, who was a subject of Sethos I; K*RI*, vol. 1, p. 309, 8–10.

122. K*RI*, vol. 4, p. 143, 10–11; see H. Kees, *ZÄS* 73 (1937): 83.

123. K*RI*, vol. 3, p. 336, 13. Another example comes from an inscription of the sculptor *ḥꜣtiꜣy*: "I was lowly of family, a little one of his town," K*RI*, vol. 7, p. 27, 8.

124. On the religious valuation of poverty in ancient Egypt, see H. Brunner, *Saeculum* 12 (1961): 319–44; idem, *Altägyptische Erziehung* (Wiesbaden, 1957), 42; R. Williams, *JSSEA* 8 (1978): 133; J. Assmann, *SAK* 8 (1980): 5, writing: "typische Selbstbezeichnungen des Menschen als Partner der Gottheit in der für die 'Persönliche Frömmigkeit' kennzeichnenden Gott-Mensch-Beziehung."

125. S. Morenz, *Egyptian Religion*, 130–33.

126. J. Assmann, in O. Keel, ed., *Studien zu altägyptischen Lebenslehren*, OBO 28 (Freiburg and Göttingen, 1979), 33–35; idem, *Re und Amun: Die Krise des polytheistischen Weltbilds im Ägypten der 18.–20. Dynastie*, OBO 51 (Freiburg and Göttingen, 1983); P. Vernus, *RdE* 30 (1978): 130–32.

127. Amenemope, 22, 5–7.

128. K*RI*, vol. 3, p. 336, 11–12.

129. *HO* I, 37 verso = J. Assmann, in O. Keel, ed. *Studien zu altägyptischen Lebenslehren*, p. 69 n. 22, with many similar examples.

130. O. Colin Campbell 4 = *HO*, pl. 39, no. 1, recto 1–3; translated by P. Vernus, *RdE* 30 (1978): 131.

131. E. Hornung, *Conceptions of God in Ancient Egypt: The One and the Many* (Ithaca, 1982), 201–2; W. K. Simpson, in J. Assmann, E. Feucht, and R. Grieshammer, eds., *Fragen an die altägyptische Literatur: Studien zum Gedenken an Eberhard Otto* (Wiesbaden, 1977), 493–98.

132. On the theme of the religious response to corruption, see H. Brunner, in W. Schuller, ed., *Korruption im Altertum: Konstanzer Symposium, Oktober 1979* (Munich, 1992), 71–72. Brunner holds that personal piety was neither the consequence of nor a reaction to corruption, but rather something that asserted itself parallel to it. See also pp. 146–47 on the appearance and spread of the practice of consulting oracles.

133. For an excellent summary, see J. Baines, in B. E. Shafer, ed., *Religion in Ancient Egypt*, 172–78.

134. P. Vernus, in *Colloques de la Société Ernest-Renan* (Paris, 1977), 149; idem, *Le Surnom au Moyen Empire: Répertoire, procédés d'expression et structures de la double identité du début de la XIIᵉ dynastie*, Studia Pohl 13 (Rome, 1986), 122.

135. There are excellent treatments by H. Brunner in *LdÄ*, vol. 4, cols. 951–63, and J. Baines, in B. Shafer, ed., *Religion in Ancient Egypt*, 179–94. See also A. I.

Sadek, *Popular Religion in Egypt During the New Kingdom*, HÄB 27 (Hildesheim, 1987).

136. A. R. Schulman, *JARCE* 6 (1967): 43–52; W. Gugliemi, *ZÄS* 118 (1991): 116–27; W. Gugliemi and J. Dittmar, in *Festschrift für Emma Brunner-Traut*, 119–42.

137. See 179 n. 25.

138. D. Valbelle, *"Les Ouvriers de la Tombe,"* 95.

139. J. H. Breasted, *Development of Religion and Thought in Ancient Egypt* (New York, 1912), 344–70; J. J. Clère, *RdE* 27 (1975): 70–77; A. Erman, SPAW 1911, pp. 1086–90; B. Gunn, *JEA* 3 (1916): 81–94; G. Nagel, *Revue de Théologie* 23 (1935): 3; R. Williams, *JSSEA* 8 (1977–1978): 131–37.

140. Cairo JE 37463; PM II, 166; A. Rowe, *ASAE* 40 (1940): 47–50 and pl. 9; *Urk.* IV, 2075–76.

141. See the penetrating study by J. F. Borghouts, in R. J. Demarée and J. J. Janssen, eds., *Gleanings from Deir el-Medîna*, Egyptologische Uitgaven 10 (Leiden, 1982), 1–70.

142. P. Vernus, *RdE* 30 (1978): 127–29.

143. Ibid., 136–37.

144. That oracles were evidently a manifestation of personal piety is shown, for instance, by their common phraseology; see ibid., 155 n. 30.

145. See p. 105.

146. The most recent and remarkable study is that by A. G. McDowell, *Jurisdiction in the Workmen's Community*, 112–38.

147. E. D. Bedell, "Criminal Law in the Egyptian Ramesside Period" (Ph.D. diss., Brandeis University, 1973), 201; J.-M. Kruchten, *Le grand texte oraculaire de Djéhoutymose intendant du domaine d'Amon de Pinedjem II*, Monographies Reine élisabeth 5 (Brussels, 1986), 346: "À mesure que la corruption et l'inefficacité des cours de justice locale croissaient, le recours à de tels arbitrages devenait plus fréquent."

148. Brought to light for the first time by the admirable historian E. Meyer, *Gottesstaat, Militärschaft und Standwesen in Ägypten*, SPAW 28 (Berlin, 1928).

149. For the modifications that the concept of theocracy brought to the institution of kingship, see P. Vernus, in E. Le Roy Ladurie, ed., *Les Monarchies: Colloque, Université de Paris-I, Centre d'analyse comparative des systèmes politiques, 8–10 décembre 1981* (Paris, 1986), 37–38.

150. See p. 21.

151. *Tanis: L'Or des Pharaons: Paris, Galeries Nationales du Grand Palais, 26 mars–20 juillet 1987, Marseille, Centre de la Vieille-Charité, 19 septembre–30 novembre 1987* (Paris, 1987), 103–4; on theocratic ideology, see also p. 104, text no. 2, and p. 108, text no. 7.

152. For the manipulation of the oracle, see p. 187 n. 87.

Appendix: Terms for Bribe

1. See 186 n. 69.

2. G. P. F. van den Boorn, *The Duties of the Vizier: Civil Administration in the Early New Kingdom* (London, 1988), 112–13, calls it an "omnibusword" [*sic*].

3. P. Vernus, *RdE* 32 (1980): 122 (a).

4. A. H. Gardiner, *RdE* 6 (1951): 122 t.

5. A. H. Gardiner, *The Wilbour Papyri*, vol. 2 (Oxford, 1948), 85 n. 5.

6. C. Eyre, in M. A. Powell, ed., *Labor in the Near East* (New Haven, 1987).

7. H. von Deines, *Wörterbuch von ägyptischen Drogennamen* (Berlin, 1959), 403; G. Charpentier, *Receuil de matériaux épigraphiques relatifs à la botanique de l'Égypte antique* (Paris, 1986), 526, no. 859.

8. H. von Deines, *Wörterbuch von ägyptischen Drogennamen*, 391–93; G. Charpentier, *Receuil de matériaux*, 506; R. Germer, *Untersuchungen über Arzneimittelpflanzen im Alten Ägypten* (Hamburg, 1979), 288.

9. On this point, see G. Charpentier, *Receuil des matériaux*, 555, 1. It would be beyond our purposes here to enter into the thorny problem posed by plant names of the type *ḥsꜣ/ḫnꜣ/ḥsy/ḥsꜣ/ḥsy*, etc.

10. K. Sethe, *Aegyptische Lesestücke zum Gebrauch in akademischen Unterricht* (reprint, Hildesheim, 1959), p. 79, 19.

11. J. F. Quack, *Studien zur Lehre für Merikare*, GOF 23 (Wiesbaden, 1992), 30.

Subject Index

Note: Italicized page numbers indicate illustrations.

Index of Egyptian Terms

in, opposed to *iṯꜣ*, with regard to communications, 190 n. 46; "go in search of," "bring," with regard to social promotion, 194 n. 45

inb, "oil," 84

inbt, "redoubt," 57

irw nfr, "do something good," 180 n. 95

ir . . . r, "distinguish (something) from . . . ," 193 n. 27

ir ḥꜣw + suffix, "dispose of," 185 n. 34

iḥ, "be plunged into darkness, drowse," 190 n. 43

iḥwty, "cultivator," 195 n. 69

iṯꜣ, opposed to *in*, with regard to communications, 190 n. 46

ꜥꜣw, "foreigner," 161 n. 24 and 168 n. 175

ꜥrk, "solemn renunciation," 178 n. 13

ꜥḥ, "to be in service," 184 n. 9

wꜣḥ, "to submit," 188 n. 93

wꜣḥ ist, "conduct an excavation," 162 n. 47

wꜥ is, "undertake the profanation of a tomb," 174 n. 54

wꜥb, "pure priest," 187 n. 78

wnḏw, "group," 161 n. 31

wsr, "rich," 142

wšbt, "reaction," 174 n. 47

bꜣkw(t), "taxes," 186 n. 67

bꜥ, "be attentive to," 195 n. 78

bꜥ, "neglect," 195 n. 78

bw, in *m bw wꜣ*, 163 n. 79

bn sw, "he has nothing," 186 n. 70

bsy, "if only!" 187 n. 81

prw, "surpluses," 194 n. 58

pḥ nṯr, "enter into contact with the divine," 190 n. 42

fꜣyt, "group of bearers," 195 n. 66

mꜣꜥt, in *m mꜣꜥt*, "truly," 176–77 n. 103

miḥꜥ(t), "cenotaph, funerary monument," 165 n. 114

mwt, "die," hyperbolic use, 172 n. 20

mnnty, part of a tomb, 162 n. 68

mryt, "riverbank," 175 n. 66

ms-ḫr, "native of the (sector of) the Tomb," 169 n. 207

mkw, "protection," in *pnꜥ nꜣ mkw*, 190 n. 58

n(i)k, "copulate," 76

nfrw, "rear, extremity," 173 n. 30

nmḥ, "poor," 198 nn. 119 and 120

nkt, "bribe," 72 and 152

rꜣ-ꜥ, "manuscript box," 176 n. 96

rꜣ-ꜥ-pd, "platform," 181 n. 69

rwḏw, "controllers," designating the "authorities" of an institution, 161 n. 45, 186 nn. 64 and 69

(r)di, "give," hence "denounce," 167 n. 162

(r)dit r tꜣ, "give birth," 184 n. 20

hꜣi (pꜣ iwr), "abort," 184 n. 15

hꜣw, "circle of acquaintances," 171 n. 250, 186 n. 65

hnn, "show one's approbation," 187 n. 89

Index of Passages Translated